Alexander th
and Pei

Alexander the Great and Persia

From Conqueror to King of Asia

Joseph Stiles

PEN & SWORD
HISTORY

First published in Great Britain in 2022 by
Pen & Sword History
An imprint of
Pen & Sword Books Ltd
Yorkshire – Philadelphia

ISBN 978 1 39909 441 2

Typeset by Mac Style
Printed and bound in the UK by CPI Group (UK) Ltd,
Croydon, CR0 4YY.

Pen & Sword Books Limited incorporates the imprints of Atlas,
Archaeology, Aviation, Discovery, Family History, Fiction, History,
Maritime, Military, Military Classics, Politics, Select, Transport,
True Crime, Air World, Frontline Publishing, Leo Cooper, Remember
When, Seaforth Publishing, The Praetorian Press, Wharncliffe
Local History, Wharncliffe Transport, Wharncliffe True Crime
and White Owl.

For a complete list of Pen & Sword titles please contact

PEN & SWORD BOOKS LIMITED
47 Church Street, Barnsley, South Yorkshire, S70 2AS, England
E-mail: enquiries@pen-and-sword.co.uk
Website: www.pen-and-sword.co.uk

Or

PEN AND SWORD BOOKS
1950 Lawrence Rd, Havertown, PA 19083, USA
E-mail: Uspen-and-sword@casematepublishers.com
Website: www.penandswordbooks.com

Contents

Acknowledgements

I would like to thank Phil Sidnell and Pen & Sword Publishing for making this book possible. Thank you to Dr John Broom at Norwich University for our long and enjoyable conversations on Alexander. Finally, thank you to my family for their support and encouragement during this project.

Ancient Sources

Main Ancient Sources on Alexander

Arrian of Nicomedia: Greek historian and Roman governor, 2nd century CE.

Quintus Curtius Rufus: Roman historian, 1st century CE.

Diodorus Siculus: Greek historian, 1st century BC.

Justin: Roman Epitomizer of Gnaeus Pompeius Trogus' History, 4th century CE.

Metz Epitome: Epitome of Alexander's life.

Plutarch: Greek biographer, 1st–2nd century CE.

Alexander Romance: Account of Alexander's life with fictional and factual elements, attributed to Pseudo-Callisthenes.

Itinerary of Alexander: 4th century CE account of Alexander's campaigns dedicated to the Roman Emperor Constantius II.

Other Relevant Ancient Sources

Aelian: Roman historian, 2nd and 3rd century CE.

Appian: Greek historian, 2nd century CE.

Aristotle: Greek philosopher, 4th century BC.

Athenaeus: Greek rhetorician, 2nd and 3rd century CE.

Ctesias: Greek historian, 5th century BC.

Demosthenes: Greek statesman and orator, 4th century BC.

Heidelberg Epitome: Epitome of the Diadochi (Successor) period.

Herodotus: Greek historian, 5th century Greek BC.

Homer: Greek epic poet.

Lucian of Samosata: Greek Satirist, 2nd century CE.

Valerius Maximus: Roman writer, 1st century CE.

Memnon of Heracleia: Greek historian, 1st century CE.

Cornelius Nepos: Roman biographer, 1st century BC.

Pausanias: Greek geographer, 2nd century CE.

Polyaenus: Greek military writer, 2nd century CE.
Polybius: Greek historian, 2nd century BC.
Strabo: Greek geographer, 1st century CE.
Theophrastus: Greek writer, 4th–3rd century BC.
Xenophon: Greek soldier and historian, 5th–4th century BC.

Preface

Soldier and Politician

Throughout history, military leaders have looked to Alexander the Great as a figure worth emulating. Notably, French Emperor Napoleon Bonaparte, while in exile on his island prison of St Helena, said the following about Alexander:

> What I admire in Alexander the Great is not his campaigns, which we cannot fully understand, but his political astuteness. At the age of thirty-three he left behind him an immense empire well established, which his generals divided among themselves. He knew the art of gaining the love and trust of conquered nations.[1]

The French emperor's comment may strike one as a bit surprising as it does not fit Alexander's popular image. The Macedonian king is remembered as one of the great commanders of history and as the man who defeated the Persian Empire. Alexander's victories on the battlefield vastly overshadow his political side. Commonly Alexander is described as a despotic drunk who gave little thought to ruling his empire. Few would call Alexander a 'politically astute' ruler who 'knew the art of gaining the love and trust of conquered nations'.

Napoleon's experiences on his ill-fated Egyptian expedition shaped his view of Alexander. One of the French emperor's great regrets was not founding a great eastern empire like Alexander. Napoleon knew first-hand what it was like to campaign in a hostile foreign land from his time in Egypt. He understood that it required more than victory on the battlefield to bring about success. The political policies of the conqueror towards the conquered were an equally critical element. In Napoleon's opinion, Alexander achieved success because he mastered the role of 'both a soldier and a politician'.[2]

Alexander the Great and Persia explores Alexander's efforts as both a soldier and politician during his campaign in Asia. It seeks to answer the following questions. How did Alexander conquer the Persian Empire? How did he maintain his rule as 'King of Asia'? Should Alexander be viewed as one of history's great empire-builders?

In making these determinations, *Alexander the Great and Persia* focuses on Alexander's policies towards Persians and Asians, a topic largely overlooked in historiography. Alexander's pro-Persian policies were an essential element of his reign and something to which the king devoted a great deal of effort. From this examination, the reader will better appreciate Alexander's kingship and gain a greater understanding of the critical role played by Persians and Asians in his empire.

Introduction

Conqueror to King of Asia

In the autumn of 331 BC, King Alexander III (Alexander the Great) of Macedonia marched his army into the heart of Mesopotamia. On the plain of Gaugamela, he engaged in battle with the army of Persian King Darius III. After a hard-fought struggle, the Macedonians emerged triumphant over their Persian foes. King Darius fled eastward with what remained of his followers, leaving the field to Alexander. Alexander's victory in battle over the Persian king marked the death blow to the Achaemenid Persian Empire. In the words of the ancient biographer Plutarch, 'the authority of the Persian empire was regarded as having been completely overthrown', and Alexander took the new title 'King of Asia'.[1]

Three years before his victory at Gaugamela, in the spring of 334, Alexander launched his campaign of conquest against the Persian Empire.[2] Since that time, Alexander had succeeded in breaking down the power of the Persian state. His numerous military victories destroyed Persian military power. The triumph at Gaugamela was the culmination of Alexander's colossal efforts in the East. From this point onwards, Alexander could rightly claim to be the ruler of Asia.

As 'King of Asia', Alexander faced the new challenge of ruling over a diverse and massive territory. The Macedonian king recognized the great difficulty of ruling over people very different from his own. Even after the victory at Gaugamela, usurpers and rebels remained in the field against him. The new empire's borders in Central Asia and India had yet to be secured. Alexander's expeditions to consolidate his empire were undoubtedly his most brutal. Those who resisted the new ruler of Asia could expect to be dealt with harshly as mere rebels who defied their king. The deaths from Alexander's subjugation of Asia numbered in the hundreds of thousands, with countless others reduced to slavery.[3] The Macedonians looted Asia of its wealth, stripped temples to its gods, and even burned the palace of Persepolis. Alexander would earn himself the nickname 'Alexander the Accursed' in Iranian traditions.[4]

Despite these great acts of brutality, the Macedonian king had no wish to annihilate the people of Asia. In the king's own words, he had not come to Asia to fundamentally destroy its way of life and make it a 'desert'. The classic view of Alexander is that he saw himself as a Hellenic civilizer of the 'barbarian' peoples of Asia. At times Alexander did indeed propagate the idea of a civilizing mission in the East. Alexander would speak before his soldiers about the need to instill 'better habits' in the Asians to 'appease their savage temper'. However, evidence of such a Hellenization programme by Alexander is limited and vastly overstated. The creation of the Hellenistic states in Asia was much more the product of his successors, such as Antigonus.[5]

More often than not, Alexander did not impose 'civilization' or 'Hellenization' on the Persians but instead adopted eastern customs. The ancient historian Diodorus Siculus refers to Alexander as an admirer of Persian traditions. In Alexander's opinion, the Persians offered many attributes 'we (Macedonians) should not blush to imitate'. Indeed, as king of Asia, Alexander began to imitate the Achaemenid rulers, much to the distaste of his Macedonian veterans. The king adopted eastern-style dress, introduced Persian practices at court, took part in great royal hunts, and started the mass recruitment of Asian youths for his army. Alexander would even take the dramatic step of encouraging mixed marriages between Greeks-Macedonians and noble Asian women, with the king himself taking one Asian and two Persian wives. These actions were in keeping with Alexander's belief that the only way for the empire to function was by incorporating aspects of the 'vanquished'.[6]

Throughout his campaign in Asia, Alexander did all he could to paint himself as a legitimate ruler. His goal was to make the people of Asia come to accept his victory without 'regret'. He hoped to win over the Persian and broader Asian elite by 'goodwill, rather than by force' and make them 'sharers in his successes'. The Macedonian ruler knew he needed to build a support base and acquire legitimacy in the eyes of the elite. Had he failed to garner this support, Alexander would have found his rule in the East far more challenging. In the end, the king's efforts paid off as he was able to eventually mollify the Persian and Asian elite, including even the family of Darius.[7]

It is a step too far, though, to declare, as some have done, that Alexander, through his policies, sought to fuse the races and unite humanity. In fact, on numerous occasions, he kept Macedonians and Persians in parallel structures apart from each other. Alexander's adoption of Persian-Asian attributes stemmed largely from consideration of the military and political realities he faced. The Macedonian ruler undertook measures to make his rule feasible and provide the Asian elite with a reason to support him. However, we should not lock Alexander's actions into a box. The king did not merely undertake what was pragmatic, practical or expedient. Alexander had a vision for his empire, and his pro-Persian policies extended beyond simple political necessity.[8]

By 324, Alexander could claim to have accomplished his goal of subduing the Persian Empire. He had succeeded in crushing all the major rebel movements against his rule. The king had carved out the borders of his empire in the north and east. The Asian elite, either out of fear of the king's wrath or Alexander's sympathetic policies, had become subservient. Alexander's sudden death in June of 323 was as stunning to the Asians as the Macedonians. They were bewildered that their conqueror, who they had deemed invincible, could be dead. The ancient epitomizer Justin writes: 'All the barbarous nations, whom he had shortly before subdued, lamented for him, not as an enemy, but as a father.'[9] The Asians and Persians were rightly worried about what was to come. They knew that Alexander's successors might not share his tolerance for their ways.

Alexander's death came as a great shock to the family of the former King Darius. Since their capture a decade earlier, the Macedonian ruler had treated them with respect and kindness. Darius' mother Sisygambis had formed a close bond with the conqueror, becoming his 'quote, unquote' mother. Hearing the news of Alexander's demise, Sisygambis 'put on mourning garb and, tearing her hair, threw herself on the ground'. Sisygambis, at that moment, wondered about the fate of herself and her family. The Persian noblewoman felt as if she had been taken prisoner for a second time and again 'had lost royal rank'. Sisygambis, in her life, had witnessed her fair share of bloody regime changes and accurately predicted that Alexander's death would mean the destruction of her family. The Persian matriarch felt no more reason to live and chose to starve herself to death. As the Roman historian Quintus Curtius Rufus wrote: 'Surely her death is strong testimony to Alexander's indulgence towards her and to his just treatment of all the captives; for she who had had the fortitude to live after Darius was ashamed to survive Alexander.'[10]

Chapter One

Persia and Macedonia

The Achaemenid Persian Empire was one of the ancient world's most powerful states. At its height, the empire stretched from south-eastern Europe to the borderlands of India. As the saying went, the Persian state extended 'toward the south to a region where men cannot dwell by reason of the heat, and to the north to a region where they cannot dwell by reason of the cold'.[1] It possessed some of the most splendid cities of the ancient world: Babylon, Ecbatana, Susa and Persepolis. The Persian Great King ruled this vast land with the blessing of the supreme god Ahura Mazda. By the king's will, his loyal satraps and officials managed the provinces. The much-vaunted Persian army stamped the king's will across Asia.

While the Persians ascended to great power, Macedonia was merely a minor kingdom in northern Greece. When the Persians marched into Europe in the late fifth century, they quickly subdued the Macedonians and made them vassals of the empire. Their arrival in Macedonia would have a defining impact on the kingdom's development. The Macedonians would play a critical role in the Greco-Persian wars contributing to the efforts of both sides. The Macedonian kingdom had been pushed progressively forward and brought into the wider world by the war's end.

Foundation of the Persian Empire

Cyrus the Great brought about the rise of the Persian Empire. At the time of Cyrus' birth, the Medians were the dominant force on the Iranian plateau. Persis (Persia), from where Cyrus hailed, was merely a subject state of the Median Empire. In 559 BC, the Persians, under the leadership of Cyrus, rejected the rule of the Median king and revolted against him. The Persians would emerge victorious in this war, liberate their homeland and conquer the Medes. The Achaemenids, the clan to which Cyrus belonged, would play the leading role in the new Persian state.[2]

King Cyrus, now at the head of this extensive empire, sought to expand his rule further. In 547, the Persians entered into war against the powerful Lydian kingdom of western Asia Minor. Cyrus would defeat the Lydian king and capture his capital of Sardis. Cyrus next turned his attention to the Babylonians, and in 539 this mighty kingdom succumbed to invading Persian armies. With the defeat of Media, Lydia and Babylonia, Cyrus had established the Persians as the rulers of western Asia. The Persian founder himself would die fighting the nomadic Scythians in 530, but his empire would endure and expand further in the period to come.[3]

The great conqueror's son Cambyses would inherit the empire. Cambyses would become infamous in Greek sources for his immorality and supposed mental instability. They attribute to Cambyses a variety of crimes such as murdering his brother and illegally marrying his sister. Greek histories stereotypically paint Persian rulers, other than the 'noble' Cyrus, as debauched. As the famed Greek historian Herodotus writes, 'Cambyses was harsh and arrogant, Cyrus was merciful and always worked for their [the Persians] well-being.'[4]

Despite his alleged instability and moral bankruptcy, Cambyses would prove successful as a conqueror. In the image of his father, Cambyses led a campaign bringing Egypt under the Persian yoke in 525. The Persian ruler did not have long to celebrate as, following the Egyptian conquest, Cambyses would soon die in mysterious circumstances. The period that followed was one of political unrest. Rule over the empire fell to Smerdis, who was either the younger son of Cyrus or an imposter. A conspiracy of seven powerful Persian clans murdered Smerdis soon afterwards.[5]

The conspiracy's leader Darius then assumed the Persian throne. King Darius I 'the Great' is held to have been the Persian Empire's greatest ruler. He would provide the empire with stability following the rule of Smerdis. Under his thirty-year rule, the empire grew to its height of power and influence. According to Herodotus, the king earned the nickname 'Darius the Merchant' because of the empire's newfound wealth.[6]

One of Darius' most outstanding contributions was the building of the Persian royal road. This road ran between the important centres of Sardis and Susa, connecting the territories between western Asia Minor to the Persian heartland. According to Herodotus, those who journeyed along the route could expect safe and speedy travel. The military implications of the road were significant. It allowed for the prompt deployment of soldiers, relaying of messengers and a stable logistical route. Darius' son and successor, King Xerxes, would use the road when marching his massive army to invade Greece.[7]

Darius also created the satrapal system as a solution to governing the massive Persian state. He divided his empire into some twenty parts, each headed by a satrap. The satraps would have a certain level of autonomy to manage their affairs and raise mercenary forces. The system proved to be a simple way of ruling a large, diverse empire as the satraps could crush local rebellions and assist foreign allies. On the other hand, the satraps could prove incompetent or even rebel against the Persian ruler. Despite drawbacks, the system created by Darius would stand the test of time.[8]

In addition to being a great reformer of the Persian state, Darius was also an able military leader. He was able to subdue all rebellions at home and turned his attention towards expanding the empire. He advanced in the east up to the Indus River and in the west into Europe. In 510, during Darius' European campaign, the Persians first came into close contact with the Macedonian kingdom.[9]

Macedonian Vassalage to Persia

Darius sent messengers to the Macedonians demanding the usual tribute of 'Earth and Water'. The Macedonians were also to provide hostages to guarantee future peace with Persia. The reigning Macedonian King Amyntas I did not have the military capabilities to resist the Persians. The Macedonians chose to submit and became vassals to the Persian Empire.[10]

Controversy soon arose between the two allies. Herodotus provides us with a story of a banquet hosted by Amyntas for Persian officials. While attending the dinner, the Persians asked their hosts to provide women for their entertainment. At Persian feasts, it was commonplace for women to sing and amuse the guests. Amyntas agreed to the Persian request and ordered women brought forth. As per Macedonian custom, the female attendees took their places in the opposite row from the Persians. The situation displeased the Persian guests who wanted the women's close company. Amyntas reluctantly ordered the women to sit by the Persians.

The new arrangement prompted revulsion from the Macedonians and particularly from Amyntas' hot-blooded son Alexander. Alexander intended to take action against the Persians and asked his father to leave.

Amyntas, clearly aware of his son's intentions, did not want to be connected with the affair. Alexander then had the women withdraw, replacing them with male warriors dressed in women's clothing and armed with daggers. The Macedonians proceeded to murder their Persian guests; a shocking beginning to the relations between the two nations.[11]

Following the massacre, the Persians sent a general named Boubares to investigate the matter. Had the Persians learned the truth, Macedonia could expect harsh punishment. Amyntas, however, skilfully managed the situation and kept the murders a secret. To buy his silence, Boubares was bribed with gold and given his sister Gygaea in marriage.[12]

The marriage between Boubares and Gygaea foreshadows Alexander the Great's mixed marriages between Persians and Macedonians. In the case of Boubares and Gygaea, it was a Persian marrying a Macedonian noblewoman, the reverse of Alexander's unions. This dynamic reflects how Persians held the dominant position in the sixth century while Macedonia held all the power in Alexander's era. The partnership further demonstrates the significance placed on political marriages by both Macedonian and Persian society.

As the preceding story illustrates, the Macedonian elite was unhappy with their position as vassals. They were not pleased to see the Persians' infringement of their rights. Nonetheless, the Macedonians had a great deal to gain from their Persian overlords. During this period, Persian influence began affecting Macedonian institutions. One of the clearest examples of Persian inspiration was the Macedonian page system.

The Macedonian royal pages were young men drawn from elite Macedonian families. They were taught martial skills and educated to prepare them for future leadership positions. The pages had the critical task of watching over the king. The Macedonian page system has a great deal of similarity to the Persian model. From descriptions of the Persian page system provided by Xenophon, we can see numerous points of comparison. The historian Arrian also states how Macedonian pages 'in Persian fashion' assisted Macedonian rulers in mounting their horses. From these accounts, one can assume that the Macedonian court had taken on some Persian attributes before Alexander the Great's reign.[13]

The Persian alliance would have other more direct benefits for Macedonia. The Persians would increase Macedonia's territorial holdings and improve its road system. The collaboration with Persia brought

Macedonia into contact with the Near Eastern world. Macedonia was no longer merely a remote city-state but connected to a multi-continental empire. The opening of Macedonia had a positive effect on the kingdom's economy as they could now actively trade with the Persians and their allies. From the reverse perspective, the Persians viewed the Macedonian alliance as extremely important due to the country's strategic position. The Persians sought to expand their holdings into Greece, and Macedonia served as a critical support base for these efforts. While mutually beneficial to Macedonians and Persians alike, the alliance would find itself severely tested when Darius the Great began his invasion of Greece.[14]

Macedonia's Role in the Greco-Persian Wars

In 492 BC, a Persian force under the command of Darius' son-in-law Mardonius arrived in Macedonia. The Macedonians, as part of their agreement with Persia, offered their assistance to the arriving army. Mardonius planned to take the war into Greece itself through Macedonia. Plans changed, however, when Thracian tribes attacked the Persians and Mardonius fell wounded. Following these attacks, the Persians were determined to subdue the local Thracians. With Macedonian support, Mardonius launched a campaign against the Thracians and pacified them. The Persians had taken significant losses in this sideshow and departed back to Asia for the time being.[15]

Following this failed effort in northern Greece, Darius shifted his attention towards launching an amphibious expedition against Athens. This renewed effort would ultimately lead to the disastrous Persian defeat at the Battle of Marathon in 490. The loss temporarily ended significant Persian efforts against Greece. Darius would die four years later, leaving the empire to his son Xerxes. Xerxes would again set his sights on Greece, preparing for another war. In 480, the Persian ruler had assembled a massive army and crossed the Hellespont into Greece. This new conflict again put Macedonia in the crosshairs.[16]

By the time of Xerxes' invasion, Macedonian King Amyntas had died and rule over the kingdom had passed to Alexander. Alexander had no love for Persia as he had already proven in his murder of their officials. The king's sympathy was with the other Greek states, and he would come to be known as the 'Philhellene'. At the same time, Alexander must have feared Xerxes' power and could not openly oppose him.[17]

When Xerxes' host arrived, the Macedonians co-operated and provided the Persians with assistance. The kingdom's soldiers even joined the Persian invasion force as it marched south through the Macedonian mountains. Xerxes was pleased by the Macedonians' collaboration and awarded Alexander all the land between Mount Olympus and Mount Haemus. Despite any personal animosity, Alexander and his kingdom gained much from the Persian alliance.[18]

Accompanying the invading Persian army, Alexander chose to warn his fellow Greeks of the approaching menace. Particularly the king sent word to the Greeks about its overwhelming size. This information spurred the Greeks to retreat from their forward positions in Thessaly. After redeploying, the Greeks led by the Spartan King Leonidas would make their epic stand at the pass of Thermopylae. The Spartans held up the Persians for a brief period before being overrun.[19]

As the Persians advanced deeper into central Greece, King Alexander sought to protect cities in Boeotia from being ravaged. He sent Macedonian soldiers ahead of the advancing Persians to warn the citizens. The Macedonians were then able to trick the Persians into thinking people had submitted to Xerxes. After clearing the Boeotian plain, the Persians marched onwards to Athens. Xerxes brutally sacked Athens to avenge his father's failure at Marathon. The Persians did not have long to cherish the victory as they subsequently suffered a critical naval defeat to the Greeks at Salamis. Alexander may have hedged his bets against the Persians, providing the Athenians with Macedonian timber for their ships.[20]

Alexander was playing both sides in the conflict. The Macedonians supported the Persian militarily and benefited from territorial gains. At the same time, Alexander assisted his fellow Greeks when he had the opportunity. The Persians, to some extent, were aware of Alexander's friendliness with the Greek states, especially Athens. Mardonius, now serving as Xerxes' general, dispatched Alexander to the Athenians on a diplomatic mission. Mardonius hoped that Alexander could convince the Athenians to abandon the other Greek states and ally with Persia. Alexander went before the Athenians offering generous terms and advising them to submit due to Persia's overwhelming strength. The

Athenians, as Alexander likely expected, rejected such terms and sent him back to Mardonius.[21]

Ultimately the Persian and Greek armies would come face to face at Plataea. During the engagement, the Macedonians lined up on the Persian side, opposing the Athenians. The night before the fighting, Alexander again showed his true sympathies and rode over to the Greek side, warning them that the Persians intended to attack at dawn. The ensuing battle would result in a decisive Greek victory and spelled the end of Persian power in Greece.[22]

Following the Persian defeat, Alexander headed back to Macedonia. The Persian-Macedonian alliance was officially over, and Alexander readied his forces to liberate the kingdom. The Persians retreated from Plataea northwards, having to pass back through Macedonia to reach the Hellespont. Alexander used the opportunity to attack the retreating Persian columns near Amphipolis, taking many prisoners. With Macedonia now liberated, Alexander used the opportunity to expand his territory, further seizing critical silver and gold mines. The defeat of the Persians left Macedonia larger and more prosperous than ever before.[23]

The conclusion of the Greco-Persian Wars brought this first phase of Macedonian and Persian relations to an end. Alexander skilfully managed to play the Persians and Greeks off against each other. The Macedonians gained much from the Persian alliance and even more by taking advantage of Persian weakness. The next significant encounter between the two powers would come in the mid-fourth century, in the time of Macedonian King Philip II and the Persian King Artaxerxes III Ochus.

Chapter Two

Philip and Artaxerxes Ochus

Philip II of Macedonia and Artaxerxes III Ochus were monarchs of exceptional skill and ability. Philip, the father of Alexander the Great, reformed the Macedonian kingdom in its entirety and led his people to greater heights of power than ever before. Ochus brought about a revival of Persian political and military strength. These two dynamic rulers would clash on several occasions as each jockeyed for power. It was Philip and Ochus who did the most to lay the foundations for Alexander's world.

Philip the Great

When Philip came to power in 359 BC, the Macedonian kingdom was in a state of crisis. King Perdiccas III, the older brother of Philip, fell in battle against the Illyrians along with much of the Macedonian army. This defeat crippled Macedonia and left her open to foreign invasion. Philip would inherit the throne on the death of his brother. The chances of Philip, perhaps even the kingdom itself, surviving the chaos looked slim. However, Philip did not lose heart at the challenges he faced and would prove himself capable of meeting the dangers. As Diodorus states, Philip would raise Macedonia 'from the most insignificant beginnings' and build his kingdom into 'the greatest of the dominions in Europe'.[1]

Philip's unique abilities as a leader have their roots in his time in the city of Thebes. During his brother's reign, Philip had lived as a hostage in Thebes as part of a peace agreement. Thebes was the foremost Greek military power of the period, and Philip observed their army in action and its great commanders up close. On assuming the throne, Philip used his experience in Thebes to reorganize the Macedonian army.[2]

Philip's most significant military innovation was the introduction of the long pike known as the sarissa. This was a two-handed weapon and could be upwards of 15ft long. One ancient writer compared the sarissa in size to a tall male tree. This lengthened spear gave the Macedonians an advantage over other Greeks wielding the traditional 8ft hoplite spear. Philip's new sarissa-armed soldiers did not fight in individual actions, but rather in a tight formation known as the Macedonian phalanx.[3]

However, Philip's future success on the battlefield was not solely due to the sarissa. Demosthenes, Philip's great Athenian rival, attributed Macedonian success not to the phalanx alone but also to the accompanying light troops and cavalry. The Macedonian cavalry, in particular, expanded its capabilities under Philip. The horsemen began to employ the wedge formation armed with their cavalry sarissa. The introduction of siege techniques and equipment proved a crucial factor in Philip's and later Alexander's ability to take cities. Philip could unleash siege towers, battering rams, saps and catapults against a town's defences. Philip's reign also saw the foundation of a small Macedonian navy.[4]

It was not only in the military sphere that Philip showed his prowess. The Macedonian king proved himself a brilliant politician. According to the ancient descriptions, Philip had the skills of a professional actor with both a charming and devious personality. Diodorus reports how Philip valued his diplomatic successes even higher than his battlefield victories. The king would become infamous for his skilful political marriages.[5]

Campaigns of Philip

On coming to the throne, Philip faced multiple attempts to depose him from power. The Athenians had their selected candidate for the Macedonian kingship: a man named Argaeus. Athens backed this usurper with naval support and 3,000 hoplites. Philip engaged the Greek invaders in battle and emerged victorious, securing his throne. The Athenians were allowed to withdraw after a truce, without ransom, as Philip did not want to spark a more significant conflict. This victory helped to boost the morale of the Macedonians by giving them their first taste of success. Philip then made peace with Athens by renouncing his claim to the vital city of Amphipolis.[6]

In 358 BC, Philip turned against the 'barbarian' tribes on Macedonia's frontiers. He then marched upon the Paeonians and subjugated them. A movement against the Illyrians followed as they still occupied Macedonian territory. Philip confronted Illyrian King Bardylis in battle.

The Macedonian emerged victorious, employing a combined arms assault of infantry frontally and cavalry on the flanks. Philip forced the Illyrians to withdraw from Macedon as part of the subsequent peace terms. After only a year in power, he had restored Macedonian honour and avenged the death of his brother.[7]

Following the victory against the Illyrians, between 357 and 354 Philip moved to assert Macedonian rule over the coastal regions. The king reneged on his previous deal with Athens. Intending to drive Athenian influence from the area, he moved against Amphipolis. Philip used his siege engines to breach the defences and capture the city. He allied with the Chalcidian League, beating Athens to the punch. The major coastal centres of Pydna, Potidaea and Methone would come under Macedonian control. At the siege of the latter city, Philip would famously lose his eye.[8]

The Third Sacred War had broken out between Phocis and Thebes in 356. The war began when the Phocians seized the legendary oracle of Delphi. Their actions were viewed as a sacrilege to many Greeks. Using the money from Delphi, the Phocians hired mercenaries and raised a formidable force to fight Thebes. They gained the support of both Athens and Sparta for their efforts. Philip entered the war on the side of the Thebans. Thessaly, to the south of Macedonia, would be the battleground between Philip and the Phocians.[9]

The Phocians sent an initial expeditionary force which found itself swiftly defeated by Philip and driven from Thessaly in 353. The Phocians regrouped under Onomarchus and re-entered Thessaly with a large army that outnumbered Philip's two to one. Onomarchus defeated Philip in two consecutive battles, pushing him back to Macedon. Onomarchus then turned his attention to the Thebans, giving Philip time to regroup. Philip raised a new army which included the famed Thessalian cavalry. The Thessalian horsemen would later fight heroically in the campaigns of Philip's son Alexander.[10]

When ready, Philip again moved into Thessaly to challenge Onomarchus. The two sides' armies of roughly equal numbers met at the Battle of Crocus Field in 352. Philip had his men wear laurel crowns in recognition of their sacred mission to avenge the sacrilegious looting of Delphi. Philip used his Thessalian cavalry to turn the Phocians' flank and win the battle. The slaughter is said to have been immense, with some 6,000 dead on the Phocian side. The Phocians were driven into the sea, desperately trying to reach the Athenian navy off the coast.[11]

Following his victory over the Phocians, Philip brought Thessaly entirely under his control. In 352, he advanced to the famed pass of Thermopylae, intending to move into central Greece. The Athenians swiftly moved to block his advance, and Philip did not attempt to force the position. The Athenians had grown fearful of continued Macedonian expansion urged on by the fiery orator Demosthenes.[12]

Philip, having been blocked from moving further into Greece, turned his attention towards Thrace. The region was rich in silver mines that Philip wanted for Macedonia. He moved to gain the goodwill of the Greek cities lining the Thracian coast and drove back the Thracian tribes who raided their territory. The king's previous alliance with the Chalcidian League had fallen apart, and in 349 Philip captured their primary centre of Olynthus.[13] Over most of the next decade he worked to consolidate his gains.

In 340, Philip set out to capture the city of Perinthus on the Thracian coast due to its friendliness to Athens. The siege foundered in the face of stout defences, and the Persians soon intervened on the Perinthians' behalf. Failing at Perinthus, Philip turned on nearby Byzantium, besieging the city. For the second time, the Macedonians' siege efforts proved unsuccessful and, with the arrival of an Athenian-led fleet, Philip withdrew. Notably, while Philip campaigned in Thrace, a teenage Alexander had been left as regent of Macedonia. Alexander would fight a minor campaign against the Maedi tribe and found a city.[14]

Philip, having failed to take Byzantium, directed his wrath upon the Scythians in 339. After ravaging them, Philip marched home with a significant amount of slaves and treasure. On his return march from Scythia, a Thracian people called the Triballians ambushed Philip's army. In the engagement, the Triballians came out on top, seizing the Macedonian baggage. Philip received his second most famous injury, taking a spear wound that left him with a limp. A young Alexander would joke with his father, 'Be of good cheer, Father, and go on your way rejoicing, that at each step you may recall your valour.'[15]

In 338, after recovering from his wound, Philip was determined for a final war with Athens to gain hegemony over Greece. The Athenians turned to Thebes for aid in repulsing the Macedonian threat. The combined Athenian and Theban armies united at Chaeronea. The allies offered Philip the decisive battle he craved. The Battle of Chaeronea resulted in a decisive Macedonian victory. Alexander would play a prominent role in the fighting. With the destruction of the Athenian-Theban army, the Macedonians established their hegemony over Greece.[16]

Artaxerxes Ochus

As Philip's Macedonia rose to supremacy in the Hellenic world, the Persian Empire underwent a resurgence in power. At the close of the fifth century, Egypt broke off from the empire and internal civil war erupted. Later attempts to retake Egypt proved to be a failure, and further revolts plagued the kingdom. Like his Macedonian rival Philip, Artaxerxes III Ochus, on assuming the throne, faced numerous obstacles to rebuilding Persian power.

Artaxerxes Ochus had inherited the throne at roughly the same time as Philip. His path to the throne had been difficult as his aged father, Artaxerxes II, had two other favoured sons. The future Persian king first had to outmanoeuvre his brothers to gain the kingdom. Ochus set up the crown prince's execution and the suicide of the younger son. The elder Artaxerxes died soon after, distraught by the events, leaving the throne to Ochus. The latter's reign began in an infamously bloody fashion, slaughtering all other potential rivals.[17]

The ancient Greco-Roman historians present Ochus as nothing short of a monster. They depict him as savage, bloodthirsty and jealous, but at the same time effeminate and incapable as a warrior. The historiography surrounding Ochus is similar to that of Cambyses. Putting aside the ancient biases, Ochus would prove himself to be a highly competent leader. The Persian Great King undertook to unify his realm and crush all separatist elements. Over his two decades on the throne, he reduced satrapal power in Asia Minor, suppressed rebellions in Cyprus and Phoenicia, and reconquered Egypt.[18] The fact that Artaxerxes was able to overcome the Egyptians where his predecessor Artaxerxes II had failed is testament to his military power and personal leadership.

War with Artabazos

During the period of 356 to 353 BC, Philip and Ochus first came into contention during the latter's campaign against Artabazos, the rebellious satrap of Hellespontine Phrygia. Artabazos was a veteran figure of the empire by the time of Ochus' accession. He had helped Artaxerxes II in his suppression of a rebellion in Cappadocia. Artabazos turned against Ochus over the king's attempts to curb his independence and reduce his military power. Ochus' struggle against Artabazos would ultimately put him at odds with the major Greek states, including Macedonia.

The Persians would have difficulty in suppressing the satrap. Artabazos had turned for support to Athens, who obliged by sending an expeditionary force. The satrap also had at his disposal the services of the Rhodian mercenary brothers Mentor and Memnon. The brothers proved to be two of the most talented generals of their era. Artabazos had brought the mercenaries into his household by marrying their sister.[19]

Ochus ordered the satraps of Asia Minor to crush Artabazos. According to Diodorus, they assembled an overwhelming force for the attempt. Despite the alleged massive size of the satrapal army of some 70,000 men, Artabazos and the Athenians managed to repel them. Failing on the battlefield, Ochus turned to diplomacy and opened negotiations with Athens. The Persian king sought to separate Artabazos from this ally. The Persians vowed to aid Athens' enemies and send a fleet against Athens if they continued to assist Artabazos. The Athenians, frightened by the Persian threats, chose to abandon Artabazos.[20]

Having lost the aid of Athens, Artabazos now turned to Thebes for assistance. The Thebans obliged, readying an expeditionary force. Sympathetic to the Theban efforts, King Philip escorted the Theban army through his territory and facilitated its crossing into Asia. With Thebes' help, Artabazos retook the initiative, winning several battles against the Persians. Ochus again turned to the use of diplomacy against Artabazos. The Thebans were in desperate need of money for their continued wars in Greece. Ochus promised to provide the funds necessary if they would abandon Artabazos. The Thebans obliged and betrayed their former ally.[21]

Without the aid of Athens and Thebes, Artabazos would eventually be defeated and driven from Asia Minor. In 352, the deposed satrap fled to the safety of Philip's court in Macedonia. Artabazos brought with him his close relatives, Memnon of Rhodes, and his many children, including his daughter Barsine. At Philip's court, they would meet a young Alexander, a figure with whom their lives would become deeply intertwined.[22]

Mentor did not join his relatives in Macedonia. Instead, he continued the fight against the Persians in Egyptian service. The Rhodian, however, soon betrayed his new masters and joined Ochus. He would then play a significant role in the Persian conquest of Egypt in 343. For his services, Ochus awarded him the Rhodian command over the coast in Asia Minor and allowed his relatives to return home.[23]

Settling into his new position, Mentor set about enforcing Ochus' control over the region. The Rhodian targeted Hermias, ruler of Atarneus in western Asia Minor. Hermias was an ally of King Philip and could potentially provide Philip with a bridgehead in Asia. The Rhodian employed trickery to achieve his objective. Mentor invited Hermias to attend a meeting with a promise of amnesty. When the ruler arrived, Mentor took him back as a prisoner to Susa. Mentor tortured Hermias to death for information on Philip. He then used Hermias' seal to gain the submission of his territory. With Hermias dealt with, Mentor could boast of having secured the coast for the Great King.[24]

Persian Reconquest of Phoenicia, Cyprus and Egypt

In 345 BC, Ochus turned his attention to restoring Persian rule in Phoenicia, Cyprus and Egypt. Ochus assembled a massive army for the war, by Diodorus' estimate 30,000 cavalry, 300,000 infantry, 300 warships and 500 merchant craft. The Persian Empire of this period was hardly the weak declining state alleged by many. The Great King was determined to take the field in person and squash all opposition.[25]

Ochus marched upon the rebellious Phoenicians. Sidon, a wealthy trading city, was the centre of the rebellion in the region. The city's ruler had appealed to the Egyptian Pharaoh Nectanebo II for aid against the Persians. The Egyptians dispatched mercenaries under the command of Mentor to aid Sidon's struggle. Mentor defeated the local satraps, driving them from the territory. In defiance of the Persians, the citizens destroyed the city's royal park, a favourite spot of the Persian kings.[26]

Ochus marched against the rebellious Sidonese, calling upon his satraps for support. Belesys, satrap of Syria, and Mazaeus, satrap of Cilicia, marched to the king's aid. Two decades later, Mazaeus would become one of Alexander's great foes and subsequent ally. Taking Sidon proved to be an easy task. Its king betrayed the city and Mentor defected to the Persians. According to Diodorus, the Persians plundered and burned the city. Some 40,000 Sidonians perished in the massacre. Ochus is then said to have sold the ruins for a great sum of money.[27]

While Ochus advanced upon the Phoenicians, his Carian satrap Idrieus operated against Cyprus. The island's nine kings had united in rebellion against Ochus. Idrieus would invade the island at the head of some 8,000 mercenaries and besieged its most significant city of Salamis. The king of Salamis held out for some time, but eventually surrendered. Ochus proved merciful and allowed the king to retain his throne. With Salamis' capture, Idrieus restored Cyprus to Persian rule.[28]

Ochus, having dealt with Sidon and the Cypriot revolt, marched upon Egypt in 344. Egypt's defences were a challenging obstacle as the Persian king had previously failed to capture the region in 351. Nectanebo was well prepared to meet the Persian invaders. The Egyptians had assembled a force comprising 60,000 Egyptians, 20,000 Greek mercenaries and 20,000 Libyans. Nectanebo had taken the precaution of fortifying the approaches to Egypt and filling the Nile with a fleet of river craft. Ochus faced the most challenging campaign of his military career.

The Egyptian border town of Pelusium was Ochus' first objective. The city had been the site of the great Persian victory under King Cambyses, something that Ochus surely hoped to repeat. Some 5,000 Spartan mercenaries hired by Nectanebo defended Pelusium. Both sides made wide use of Greek mercenaries with Thebans spearheading Ochus' army. The Spartans and Thebans fought particularly hard because of the rivalry between their two states. Initially the city held out, mainly due to a large ditch blocking the advance. The Persians ingeniously diverted a canal, allowing them to fill the trench and begin siege operations. These new circumstances compelled the Spartan garrison to surrender.[29]

The victory at Pelusium now left Egypt open to invasion. Nectanebo, instead of supporting his men at Pelusium, retreated with the main Egyptian army. The Egyptian leader had become uneasy about the risk of meeting the enemy in a pitched battle. He instead chose to disperse his army into garrisons and prepare for a siege of the capital Memphis. In Diodorus' opinion, Nectanebo's ultimate defeat was not due to his preparations but his poor generalship and lack of military experience. As the Persian army advanced into Egypt, Mentor and Ochus' chief eunuch Bagoas took on a leading role in the operation. The two men waged a propaganda campaign to convince the Egyptians to surrender in exchange for amnesty. With the example of Sidon all too recent, the Persian strategy looks to have been successful and Egyptian resistance collapsed.[30]

Egypt's cities surrendered one by one to the Persians out of fear. Nectanebo's plans for the defence of Memphis never materialized. The Egyptian leader still seemed reluctant to fight the Persians. Instead, the pharaoh fled south, taking his wealth with him, to Ethiopia. Egypt again became part of the empire with Nectanebo's departure, and Ochus installed a new Persian satrap. The Persian king took his wrath out on the Egyptians, raiding their temples and tearing down their walls to prevent further resistance. With his Egyptian victory, Ochus could now claim to have restored the Persian Empire to its former glory.[31]

Philip had supported both the Cypriot rebels and the Egyptian pharaoh, the idea being that these rebels would keep the Persians busy and allow Philip to conquer Greece without their interference. However, taken aback by Ochus' rising power, Philip had a change of heart and decided to cut his allies loose. Macedonia was not yet ready to face Persia and Philip preferred to make peace with Ochus. The Macedonians and Persians would come to an agreement concluding with a non-aggression pact. The pact would be short-lived and the two sides openly clashed during the siege of Perinthus.[32]

Siege of Perinthus

In 340 BC, Philip put the coastal city of Perinthus under siege in his effort to subdue the coast. He attacked the city with all manner of siege equipment, but the Perinthians held out bravely, beating off the assaults. Despite the resistance, the city still expected to run out of supplies and surrender looked imminent. It was at this desperate hour that the siege caught the attention of King Ochus.[33]

In an 'unexpected move', Ochus chose to aid the Perinthians. The Persian king ordered his satraps in Asia Minor to support the Perinthians and break Philip's siege. The satraps obeyed and began to transfer money and supplies to the assistance of the defenders. Arsites, the satrap of

Hellespontine Phrygia who would later fight against Alexander's invasion, led the relief efforts. The Persians sent to Perinthus a mercenary force led by a hired Athenian general.[34]

This assistance by Persia proved too much for Philip, who broke off the siege and withdrew. Philip's lack of a large navy to match Persia remained an especially critical issue for the Macedonians. Had the Macedonians possessed such a navy, Philip could have blockaded the city by water and prevented Persian intervention. Without this naval strength, the Persians could defeat Philip without even using the main Persian army, only hiring mercenaries and sending supplies. Ochus had again reasserted Persian power by crippling Macedonian efforts.

Persian intervention at Perinthus would leave a lasting impression on the Macedonians. Following the Battle of Issus, Darius, in a letter to Alexander, would claim that the Macedonian invasion was unprovoked as they had 'suffered no ungracious treatment' from the Persians. Alexander remembered Perinthus well and used it to justify his military actions. The king wrote to Darius: 'It was you who began the mischief. You assisted Perinthus, which wronged my father; and Ochus sent a force into Thrace, which was under our sovereignty.' Alexander was, in effect, alleging that the Persians opened hostilities by supporting Macedonia's enemies.[35]

Philip's Asian War

Philip, undeterred by the defeat at Perinthus, began planning a campaign into Asia. According to Aelian, the Athenian orator Isocrates first gave Philip the idea for such an invasion. Under Isocrates' influence, Philip envisioned himself leading a united Hellenic effort against the Persian Empire. The goal of such an expedition was one of revenge on Persia for their crimes under Xerxes. Philip, in particular, wanted to punish them for their desecration of Greek temples.[36]

Following the victory at Chaeronea, Philip was finally in a position to lead a Greek coalition against the Persians. On the bloody battlefield, a drunken Philip celebrated over the dead until an Athenian captive reminded him that he now had the chance to play the role of Agamemnon. It was Agamemnon who, in Homer's *Iliad*, led a united Greece against Troy. Philip got the prisoner's message recognizing that he would need to appease those Greeks he had defeated in war and get them on board for the invasion of Persia.[37]

In preparation for the war, Philip called together a council of the Greek states at Corinth. At the council, all the Greek states, except for Sparta which did not attend, elected Philip as 'Hegemon' (supreme leader) of Greece. The Greek states each pledged to provide support for the endeavour against Persia. Philip had gained the political support and manpower he needed to open his war.[38]

In 336, Philip sent a 10,000-man expeditionary force to Asia under the command of Parmenion, his most trusted general, and Attalus, the uncle of his latest wife Cleopatra. Philip later planned to lead a much larger force into Asia, building from his lieutenant's gains. Alexander would later be critical of Philip not leading the army and attending to duties in Greece 'at a time when Asia should have been laid waste by fire'. Parmenion and Attalus' primary goal was to establish a bridgehead in Asia and 'liberate' the Greeks of Asia Minor. The Macedonian generals proved successful in establishing their foothold, but failed to accomplish much else in the region.[39]

Assassinations of Ochus and Philip

While Philip was uniting Greece for war in Asia, the Persian Empire suffered a critical blow. In 338 BC, the aging Artaxerxes Ochus was poisoned by his eunuch Bagoas, who was not a mere court official, having held both military commands and administrative positions. With Ochus out of the way, Bagoas set himself up as de facto ruler of the empire and installed the Persian king's son Arses on the throne. The eunuch then proceeded to murder Arses' brothers and isolate the young prince. Arses, however, proved disobedient to Bagoas' wishes and was also eliminated by the eunuch. The throne would pass into the hands of Darius III.[40]

Darius was not 'in the direct line of descent', but both his mother Sisygambis and father Arsames were of the Achaemenid house. Darius is known to have been an exceptionally brave man; hardly the coward that history has made him out to be. Darius had accompanied Ochus during a campaign against the warlike Cadusians. In this campaign, a Cadusian warrior of some renown challenged any Persian who dared to duel him. None answered the call except for Darius. He fought the Cadusian, cheered on by the Persian army, and emerged victorious, slaying his opponent. For this bravery at war, the Persians deemed Darius 'worthy to take over the kingship'.[41]

Not long after his accession, Darius would have a falling-out with the eunuch. Bagoas now planned to murder Darius through the use of poison. Darius would uncover Bagoas' plot and force the eunuch to drink his own poison. Despite the removal of Bagoas, Darius could not shake the fact that he had come to power through unsavoury means. Alexander would later use this fact to his advantage, labelling Darius a 'usurper' to the Persian throne. The main threat facing Darius at the onset of his rule centred on Egypt. The Egyptians had risen in revolt under a leader named Khababasha. They were still rebellious, despite the recent victories by Ochus. Darius invaded, restoring order, and had himself recognized as ruler of Egypt.[42]

Like Ochus and Arses, Philip would also soon fall victim to an assassin. According to Diodorus, the priestess at Delphi had predicted Philip's death, remarking that 'wreathed is the bull. All is done. There is also the one who will smite him.' Philip had misinterpreted the oracle's meaning as the slaughter of the Persians when, in fact, he would be the victim. In the autumn of 336, an assassin stabbed Philip to death at his daughter's wedding. The assassin's most likely motive was personal anger towards Philip. However, ancient and modern historians have long speculated about a larger plot involving Alexander and his mother Olympias. Alexander himself tried to blame the murder on a Persian-led conspiracy. Initially, on hearing of Philip's death, Darius was pleased. His opinion soon changed when news arrived of 'Alexander's vigour and rapidity'. In response, Darius increased the size of his military forces in preparation for a potential conflict.[43]

By this time, Mentor had died and his brother Memnon had ascended to his command. By Darius' orders, Memnon resisted Parmenion's efforts on the coast. Memnon, despite inferiority in numbers, fought a dogged campaign against the Macedonians. He defeated them in an engagement at Magnesia and drove Parmenion's subordinate Calas back to the Hellespont. Memnon marched across Mount Ida and fell upon Cyzicus, a Macedonian ally, almost capturing the city. Memnon succeeded in effectively keeping the Macedonians bottled up on the coast. The situation would not change dramatically until the arrival of Alexander in the spring of 334.[44]

Philip and Ochus both left a lasting legacy on the region. Philip built the military system that Alexander would use to conquer the Persian Empire. Critically, Alexander's father broke down the power of the Greek states and established a Macedonian presence in Asia. Without the groundwork laid by Philip, Alexander's conquests would hardly have been possible. Ochus succeeded in rebuilding Persian military power by reconquering Egypt and crushing his internal adversaries. At Perinthus, he demonstrated that the Persian Empire was still a force to be reckoned with that could repulse the Macedonians. Without Ochus, Alexander would have faced a divided and much weaker Persian state.

Chapter Three

Alexandropaedia

On 20 July 356 BC the Temple of Artemis at Ephesus, one of the marvels of the ancient world, burned in a great fire. The distraught temple priests predicted the inferno as a sign of a coming 'great calamity for Asia'. According to Plutarch, it was on the day of this catastrophe that Alexander the Great was born. Justin records a similar birth omen, alleging two eagles perched on the roof of King Philip's home as foretelling an empire of both Europe and Asia. Plutarch and Justin wrote their accounts of Alexander's birth with all the benefits of hindsight. Nonetheless, they are an essential illustration of how the ancients linked Alexander's destiny with that of Asia from his birth.[1]

Alexander's upbringing (356–336) is not a thoroughly documented period of his life, and the accounts are primarily anecdotal. From our sources, what can be certain is that the young Alexander took a great interest in the East and the Persian Empire. During his upbringing, Alexander had numerous opportunities to learn about the East from visiting Persian dignitaries, his tutor Aristotle, literary works, historical figures and Greek legends. This chapter will demonstrate that the knowledge gained by Alexander during his youth shaped his later actions as king.

Persians at the Court of Philip

Plutarch recounts how a boyhood Alexander received a group of Persian ambassadors during his father's absence. The young man enquired of the Persians about a variety of topics related to their empire. These included questions on its road system, the army's size, and where the Great King took up position in battle. Alexander 'was completely engrossed with the most vital concerns of the dominion' and eager to learn about the Persians.[2]

The Persian envoys were surprised by Alexander's questions. They expected the prince would ask them childish things about Persia's famed wealth or the Hanging Gardens of Babylon. Alexander proved that he was certainly not an average child. Valerius Maximus recounts how a boyhood Alexander suffered a burn from a piece of hot coal, but did not recoil from the pain. Maximus further remarks that had Persian King Darius seen the unflinching Alexander, he would not have challenged him. Perhaps the Persian ambassadors left with a similar feeling about the young prince.[3]

The encounter with the ambassadors was not the only opportunity for Alexander to meet Persians in his youth. Several Persian officials sought asylum at Philip's court. The deposed satrap Artabazos lived at Philip's court when Alexander was a child. In Macedonia, Artabazos lived with his brother-in-law Memnon and his daughter Barsine. It is not improbable that the curious Alexander would have engaged in conversation with these foreigners as he did with the Persian ambassadors.[4]

Alexander, as king, would become intimately connected with Artabazos, Memnon and Barsine. Artabazos would become a close advisor of King Darius, serving him during the war against Alexander. Following Darius' death, Artabazos would then join Alexander and serve as his satrap in Bactria. Memnon would play a leading role in the resistance to Alexander's invasion of Asia, proving to be one of his most formidable enemies. Finally, Barsine would fall captive to the Macedonians. She then became Alexander's first female lover and the mother of his son Heracles of Macedon.[5]

Another Persian at the court of Philip was the official Sisines. The satrap of Egypt had dispatched Sisines on a diplomatic mission to the Macedonian court. During his stay, Philip spoiled Sisines with gifts and praise, hoping to win him over. Philip's ploy was a success and Sisines chose to remain at court, switching his loyalty to Macedonia. He would stay at the Macedonian court into the reign of Alexander and accompany the king on his invasion of Asia.

Before the Battle of Issus, Sisines received a letter from the Persians. Darius' grand vizier Nabarzanes wrote to Sisines, testing his loyalty. Nabarzanes promised Sisines rewards if he betrayed Alexander and returned to Persian service. Despite the enticing benefits, Sisines remained loyal to Alexander and sought to give the king Nabarzanes' letter. However, Sisines, not wanting to interrupt the military preparations, delayed handing in the letter. Unfortunately for the Persian, Alexander already knew about the letter in advance and was suspicious of Sisines' loyalty. Alexander had Sisines executed before he had a chance to explain, bringing a tragic end to his tale.[6]

Alexander may have known the Parthian Amminapes growing up at court. Amminapes, like Artabazos, had fled from Ochus' wrath to go to the court of Philip. He later returned to Persian service, likely after Ochus' death. By the time of Alexander's invasion, he was serving as an official in Egypt. When Alexander's army entered Egypt, Amminapes quickly surrendered to the king. Alexander doubtless remembered Amminapes from his youth and rewarded him with a posting in his native Parthia.[7]

The Pixodarus Affair

In 337, a teenage Alexander became involved in the so-called 'Pixodarus Affair'. King Philip was interested in winning over the Hecatomnid rulers of Caria. The Carian royals controlled the vital port city of Halicarnassus and their support would greatly assist his plans in Asia. The Carians themselves had reason to entertain Philip's offers to achieve greater autonomy from the Persian king with Macedonian backing.

The Carians had just undergone a period of internal instability. Idrieus, the satrap of Caria, had died and was succeeded on the throne by his wife Ada. Ada was in turn swiftly deposed by her younger brother Pixodarus. Taking advantage of this change in power, Philip hatched a scheme to have Alexander's mentally disabled brother Arrhidaeus marry Pixodarus' daughter. This marriage would unite the Macedonian and Carian houses and help pave the way for the Macedonians' planned invasion of Asia.[8]

Alexander got word of this and misinterpreted it as a threat to his succession. He intervened, sending someone to negotiate a marriage between himself and the daughter of Pixodarus over his brother. Before Alexander could come to an agreement with the satrap, Philip confronted his son, forbidding him to marry a mere servant of the Persians. Alexander's interference seems to have derailed the whole negotiation process and neither he nor Arrhidaeus married the Carian princess.[9]

Aristotle

The philosopher Aristotle undoubtedly shaped Alexander's views on Persia. For five years, Aristotle served as a tutor for Alexander and his childhood companions. Together they would take long walks as Aristotle lectured the students about the world. Aristotle nurtured Alexander's intellectual nature, encouraging his interest in philosophy, medicine, biology and literature. For a time Alexander came to admire and love Aristotle even more than his father Philip.[10]

During his lessons, Aristotle taught Alexander about the East's geography. Aristotle believed that a great outer ocean existed at the edge of Asia beyond the Indian Caucasus (Hindu Kush) Mountains. This faulty geography might have impacted on Alexander's thinking during his Indian campaign. The Macedonian king imagined that he could reach this distant ocean when, in fact, none existed.[11]

According to Plutarch, Alexander received lessons on 'ethical and political doctrines' from Aristotle. Alexander learned to behave 'like a philosopher'. Aristotle likely passed on to Alexander the teachings on kingship found in his work *Politics*. Aristotle believed that for a monarchy to endure and gain the support of its subjects, it had to be limited in nature. The philosopher believed in a clear distinction between Greek freedom and supposed Eastern despotism.[12]

While in the East, Alexander seems to have had little difficulty in adapting to the habits of Eastern monarchies. Our ancient historians portray Alexander as forgetting that power corrupts. As Justin would put it, Alexander, by embracing the Persian ways, was 'being utterly unmindful that power is accustomed to be lost, not gained, by such practices'. Alexander did not come to adopt Aristotle's prejudice towards the Persians.[13]

Aristotle strongly believed that Greeks were superior to non-Greeks. In *Politics*, the philosopher speaks of how the 'barbarians' of the East, though intelligent, lacked 'spirit' compared to their Greek counterparts. In his opinion, Asian peoples such as the Persians should be slaves or serfs to the Greeks. Alexander did not take Aristotle's viewpoint to heart and instead found much to be admired in the Persians.[14] As Plutarch relates:

> For Alexander did not follow Aristotle's advice to treat the Greeks as if he were their leader, and other peoples as if he were their master; to have regard for the Greeks as for friends and kindred, but to conduct himself toward other peoples as though they were plants or animals, for to do so would have been to cumber his leadership with numerous battles and banishments and festering seditions.[15]

This impasse between Alexander and Aristotle would boil over years later. Aristotle's great-nephew Callisthenes accompanied Alexander on his campaigns as the official court historian. A disagreement would eventually break out between Callisthenes and the king over Alexander's adoption of the Persian submission ritual called proskynesis. Callisthenes was ultimately imprisoned for his supposed involvement in a plot to kill Alexander and he subsequently perished. The death of Callisthenes must have deepened the divide between Aristotle and Alexander. Incredibly, our sources mention Aristotle's possible involvement in Alexander's mysterious death. Allegedly Aristotle provided poison that was smuggled to Asia and then used to murder the king. The story is improbable, but represents the frayed relationship that existed between Aristotle and Alexander in the end.[16]

The Trojan War

Plutarch asserts that Alexander was 'by nature a lover of learning and a lover of reading'. The king was exceptionally knowledgeable about Greek literary works such as the 'tragedies of Euripides, Sophocles, and Aeschylus'. The piece of literature that did most to shape Alexander's views was Homer's *Iliad*. Alexander kept a unique copy of Homer's epic poem, compiled by Aristotle, under his pillow when he slept. He later placed his copy of the *Iliad* in a chest captured from the Persian Great King Darius. Alexander viewed the *Iliad* as beneficial to the study of warfare. He was known to have been able to quote from Homer's work at will.[17]

Before crossing his army into Asia, Alexander travelled to the town of Elaeus in the Hellespont. At Elaeus, he visited the grave attributed to the Greek hero Protesilaus, famous for being the first Greek killed during the Trojan War. Alexander, in a symbolic act, sacrificed to the Greek hero. The king hoped that the Macedonian army would have a safer crossing than Protesilaus.

When he crossed over the Hellespont into Asia, Alexander visited the supposed ruins of Troy. Alexander took relics from the ruins, including a 'sacred' shield that later saved his life in India. Together with his lover Hephaestion, Alexander visited the graves of Achilles and Patroclus. The trip concluded with a symbolic ritual in which Alexander and his comrades, crowned in garlands, ran a race naked. Alexander's visit to Troy served to inspire the king before his coming struggle for control of Asia.[18]

Achilles is a figure from whom Alexander took great inspiration. Comparisons between the two warriors are commonplace then and now. One of Alexander's childhood tutors flattered the young prince and his father by referring to Alexander as Achilles and Philip as Achilles' father Peleus. The maternal family of Alexander was even said to have descended from Achilles.

The strong connection between Alexander and Achilles has led to the two becoming almost synonymous with each other. This connection to Achilles has served to distort perceptions of Alexander, leading to the portrayal of him as something akin to a heroic warrior on an epic quest in search of glory. Seeing Alexander as simply the embodiment of Achilles diminishes his standing as a great strategist. While Alexander undeniably has a resemblance to Achilles, the two are not identical copies.[19]

The prince's admiration for Homer's King Agamemnon has garnered less attention from historians. According to Plutarch, Alexander's favourite line from the epic was 'Both things is he: both a goodly king and a warrior mighty.' Alexander believed that Homer, by these words, had 'honoured the manly courage of Agamemnon and prophesied that of Alexander'. The comparison between Alexander and Agamemnon is perhaps more fitting than that of Achilles. Alexander, like Agamemnon, led a Greek coalition to Asia; he was not merely a warrior on the battlefield but a great strategist.[20]

If Alexander indeed felt like he was undertaking his own Trojan War, it is not without analogies. The *Iliad* mentions many locations the king would encounter in Asia, such as Mount Ida where Zeus watched the fighting at Troy, and the Granicus River where Alexander would win his first victory over the Persians. It is even more ironic that Alexander's opponent in the opening stages of his Asian campaign was named Memnon. In the Trojan War, one of the legendary participants was Memnon, King of Ethiopia.[21]

According to the ancient Greek geographer Pausanias, King Memnon had set out to subdue those peoples East and returned from Susa to fight at Troy. Achilles engaged in a fierce battle with the great Ethiopian king and slew him. King Memnon's supposed tomb was located in the

Hellespont and was visited every year by the locals. As per Curtius, Alexander knew of Memnon's existence and had a 'longing' to explore his homeland of Ethiopia. Alexander would have to defeat his own Memnon in Asia, as had his 'ancestor' Achilles.[22]

According to Herodotus, the Persians viewed the Trojan War as the first great conflict between Europe and Asia. The Persians allege that the Greeks of Agamemnon's time were the first to invade Asia and thus were the initial aggressor. If the Trojan War is taken as the first great conflict between Europe and Asia, Alexander's campaign would be merely the latest in a long line of wars.[23]

Xenophon's *Cyropaedia* and *Anabasis*

Alexander, in his youth, probably gained much of his knowledge about Persia from the works of Xenophon. Xenophon's books *Cyropaedia* and *Anabasis* would have served as a valuable source for Alexander regarding Persia. Echoes of these two texts are visible in many of his actions as king. According to Arrian, before the Battle of Issus, Alexander alluded to Xenophon and his expedition against the Persians.[24] The story of Xenophon was a way of inspiring the Greeks to resist the Persians.

Xenophon's *Cyropaedia* is a semi-fictional biography of Cyrus the Great, founder of the Persian Empire. In the *Cyropaedia*, King Cyrus gives the impression of a noble philosopher-king who the reader should seek to emulate. Xenophon's Cyrus is courageous in battle, respects his conquered enemies, and is courteous to female prisoners. In a similar vein to Herodotus, Xenophon uses his account of Cyrus' life to demonstrate how the Persians of his day have fallen far since that king's era, becoming 'effeminate'. He attributes the deterioration of the Persian Empire to their own moral degradation. As Xenophon concludes at the end of the *Cyropaedia*:

> I think now that I have accomplished my task that I set before myself. For I maintain that I have proved that the Persians of the present day and those living in their dependencies are less reverent towards the gods, less dutiful to their relatives, less upright in their dealings with all men, and less brave in war than they were of old.[25]

When reading the *Cyropaedia*, one cannot help but notice several striking parallels between Cyrus and Alexander's actions. Cyrus went into battle in dashing attire with a white plume atop his helmet. Alexander also wore a helmet with a plume of 'wonderful size and whiteness'. After defeating Media, Cyrus adopted Median dress to appease the conquered and ordered his officials to wear it. After seizing the Asian throne, Alexander took a similar approach, adopting Persian dress and ordering his companions to wear it as well. When Cyrus entered Persis, he awarded gifts to the populace. Alexander would again repeat Cyrus' actions when he entered the territory.[26]

Even more significantly, Xenophon's Cyrus reflects Alexander's humane treatment of captive women. In the *Cyropaedia*, Cyrus captured Panthea, the wife of the Susian King Abradatas. Panthea was considered one of the most beautiful women of her time. Cyrus declined to gaze upon his captive and treated her courteously. Ultimately Cyrus used Panthea as a bargaining chip to get Abradatas to submit to his rule before reuniting husband and wife. This story has similarities to Alexander's favourable treatment of Darius' wife Stateira. After the queen's capture, Alexander allegedly refused to gaze upon her, not wanting to be tempted by her beauty. Some have speculated that Alexander may have employed a similar strategy to Cyrus by using Darius' wife to entice the Persian king to surrender.[27]

It is perhaps due to the *Cyropaedia* that Alexander developed a long-lasting admiration for King Cyrus. The ancient sources include numerous references pairing Alexander and Cyrus. After returning from India, Alexander had Cyrus' tomb restored and personally paid tribute to the king. Alexander sought to spare the city of Cyropolis due to its namesake. He honoured an Asian people known as the Euergetae because they had assisted Cyrus. Alexander's admiral Nearchus states that the king crossed the Gedrosian desert to outdo Cyrus, who failed in the attempt. The ancient sources were eager to draw comparisons between Cyrus and Alexander. Plutarch relates that Alexander 'possessed the high spirit of Cyrus'. The geographer Strabo attributed to Alexander the nickname 'Philo-Cyrus' ('Cyrus Lover'). According to Strabo, Alexander's title 'King of Asia' was even used by Cyrus, though perhaps written with the benefit of hindsight.[28]

Xenophon's work, the *Anabasis*, recounts his journey as one of the 'Ten Thousand', a group of Greek mercenaries in Asia. The Ten Thousand marched into Mesopotamia on behalf of Cyrus the Younger, not to be confused with his ancestor Cyrus the Great, in a fraternal war against his brother, the Persian King Artaxerxes II. Ultimately, Xenophon and his comrades fought against the Persians at the Battle of Cunaxa. Though the Greeks got the better of their foes, their patron Cyrus fell in the melee. The death of Cyrus left the Ten Thousand stranded, and they had to endure a harrowing march home through hostile territory.

The *Anabasis* included many details about the Persian Empire for Alexander to digest. In Xenophon's opinion, the weakness of the Persian state was in its great size. The empire's military forces spread out over a vast area. Thus it took a significant time for the empire to assemble a large army and Persian defences could be vulnerable to a quick thrust.[29] It is intriguing to speculate if Alexander planned his campaign with this idea in mind.

Xenophon's account of the engagement of Cunaxa would also have provided Alexander with a great deal of insight into Persian military capabilities. The *Anabasis* would have informed Alexander that the Persian Great King and his leading nobles traditionally took up a position in the centre of the Persian line. Xenophon describes the vast size of the Persian army with its infantry, cavalry and equipment. In particular, Xenophon describes the Persians' scythed chariots that Alexander himself would have to face at Gaugamela. Xenophon's account would have given Alexander a better picture of what he would later be facing in Asia.[30]

Alexander looks to have taken direct inspiration from Xenophon's patron Cyrus the Younger. The *Anabasis* presents Cyrus as a skilful and daring commander. The prince's style of warfare was to personally lead his men into battle against the enemy. At Cunaxa, Cyrus' boldness ended in misfortune when he died at the head of a cavalry charge aimed at the Persian king.[31] Charging the enemy leader was a favoured tactic used by Alexander at the battles of Issus and Gaugamela, fighting his way to King Darius. In these battles, he may have been mimicking Cyrus in his actions.

Alexander's court historian Callisthenes indeed recognized the similarities between Alexander and the younger Cyrus. The historian was keen to make connections between the two figures. Xenophon recounts a story in which the River Euphrates was diverted before Cyrus. The water was thus paying homage to the rightful king. As per Callisthenes, when

Alexander passed Mount Climax on the coast of southern Asia Minor, the water receded before him. Callisthenes made a direct comparison between the two men, thus furthering Alexander's legitimacy to rule Asia.[32]

Dionysius of Syracuse

According to Plutarch, Alexander read works by the Sicilian historian Philistos and the poet Philoxenus. Philistos and Philoxenus are both known to have served at the court of the tyrant Dionysius of Syracuse. Alexander is likely to have known the history of Dionysius' reign, and it's intriguing to speculate whether Alexander admired Dionysius in the same way he did Cyrus. Dionysius is known to history for having built up Syracuse's power and fought the Carthaginians. The Sicilian leader and Alexander were not without their similarities. Both men were great military leaders and could be overly fond of drink. Plutarch compares Alexander embracing godhood in Egypt as 'son of Ammon' with Dionysius, referring to himself as 'son of Apollo'.[33]

The connection between Dionysius and Alexander is fascinating because the Sicilian leader adopted Eastern ways as Alexander would later. In the vein of an Eastern monarch, Dionysius used a 'chariot drawn by four white horses'. The tyrant is also said to have worn 'the diadem, and the purple and all the rest of the royal apparel', imitating the Eastern model. The Greek rhetorician Athenaeus notes similarities between Dionysius' dress and the Eastern attire Alexander would later adopt: 'Dionysius, the tyrant of Sicily, adopted a theatrical robe and a golden tragic crown with a clasp. And Alexander, when he became master of Asia, also adopted the Persian dress.' Dionysius' example perhaps further served to encourage Alexander's embrace of Persian ways.[34]

Figures of Greek Myths

On numerous occasions in our sources, Alexander's actions in the East were allegedly motivated by the example of famed mythical heroes and gods. The extent to which these figures impacted on Alexander's moves has undoubtedly suffered from exaggeration. Nonetheless, they still played an intriguing role in Alexander's thinking and should not be overlooked.

Heracles was one such figure who Alexander idolized and constantly compared himself to. As with Achilles, Alexander claimed descent from the line of Heracles. Flatterers at Alexander's court would compare his exploits to those of Heracles. Heracles had legendarily travelled into the East, visiting places such as the Siwa oracle of Ammon in Egypt. Alexander would venture to Siwa in part due to Heracles' example. Later in India, Alexander came upon a fortified mountaintop called the Rock of Aornos, which Heracles had failed to capture according to local legends. Alexander took up the challenge and overcame its defences. Alexander would name his first-born son Heracles after the legendary hero.[35]

According to legend, the Greek god of wine Dionysus travelled to India. According to Arrian, the Greeks attributed the Indians' fondness for song and dance to Dionysus' visit. In embarking on his Indian expedition, Alexander had the story of Dionysus' journey on his mind. The king benevolently treated an Indian city called Nysa because of its claimed foundation by the god. Alexander was proud to have equalled Dionysus and travelled across the Indus. Following his departure from India, Alexander supposedly engaged in drunken revelry in honour of Dionysus and his exploits.[36]

Queen Semiramis was an important figure in Greek legends concerning the East. Alexander may have had an opportunity to learn about her from the works of the historians Ctesias and Herodotus. As per Greek histories, Semiramis was a bygone ruler of the famed city of Babylon. The Greeks attributed the city's awe-inspiring sights to her rule, as Diodorus refers to Semiramis as 'the most renowned of all women of whom we have any record'. In part, Alexander's decision to cross the Gedrosian may have been due to Semiramis' own failed crossing. The legend of Semiramis may also have impacted on Alexander's later decision to support female rulers in Asia, such as Ada of Caria. As Arrian notes, the view in Alexander's time was that women like Semiramis were destined to rule Asia.[37]

The Greek hero Perseus is another figure allegedly emulated by Alexander. Greeks considered the Persians to be descendants of Perseus' line. According to Herodotus, the Persians took their name from Perses, the son of Perseus. King Xerxes knew the Perseus legend and spoke of his alleged Perseid ancestry in communication with Argos. The Persian ruler likely thought the connection with Perseus would help him gain the favour of the Greeks. Alexander's interest in Perseus is understandable given his association with Persia.[38]

Alexander's youth was a formative period in the conqueror's life. The future king had opportunities to meet Persians and develop his views about the East from first-hand accounts. Aristotle laid the foundation for philosophical opinions, and his disagreements with the philosopher regarding Persians shaped his outlook. His reading of Greek literary works such as those of Homer and Xenophon left a lasting impression on the young prince. The legendary Greek heroes and gods provided Alexander with examples to emulate. Assessing Alexander's education provides us with a better understanding of his action in Asia while king.

Chapter Four

Prelude to the Conquest

Following the assassination of Philip in the autumn of 336 BC, Alexander found the responsibilities of kingship thrust upon him. The young monarch wished wholeheartedly to continue his father's war by crossing over into Asia. These plans would have to wait as Alexander became burdened by 'countless distractions and delays'. The opening of Alexander's reign would be a difficult period for the king as he found his new kingdom threatened from all sides.[1] Alexander had to eliminate potential rivals to the throne and crush rebellions throughout his father's empire. He had to deal with these internal issues before he could turn his attention back to Asia. In preparing for his Asian war, Alexander would continue the Pan-Hellenic propaganda of his father, calling for a united Greek war of vengeance against the Persian Empire. Alexander's true political and military aims are a much-debated subject. A study of his aims from the Persian perspective has yielded new interpretations.

Eliminating Rivals

Alexander moved quickly to secure his throne and deal with any potential threats on taking power. Philip's young children by his young wife Cleopatra presented an unmistakable danger, and Alexander's mother Olympias eliminated them. The son of Alexander's uncle, the previous King Perdiccas III, presented another threat. The Macedonian prince soon found himself accused of forming a treacherous plot against Alexander and was executed.[2]

The greatest potential danger to Alexander came from Attalus, the uncle of Cleopatra. Attalus had infamously insulted Alexander as being illegitimate, something the young king would not have forgotten. At the time of Alexander's accession, Attalus still held joint command, with Parmenion, of the army in Asia Minor. The general could prove formidable if he rallied the Asian army to his banner against Alexander.

A potential plot by Attalus looks to have been a real possibility as he was popular with the troops and was married to one of Parmenion's daughters. Any civil war could prove disastrous for Alexander's future plans in Asia.[3]

Alexander sent men to the Macedonian camp in Asia with instructions to capture or eliminate Attalus. Attalus, in the meantime, had entered into a conspiracy with the Athenian orator Demosthenes against Alexander. However, the general had a change of heart and sent Alexander Demosthenes' letters to prove his loyalty. Alexander was not dissuaded and allowed his assassins to proceed with their mission. Parmenion may have been privy to Attalus' murder and acquiesced, regardless of his marriage bond with the general. It may have been that Parmenion sought sole command of the army or simply that he was 'completely devoted to Alexander'.[4]

Philip's influential general Antipater presented another challenge for Alexander. According to Plutarch, Antipater had an ambitious nature – '(he) wears white clothes, but within he is all purple' – meaning that the general acted modestly, but wished to wear the purple of kingship. Antipater's daughter was also married to Alexander of Lyncestis, whose brothers king Alexander had executed for involvement in Philip's murder. Regardless of any bad blood between them, Alexander was able to win Antipater's loyalty. The king appeased the general by appointing him regent of Macedon in his absence, leaving him 12,000 infantry and 1,500 cavalry with which to hold the country. The appointment of Antipater proved a wise decision on Alexander's part. The regent successfully defended the kingdom and defeated the Spartans in the king's absence.[5]

Suppressing Rebellions

Philip's sudden death provided those he had conquered with an opportunity to reassert their independence. Alexander first made a foray south to snuff out any Greek attempts to challenge his hegemony. The Thessalians attempted to block Alexander's advance at the Vale of Tempe, but found themselves swiftly outmanoeuvred. With Alexander's arrival, the Greek states, including Athens, promptly gave in to Macedonia. More pressing concerns came in the north, where the Thracian and Illyrian tribes had risen in rebellion against Alexander. In the spring of 335, Alexander marched out against the tribes. Alexander's Balkan expedition would be the first significant campaign of his legendary military career. The king's experience had been limited to a minor campaign against the rebellious Maedi tribe and a not insignificant role in Philip's victory at Chaeronea.[6]

In opening his northern campaign, Alexander first marched against the Thracian Triballians. The king subdued them in a campaign that took his army to the River Danube. Alexander briefly crossed the Danube, conducting a punitive expedition against the Getae to shore up his kingdom's northern frontier. The king then turned his gaze to the Illyrians and, after a hard-fought action at Pelium, brought about their submission as well. Following these victories, Alexander had settled matters on the periphery of his kingdom and could turn his attention elsewhere.[7]

Plots in Greece were again brewing against Macedonian dominance. According to Plutarch, Persian gold 'flowed freely through the hands of the popular (anti-Macedonian) leaders everywhere'. Political exiles returned to their native cities to incite uprisings against Macedonia. Demosthenes, perhaps himself in Persian pay, attempted to rally the Greeks to resist Macedonia. The Athenian leader spread the rumour that Alexander had died fighting in the north against the Thracians. The greatest centre of resistance against Macedonia proved to be Thebes. The city was unhappy with its reduced status following their defeat at Chaeronea. Returning from his victorious campaigns against the tribes, Alexander marched upon Thebes. The king hoped to crush the disorder in Greece before it spread any further.[8]

However, Alexander had no interest in a long-drawn-out siege of Thebes and wished to compromise 'so that he might without disturbance pursue the war with Persia', but the Thebans refused to yield and the city had to be stormed by Alexander's army. The slaughter was great, with 6,000 Thebans killed and another 20,000 sold into slavery. Alexander then took the dramatic step of allowing the city's wholesale ruin. The primary justification given for the destruction of Thebes was their previous and apparent current support for Persia.[9]

In the fifth century, Thebes had allied itself with Xerxes' invading Persian army. The Thebans had been 'honoured as benefactors by the Persian kings'. Following the Persian war, the Greeks had even contemplated Thebes' annihilation for aiding Persia. Thebes' neighbours now wanted the city punished for their alliance with Persia. It did not help that a group of Thebans had shouted from the city's towers during the siege, asking men to join the Persian Great King in resisting the 'tyrant' Alexander. Alexander acquiesced to the demands of Thebes' neighbours for the city's destruction. The king's actions were hypocritical since Macedonia itself had previously submitted to Persia and assisted their efforts against Greece.[10]

In Plutarch's opinion, Alexander's true goal in destroying Thebes was to terrify the Greeks. Alexander's logic was that by razing Thebes, it would lessen the chance of the Greeks rebelling in the future. In theory, Alexander would be able to depart for Asia without fear of trouble in his rear. Alexander's scheme worked to an extent as the majority of the Greek states would affirm Alexander as their leader.[11] The Spartans, however, proved problematic and undeterred by Alexander's brutality at Thebes. They still refused to acknowledge Macedonian hegemony and would wage war against the kingdom in Alexander's absence.

Pan-Hellenic Propaganda

As espoused by his propagandists, the official reason for Alexander's Persian war was a Pan-Hellenic crusade of revenge. Alexander had inherited this Pan-Hellenic platform from Philip. Alexander, like his father, was said to have been influenced by the words of Isocrates. Alexander presented himself as the 'chosen avenger of Greece', destined to defeat Persia.[12] The goal was to punish the Persians for their aggression against Greece under King Xerxes and free the Greeks of Asia Minor. Alexander stated his official reasons for the war in a letter to King Darius:

> Your ancestors invaded Macedonia and the rest of Greece and did us much harm, though we had done none to them; I have been duly appointed Commander-in-Chief of the Greeks, and invaded Asia desiring to take vengeance on Persia.[13]

The Macedonians themselves were said to have been eager to follow Philip's vision and take up the war against Persia. The Macedonian soldiers 'set out, not more under his lead (Alexander's) than their own, to subjugate Asia'. Men from the Greek states joined Alexander with the hope of 'seeking satisfaction for the offences which the Persians had committed against Greece'. Before the Battle of Issus, Alexander encouraged his Greek soldiers, asking them to remember the crimes of the hated Persians:[14]

> Whenever he came to the Greek troops, he reminded them that it was by these nations that war had been made upon their country... their temples had been overthrown and burned, their cities stormed, and the obligations of human and divine law violated.[15]

At various times in his Asian war, Alexander attempted to demonstrate his commitment to Greece and the Pan-Hellenic agenda. After his victory at the Granicus River in 334, Alexander sent some 300 captured sets of armour back to Athens as spoils of war with the inscription 'Alexander son of Philip and the Greeks, save Lacedaemonians (Spartans), these spoils from the Persians in Asia.' According to Plutarch, Alexander sent these armour pieces out of a desire to 'make the Greeks partners in his victory'. He recovered the statues of Athenian heroes Harmodios and Aristogeiton taken by Xerxes, and sent them back to Athens. On one other occasion, Alexander insulted a fallen statue of Xerxes 'as if it had been alive'.[16]

Holding together a coalition of Macedonians and Greeks was no easy task for Alexander. Greek intellectuals looked upon the Macedonians as semi-barbaric and only partly Greek. Callisthenes, for example, would irritate the Macedonians at Alexander's court by pointing out their 'faults'. Alexander himself, on one occasion, remarked, 'Do not the Greeks appear to you to walk about among Macedonians like demi-gods among wild beasts?'[17] Macedonians always dominated Alexander's inner circle, but the king had several prominent Greek comrades such as his secretary Eumenes of Cardia and the admiral Nearchus.

An example of the Greco-Macedonian tension is the duel between the Athenian Olympian athlete Dioxippus and the Macedonian soldier Corrhagus. The Macedonian came splendidly dressed in full body armour, while his Athenian adversary showed up half-dressed with a club, resembling Heracles. The contest ended in a victory for the Athenian Dioxippus. The Macedonian Corrhagus would have been killed if not for the intervention of Alexander. Alexander was angered not only by the defeat of the Macedonian, but also because Asians had witnessed the bout. The duel made the Macedonians look weak in front of foreigners.

Not long after the embarrassing contest, Dioxippus, to Alexander's regret, committed suicide.[18]

One of the great Greek champions of Alexander's Pan-Hellenic efforts was Demaratus of Corinth who accompanied Alexander on his Eastern crusade. The Corinthian was in the thick of the fighting against the Persians at the Battle of the Granicus River. When Alexander's spear broke during the melee, Demaratus handed the king his own. Later, after Alexander captured Persepolis, Demaratus accompanied the king into the royal palace. Entering the imperial quarters, Alexander took a seat on the Persian throne. Demaratus then began to cry for the Greeks who did not live to see Alexander on the throne of Persia.[19]

Not all Greeks shared Demaratus' love for Alexander. In Plutarch's opinion, the Greeks may have had more reason to cry because the honour of sitting on the Persian throne was left to Alexander. Thousands of Greeks chose to serve in Persia against Alexander. In Alexander's eyes, these Greeks in Persian service were the worst kind of traitors. According to Arrian, Alexander justified acts of brutality against them because 'they, as Greeks, had infringed on an accord made in common by the Greeks by fighting for the barbarians against Greece.'[20]

At the Battle of Granicus, the Persians brought thousands of Greek mercenary infantry. These men were kept to the rear of the fighting and took no part in the main engagement. After routing the Persians, Alexander advanced upon the mercenaries. The latter asked for mercy, but Alexander bluntly refused. The Greeks were then surrounded by the Macedonians and massacred. Any survivors were put in irons and sent to serve as forced labourers in Macedonia. Alexander had sent a clear message as to what he thought of 'traitors'. At the subsequent battle near Issus, the Persian Greek mercenaries and the Macedonians again engaged in heavy fighting. According to Arrian, the two sides had a clear animosity, resulting in excessive losses.[21]

Greek ambassadors captured in Asia could find themselves subject to punishment by Alexander, who seized several Athenian ambassadors to the Persians. When Athens asked for their ambassadors' return, Alexander refused because he 'did not think it wise, with the Persian war still in progress, to relax any terrors for the Greeks who had actually fought with foreigners against Greece'. It was only later when the Persian threat had passed that Alexander allowed the Athenians to depart. However, he did make exceptions for those Greeks who were still subject to the Persian king. Ambassadors from Sinope, a city in northern Asia Minor, were allowed to go free because they had not joined his Hellenic alliance. In Alexander's mind, the Sinope ambassadors had done nothing wrong by sending emissaries to their sovereign Darius.[22]

Rules of War

It is important to gain an understanding of the rules of war as Alexander understood them. For a summary of the ancient rules of warfare, we can turn to Xenophon's *Cyropaedia*. Cyrus stated that when an army conquers a city

> ...it is a law established that for all time among all men that when a city is taken in war, the persons and property of the inhabitants thereof belong to the captors; it will, therefore, be no injustice for you to keep what you have, but if you let them keep anything, it will be only out of generosity that you do not take it away.[23]

Cyrus does not mention if killing the city's population was to be permitted. However, since everything in the city belonged to the victor, it was probably up to him.

Alexander effectively kept to Cyrus' standard during his Asian war. When he captured a city by storm, his soldiers plundered its treasures. Alexander could also order the adult male population massacred while enslaving the women and children. On other occasions, as was his preference, Alexander could spare certain citizens. For example, when he captured Miletus, he enslaved the populace but not those who held out olive branches. On another occasion, when he stormed Halicarnassus, Alexander spared those who remained in their homes.[24]

By modern standards, Alexander's actions on many occasions would be considered monstrous. However, by the standards of the ancient world, Alexander looks to have conformed to typical practice. This is especially true if we judge Alexander by Persian standards to which he was trying to conform. We must remember that Ochus had no issue with massacring 40,000 people at Sidon. All the Persian kings would not have hesitated to massacre cities that resisted their rule or rebellious populations.[25]

Political-Military Aims

Alexander's political and military aims in Asia have always been a topic of great debate. In Plutarch's fanciful recounting, Alexander 'scarcely older than a boy, had the daring to hope for Babylon and Susa; nay more, to conceive the project of dominion over all the world'. The traditional viewpoint of Alexander's aims is that he had no long-term strategic objectives. By this interpretation, Alexander simply took up Philip's war in Asia without much thought for the long game. The king, guided by events, expanded his aims to the entire Persian Empire and the world itself.[26]

This interpretation of Alexander's aims, however, denies his skill as a planner and strategist. Recent scholarship, looking at Alexander's policies from the Persian perspective, has challenged this classic viewpoint of Alexander's aims. It is more probable that Alexander, rather than mimicking Philip's limited war, had his own long-term plans. When Alexander set out for Asia, he may have always intended to conquer the entire Persian Empire and carve out a kingdom from Macedonia to the River Indus in India.

From the opening of his expedition to Asia, Alexander attempted to present himself as a viable alternative to Darius. The king was clearly familiar with the Achaemenid ruling system and knew how to play by its rules. The same tribute given to the Persian king, Alexander required to be sent to him. Alexander minted his own coins just as the Achaemenid kings had before his arrival and may have employed the same men. He labelled Darius as an illegitimate ruler for his relationship with Bagoas to further his claim to the lordship of Asia. At the same time, Alexander sought to ingratiate himself with local hierarchies to wean them away from supporting Darius. Alexander's pro-Persian policies and his imitation of the Achaemenid kings did not simply emerge with the death of Darius but had existed all along.[27]

It is also essential to emphasize that Alexander's objectives were likely more limited than is usually surmised. He demonstrated that contrary to being an aimless world conqueror, he had clear ideas about fixed borders throughout his campaigns. During his march through the Persian Empire, he stuck close to the established Persian road system. In Central Asia, he delineated a clear border at the River Jaxartes and built the city of

Alexandria Eschate. His invasion of India was perhaps merely an attempt to retake the provinces held by Darius the Great and shore up his Eastern borders. Alexander may not have been on a quest for the outer ocean or trying to conquer the entire subcontinent.[28]

The question arises of how much Alexander's soldiers knew of his plans in Asia. The answer is likely to have been very little. The Macedonians were merely fed the king's propaganda about a Pan-Hellenic war. After Persepolis was burned and Darius killed, the soldiers all expected to be heading home. From their perspective, the war of revenge was over and they had no interest in staying in Asia. On the other hand, Alexander had every intention of continuing until he subdued the entire Persian Empire. The most critical impasse between the two conflicting visions came after Darius' death; Alexander had to rally the men to continue the campaign. The excuse he used was that Darius' claimed successor Bessus would retake Asia and again threaten Greece. Alexander could not have told his soldiers from the beginning of his intention to go to India; instead, he had to draw them along slowly with new justifications.[29]

On taking power, Alexander faced numerous political and military challenges. These threats Alexander dealt with swiftly, crushing opposition at home and in his empire, before turning his attention back to Persia. Alexander's propaganda helped to justify his invasion as a Pan-Hellenic war of vengeance. The king's true aims in Asia, however, may have been very different. Rather than a short campaign of revenge, the Macedonian ruler may have sought to conquer the entirety of the Persian Empire. Alexander's goal would ultimately lead him into Central Asia and India in an attempt to establish secure borders for his Asian kingdom.

Chapter Five

Alexander Against Darius

In the words of Curtius, the war between Alexander's Macedonia and Darius' Persia was a contest between 'the most powerful kings of Europe and Asia in the hope of gaining control of the whole world'. Alexander sought to claim Asia by right of conquest and would not break from that objective. King Darius would either have to crush Alexander's army or submit before his rule. As Justin writes, 'the universe could not be governed by two suns, nor could the earth with safety have two sovereigns.' Alexander's victories at Granicus, Issus and Gaugamela destroyed the empire of Cyrus and ended Persia's three-century-long domination of the region.[1]

Spear-Won Land

In the spring of 334 BC, Alexander set out for the Hellespont, the great crossing-point into Asia. The king would finally be able to undertake his long-desired campaign. Alexander accompanied the lead ship of his fleet and was the first to disembark on Asian soil. In dramatic fashion, he flung his spear ashore, signifying his claim to Asia as a 'spear-won prize'.[2]

The size of Alexander's army is not entirely clear from the sources as our accounts provide varying numbers. The estimate of 43,000 infantry and 5,500 cavalry looks reasonable. This total would account for Alexander's field army augmented with Parmenion's expeditionary force already in Asia. Although this army may seem small for the task ahead of them, it was a highly capable force with many veterans of Philip's wars. Alexander would also have the aid of Philip's great general Parmenion, who would serve as the king's second-in-command.[3]

One of Alexander's greatest worries at this point was logistical. The kingdom was in debt, and Alexander only had the resources to supply his army for thirty days. This lack of supplies presented a danger that his expedition would dissolve just as it was getting started. Compare this to Spartan King Agesilaus II, who had gathered six months' worth of supplies before invading Asia. Alexander would need to settle the initial campaign quickly with a decisive battle. Fortunately for him, the Persian leadership would oblige him with the battle he sought.[4]

While Alexander was symbolically laying claim to Asia, the Persian leadership had yet to act against him. The Persian navy did not attempt to prevent his crossing at the Hellespont. Additionally, no Persian forces took up position to skirmish with Alexander as he advanced. Instead of directly countering Alexander, the Persians were holding a war council at the town of Zeleia. Many leading nobles were present at the meeting, including Spithridates, satrap of Lydia and Ionia, and Arsites, satrap of Hellespontine Phrygia. Arsites was the same man who had repelled King Philip at Perinthus. Memnon of Rhodes, as commander of the coastal regions, was also in attendance. The assembled Persian leaders resolved to seek battle with Alexander but Memnon advised just the reverse.[5]

Perhaps drawing upon his previous experience of fighting the Macedonians, the Rhodian did not think it wise to fight a decisive battle with Alexander. Memnon thought the army should wait for word from King Darius, 'for the sake of the office he held from the king.' He further recommended a strategic withdrawal and scorched earth campaign. According to Memnon's plan, the Persians would have to burn their foodstuffs and towns. Memnon thought this would deny Alexander anything of value and starve his army. The Rhodian's plan may have worked due to Alexander's poor supply situation. Alexander might give up the campaign and withdraw from Asia. This style of indirect warfare by the Persians was not unique to Memnon. Xenophon in the *Anabasis* reports how the Persians burned their territory to stall Cyrus the Younger's army. The Persians would employ it twice in the future against Alexander in Cilicia and Mesopotamia.[6]

Memnon's plan, though well-conceived, did not meet with the approval of the Persian leadership. From the perspective of the Persian satraps, why should they destroy their territory and run away? They were presented with an opportunity to gain glory and may even be able to kill Alexander. Arsites was said to have been the most outraged at the idea as it was his territory Memnon meant to burn. The Persian satrap declared that he would not allow one house burned in his province. Arsites, having already defeated the Macedonians once before, probably underestimated their fighting ability.[7]

As per our sources, the Persians were highly suspicious of Memnon's motives due to him being Greek. They may have believed he would switch sides and join Alexander. The fact that Memnon spent time in exile at Philip's court would not have helped. Other political reasons could also explain the tension. Arsites' dislike of Memnon could have been due to the Rhodian's kinship with Artabazos. Artabazos was Arsites predecessor as satrap, and perhaps rivalry existed between the two nobles.[8] Regardless, Arsites' position carried the day and the Persians prepared to confront the invaders in battle.

The absence of King Darius at this critical stage presented some difficulties. Had Darius been present, he might have been more willing to listen to Memnon's opinion as Artabazos was his closest confidant. Traditionally the Persian king was content to leave matters in the hands of the local satraps at this stage. The Persians had successfully contained Greek invaders in the past, most recently with Parmenion and Attalus. Darius may have expected the Hellenic invaders to be repulsed or, in a worst-case scenario, liberate some Greek coastal cities of Asia Minor before withdrawing.

It is worth noting that Justin's reconstruction of events differs from our other sources. Justin gives Darius a more significant role in the campaign and directing its strategy. In his account, rather than ordering the repulse of Alexander's army on the coast, Darius wanted to draw him inland for a decisive battle. Darius thought he could annihilate Alexander's army if it could be drawn deeper into Persian territory. Justin's account could explain the initial absence of Persian forces at the Hellespont and the massing of the army at Granicus. This alternative reconstruction would explain why the satraps were unwilling to diverge from Darius's prearranged plan, despite Memnon's idea.[9]

The Battle of the Granicus

The Persian army assembled on the Granicus River, a location Plutarch referred to as the 'gates of Asia'. Taking up a position on this river line blocked Alexander's advance along the coast road. The presence of the Persian army prevented Alexander from marching directly upon

Dascylium, capital of Hellespontine Phrygia, and Cyzicus, an allied city that Memnon had recently attacked. The size of the force awaiting Alexander varies by source. The most convincing estimates given in our sources are 10,000 Persian cavalry and 20,000 Greek mercenaries. The Persians may have actually found themselves at a numerical disadvantage. Nonetheless, the Persian leadership's bold choice to amass on the Granicus gave them a real opportunity to blunt the Macedonian invasion and perhaps kill Alexander.[10]

As the Persians expected, Alexander advanced along the coastal route, arriving before the Granicus in May 334. He was eager to bring on a decisive battle and destroy the satrapal army. However, the king faced some opposition to commencing the battle immediately. The soldiers worried because it was the month of Daesius during which Macedonian kings were not supposed to fight. Alexander got around these objections by having the men pretend it was a different month.[11]

Parmenion also advised against an immediate engagement after viewing the Persian position. The Persian army looked formidable and the river banks a dangerous obstacle. Parmenion worried that the Macedonians would be crushed as they crossed in a narrow column. He recommended that the army should encamp for the night. In Parmenion's opinion, at dawn they would be able to cross swiftly, deploy for battle and take the Persians unawares. Parmenion's plan at face value may have seemed prudent advice, but stealthily crossing the river may have been unfeasible.[12]

Alexander declined Parmenion's plan and advanced the army to battle. The Macedonian king did not want to risk losing the advantages he now possessed. Having just crossed the Hellespont, Alexander held the initiative with his army in high spirits and ready for a battle. Had Alexander halted before what he called a 'little stream', he thought it would damage his reputation. The Persians, meanwhile, might take courage from seeing the Macedonians balk at their defences. The issue of morale seems to be the most critical factor on Alexander's mind when he rejected Parmenion's counsel.[13]

The battle commenced as the Macedonians advanced into the river. The action centred on the Macedonian right wing, where Alexander and his cavalry engaged the Persian elite. Arrian remarks, 'though the battle was fought on horseback, it looked more like an infantry engagement.'

The action was fierce, with Alexander personally engaged in the fighting. The king was clearly visible to friend and foe with his Cyrus-esque white plume.[14]

The satrap Spithridates spotted Alexander in the melee. He saw an opportunity to kill Alexander and charged the king. The satrap might have succeeded in his aim if not for the intervention of Alexander's comrade Cleitus. Spithridates lost his arm just before bringing down a potentially fatal blow on the king. The river battle would turn in favour of the Macedonians as the Persian cavalry fled in disorder. Alexander then turned his attention to the Greek mercenaries whom he enveloped and destroyed.[15]

The battle's result was a stunning victory for Alexander. Macedonian casualties were light, with the highest estimate being 129 soldiers. The Persian losses were far more severe: some 2,000 of their horsemen and thousands of Greek mercenaries were captured or killed. Many of the leading Persian commanders lay dead on the field, including Spithridates and even royal family members. Arsites survived the battle and escaped capture only to commit suicide for his failure. The battle effectively eliminated the Persian satrapal leadership in western Asia Minor.[16]

The Conquest of Asia Minor

In the aftermath of the victory at Granicus, Alexander would spend the next year subduing Asia Minor. Following up on his victory over the satrapal army, he proceeded against Sardis. Perhaps Alexander remembered from Xenophon that the city had been Cyrus the Younger's 'paradise' known for its beautiful parks. The city's Persian commander Mithrenes betrayed the city to Alexander. Mithrenes' defection was significant as he would be the first Persian commander to join Alexander's cause. Keeping the Persian system of governance intact, Alexander demanded the same tribute that the populace had given to Darius. He also appointed his comrade Calas as the satrap of Hellespontine Phrygia. Calas would be the first of many satraps appointed by Alexander in Asia. The choice of Calas was a good one as he had served in Asia with Parmenion's expedition and likely knew the region well.[17]

As the Macedonian advance continued, the city of Ephesus promptly surrendered, welcoming the Macedonians. The Persian forces that remained in the region after Granicus regrouped in the coastal cities of Miletus and Halicarnassus. Parmenion, at this stage in the campaign, recommended Alexander to challenge the Persian fleet in battle. Alexander's second-in-command evidently thought it prudent to eliminate this threat. The Macedonian ruler rejected this as the risks entailed combating the larger fleet. Astonishingly, Alexander decided to disband his fleet altogether, believing that against Darius they would fight harder, knowing they had no easy escape home. Another reason on the king's mind may have been his lack of funds.[18]

On the Persian side, the issue of command now came to the forefront again with Spithridates and Arsites dead. Memnon had survived the battle and now looked to gain supreme authority in the region. The Rhodian general sent his family to the Persian king to serve as hostages and demonstrate his goodwill. Darius responded in kind, giving Memnon supreme command over 'those who dwelt next to the sea' as in the coastal territories of Asia Minor. He notably directed the local Persian commanders to obey Memnon's orders.[19] Had Memnon been given this authority earlier, the campaign may have turned out quite differently.

Departing Ephesus, Alexander marched upon Miletus. The populace attempted to persuade Alexander of their neutrality. They asked for an agreement in which both Macedonians and Persians would have equal access to the harbour. Alexander declined the Milesians' offer and took the city by siege. The Macedonians also drove the Persian fleet from its base at nearby Mycale.[20] From Miletus, Alexander marched southward, 'capturing, on the first attempt, all the cities that lay between Miletus and Halicarnassus'. He made a critical alliance with the deposed Carian Queen Ada to bolster his efforts in the territory. Alexander put the Carian capital of Halicarnassus under siege. The Persian garrison at Halicarnassus proved to be a more significant challenge for Alexander than those who held Miletus. Memnon directed the defence of Halicarnassus personally.[21]

The defenders fiercely resisted attempts to take the city. They would only abandon hope after a portion of the wall collapsed and attempts to destroy Alexander's siege equipment failed. Memnon ordered the garrison to evacuate the city, setting it on fire before withdrawing to Halicarnassus' citadel. The citadel was well fortified and would require further efforts to capture. Alexander, not wanting to be tied down, departed, leaving a contingent to continue the siege.[22]

Following the evacuation of Halicarnassus, Memnon would continue resistance in the region against Alexander. The Persians still controlled the seas and Memnon planned to use this to his advantage. He hoped to outmanoeuvre Alexander by taking the war into Greece and linking up with his Spartan allies. This manoeuvre could, in turn, entice the other Greek states to rebel against Macedonia. However, Memnon's untimely death from disease stifled these promising plans. He was succeeded in command by Pharnabazus, a son of Artabazos. The death of Memnon proved to be a critical blow to Darius as the new commander would not pursue the war with the same vigour as the Rhodian.[23]

According to Plutarch, after reducing Miletus and Halicarnassus, Alexander faced a strategic crossroads. He could either quickly advance through Asia Minor and seek a decisive battle with Darius, or he could subdue the coast of southern Asia Minor. Ultimately, Alexander chose to finish conquering the coastal regions of Lycia, Pisidia and Pamphylia before confronting Darius, this the more prudent option. Part of Alexander's strategic thinking was that by clearing the coastline, he could 'render useless the enemy's navy' by taking its supply points. This strategy of taking the bases of the Persian fleet is something he would repeat later in Phoenicia.[24]

Also during this period, Darius may have sponsored a plot against Alexander. The conspiracy hinged on Alexander of Lyncestis, commander of the Thessalian cavalry. King Alexander had executed his brothers for supposed involvement in the murder of Philip. He would have suffered a similar fate had he not been Antipater's son-in-law and prudently pledged his allegiance to Alexander before any other man. The Lyncestian had accompanied King Alexander to Asia as one of his companions. After Calas, commander of the Thessalian cavalry, became a satrap, the Lyncestian took command of the Thessalians. The Thessalians were the army's most powerful cavalry unit beside Alexander's Companions and could have posed a significant threat should they rebel. The Lyncestian, however, was quickly arrested before he had chance to act.[25]

Returning to the campaign in Asia Minor, Alexander, having cleared up the coastal regions, resolved to march north into Phrygia. Arriving before the Phrygian capital of Celaenae, Alexander again faced the potential of a long-drawn-out siege. The citadel of the city was supposedly 'impregnable' to attack. Fortuitously for the Macedonians, the city's garrison was amenable to terms. They agreed to surrender the city if no Persian aid proved to be forthcoming. Alexander left behind at Celaenae a force of 1,500 men under the command of Antigonus Monophthalmus (the One-Eyed) to oversee the surrender.[26]

Antigonus was a formidable commander and a veteran of Philip's wars. He was famous for having lost his eye in combat, and also for his giant stature. Alexander needed a capable figure like Antigonus to hold Phrygia and protect his supply lines in Asia Minor. With Antigonus in his rear, Alexander could feel confident about departing Asia Minor to confront Darius. Antigonus would prove himself up to the task of securing the region.[27]

The Battle of Issus

In the summer of 333, Alexander continued his advance onward into Cilicia. The king arrived before the pass through the Tarsus Mountains known as the Cilician Gates. The Persian garrison fled as the Macedonian army approached, giving up the critical position. Getting through the gates, Alexander advanced onto the open plain. After foiling an attempt by the local Persian satrap to burn the city, the Macedonians occupied the vital centre of Tarsus. Alexander's entrance into Tarsus holds particular significance. In Tarsus, Alexander captured the Persian mint and began to strike his own imperial coins for the first time in Asia. These coins were like those minted under Darius and Alexander may have employed the very same men.[28]

Shortly thereafter, Alexander came down with a sudden illness after swimming in a river that left him paralyzed. He was treated during his illness by Philip of Acarnania. Supposedly another Persian plot against the king emerged. Parmenion had received intelligence that the Persians were attempting to win over Alexander's doctor. The Persians had promised the Acarnanian wealth and marriage to Darius' sister if he poisoned Alexander. Surprisingly, Alexander did not act on the information as he trusted Philip. The king proceeded to drink the medicine his doctor provided, confirming him not to be a traitor.[29]

This story sounds very similar to Persian plots centring on Alexander the Lyncestian and Sisines. If we take these plots as genuine, the Persians look to have gone to great lengths to try to infiltrate Alexander's entourage to eliminate the king. For Alexander, blaming the Persians for the assassination attempts was yet another way to delegitimize the king. Alexander would later accuse Darius of plotting his death: 'He now with letters tempts my soldiers to betray me, and now with money bribes my friends to kill me, I must pursue him to destruction, not as a legitimate enemy, but as an assassin who resorts to poison.'[30]

As Alexander penetrated further into the empire, King Darius assembled the Persian army at Babylon. The Great King was now determined to take the field in person and destroy the invader. Darius called a war council with his leading nobles and Greek mercenary leaders to decide upon a plan of action. According to Diodorus, a Greek officer Charidemus advised the king not to 'stake his throne rashly on a gamble' by leading the army in person. This idea had merit, as if Darius himself were to be defeated it would certainly hurt his legitimacy and raise the stature of Alexander. Charidemus instead proposed that Darius should give him a portion of the army to go and fight the Macedonians.[31]

In an alternative version provided by Arrian, a different man named Amyntas also advised Darius not to advance against Alexander. Amyntas thought that the Persian army should remain in Mesopotamia instead of moving into the mountainous coastal region. The army could then take up a position on a plain of their choosing and destroy Alexander in the open. Amyntas' strategy also had potential as it allowed the Persian army's superior numbers to come into play.[32]

While Darius seemed receptive to the plans of his Hellenic advisors, members of his ruling circle were not. Similar to the situation faced by Memnon, Charidemus was distrusted and accused of treason by the Persian nobles. Unwisely, Charidemus responded by insulting the Persians' 'lack of manliness'. This Darius could not approve of and had Charidemus executed for insulting his comrades. It's worth noting that we should be sceptical of this account as it may be simply another attempt by our sources to demonstrate Greek intellectual superiority.[33]

Regardless of what occurred in council, Darius now looked fully determined to put aside any potential risks and personally lead the army against Alexander. He may have been further encouraged by the news of Alexander's recent illness. The Persian ruler also had to keep in mind the difficulties in supplying his large army. Winter was fast approaching, and the army had devastated the territory for food supplies. If Alexander did not advance against him, Darius would have to take the fight to Alexander.[34]

All our ancient sources place Darius' army's numbers in the hundreds of thousands. The lowest tally is 62,000 cavalry and the infantry 250,000, of which some 30,000 were Greek mercenaries. These numbers can be dismissed as exaggeration by the ancients; no doubt an attempt to make the Persian army seem like a massive horde. Regardless of its apparent size, the terrain did much to negate the Persian numerical advantage as only so many men could fit in the battle line. The Persians would find themselves facing Alexander on roughly equal terms in the confined space.[35]

Darius embarked on the campaign with all the symbols of Persian power. To the sound of trumpets, the army assembled after sunrise. In the first line of march was carried the eternal fire accompanied by the Magi priests singing hymns. The priests were followed by 365 men in 'scarlet cloaks', the royal cavalry, the 10,000 Immortals and 15,000 of Darius' 'kinsmen'. The king himself rode atop his chariot with horses of great size and was illustriously dressed, wearing the upright headdress. At the end of the column came Darius' family with numerous eunuchs, concubines and servants. It must have been a magnificent sight to behold.[36]

According to Curtius, it was 'Persian custom' to take along his family. Xenophon also reports a similar custom among Eastern kings. The royal family's presence, particularly the king's wife and daughters, gave the soldiers confidence in victory. The ordinary people held great respect for the Persian queens and princesses. Even a glimpse of them through the carriage curtains was considered a great honour. As Plutarch, in his life of Artaxerxes II, writes 'But what gratified the Persians most of all was the sight of his (Artaxerxes II's) wife Stateira's carriage, which always appeared with its curtains up, and thus permitted the women of the people to approach and greet the queen.'[37]

Alexander, meanwhile, had recovered from his illness and launched a short campaign, subduing the tribes of Cilicia. He then moved his army down the Mediterranean coastline. By the time Alexander reached the pass that led to Syria, Darius was entering Cilicia. Darius now found himself in the favourable position of being in the rear of Alexander's army. The Persian ruler could now move to interdict Alexander's line of supply and force a battle.[38]

Moving into the city of Issus, Darius found those Macedonian soldiers too ill or crippled to advance. Alexander had left them behind, thinking they would be safe. Darius allegedly tortured the Macedonians, cutting off their hands. The Persian king then had the Macedonian prisoners paraded around to witness the size of the Persian host before being sent back to Alexander. Darius may have hoped this brutality would strike fear into the Macedonians. On the other hand, this story may merely be a literary invention to demonize the Persians.[39]

In November 333 the two armies would meet in the Battle of Issus on the Pinarus River. Parmenion remarked that 'no other place was more suitable for a battle' as the terrain was narrow between the mountains and the sea. Darius' plan of battle was to attack with a mass of cavalry on his right wing along the coast to smash the Macedonians. The Persian infantry and Greek mercenaries would hold the centre against the Macedonian sarissa phalanx. Darius also deployed infantry adjacent to Alexander's right wing, hoping to outflank the Macedonians. Alexander realized Darius' plan and had his left wing reinforced with the Thessalian cavalry. The Macedonian ruler's plan was for his left to hold while he drove towards Darius himself.[40]

The battle was a hard-fought affair, and the Persians may have managed to break the Macedonian left if not for the intervention of the Thessalians. In the centre, the Persian Greek mercenaries anchored on the river held against the Macedonian phalanx for some time. Alexander's right-wing attack decided the battle, smashing the opposing Persian wing and outflanking the Persian centre. Alexander pushed at the Persian king himself, hoping to end the war in one swoop. Darius' brother Oxyathres and the royal guards put up a desperate struggle to defend the Great King.[41]

Darius was in the epicentre of the fighting, clearly visible atop his chariot. Numerous Persian nobles were 'slain by a noble death before the eyes of their king', not having turned and run but suffering 'wounds in front'. Plutarch reports that according to one version, Darius himself wounded Alexander in the thigh during the melee. Though highly suspect, this suggests the close proximity of Alexander and Darius in the fighting. Darius' horses became wounded in the melee, and his royal chariot began to swerve uncontrollably. The Persian king believed his capture to be imminent and fled the battle. He abandoned his chariot and mounted a horse that was on hand for such a contingency. Darius removed his marks of royalty, such as his cloak and shield, to assist his escape.[42]

Darius' inglorious flight may give the impression that the Persian king was a coward. The Great King's retreat further served to reinforce Greek stereotypes of Eastern effeminacy on the battlefield. When one looks at the situation objectively, the reasons for Darius' flight are clear. If the Great King were to be captured or killed, Persian efforts would collapse. On the other hand, if the Persian king could make a getaway, he would be able to raise a new army to resist Alexander. Darius was known to have fought enemies in single combat and was certainly no coward.[43]

With Darius' flight, the Persian army began to disintegrate. The Persians were 'driven like sheep' by the Macedonians and took flight in all directions. Alexander would pursue Darius until nightfall before giving up the chase. The king then entered the Persian camp and secured Darius' family as his prisoners. The highest estimate of Macedonian casualities numbers only 450 men. Like Granicus, the battle near Issus came at a far greater cost for the Persians. Diodorus puts the Persian dead at 110,000; an overstatement, but it reflects the extreme bloodshed.[44]

While Alexander captured Darius' family, Parmenion marched on Damascus. Before the engagement at Issus, the Persian elite had sent their families and valuables to Damascus for safety. Additionally, the Greek foreign ambassadors were staying in the city. En route to the city, the governor of Damascus sent a message to Parmenion offering his surrender. Parmenion was sceptical of such a proposition, sensing a trap. However, the governor was truthful and would not attempt to hold the city despite its considerable defences. He took the almost unbelievable step of scattering the treasures across the plain and getting the noble families to flee on foot. The governor departed only to be murdered by one of his officers, obviously disgusted by the display. Parmenion moved in, captured the treasury, and rounded up the noble prisoners.[45]

Curtius writes that 'hardly any house of a member of the court escaped the disaster' at Damascus. Among the prisoners taken by Parmenion were the wife and daughters of King Ochus, the daughter of Darius' brother Oxyathres, the wife, son and daughter of Artabazos, the wife of Pharnabazus, three daughters of Mentor and a son of Memnon. Securing these important prisoners was crucial to Alexander's objectives. These captured nobles would serve as hostages to give Alexander increased leverage. It is perhaps unsurprising that these three families would eventually join Alexander as his allies.[46]

For Alexander, the most important prisoner of the group was Artabazos' daughter Barsine. Barsine was Greek through her mother, the sister of Memnon, and Persian royalty through her father. Barsine was a great 'beauty' with a 'gentle disposition'. Alexander began an affair with her soon after, something Parmenion is said to have encouraged. Together they would have a son named Heracles. When he came of age Heracles, with the help of Barsine, would make his own play for the throne. Tragically the prince and his mother would be betrayed by their ally Polyperchon and murdered.[47]

Parmenion understood the importance of his mission at Damascus. The general looks to have gone to great lengths to keep hold of his prizes. If Polyaenus is accurate, Parmenion does not seem to have taken many Macedonians with him. He had to rely on 'barbarians' to guard the booty. The Macedonian general was afraid that these soldiers could abandon their post at any time. He came up with an unorthodox solution to the issue. He had horses distributed to every man and then declared the death penalty for anyone who didn't hold on to their horse. The fearful soldiers held the horses tight and, by extension, continued their guard duty.[48]

Alexander and Darius: Negotiations

After his dramatic escape, Darius returned to Babylon with the remnants of his army. The Persian king now sought to assemble another army to defeat the invader and called up soldiers from the upper satrapies. At the same time, Darius opened negotiations with Alexander by dispatching letters and envoys. As noted previously, Alexander had both Darius' family and numerous other noble prisoners to use as bargaining chips. The Persian king's most fervent wish was to recover his family from captivity.

Darius proposed to give Alexander a hefty ransom of some 30,000 talents for the return of his family. Further, the Persian king offered a peace deal in which Alexander would marry his daughter, become his ally, and gain the western half of the Persian Empire. Darius advised Alexander to accept his offer quickly. The Persian king lamented how the fortunes of war changed quickly, attributing his defeat to the narrow terrain, which he assured Alexander would not happen again.[49]

Having received Darius' terms, Alexander presented the matter before his companions. Parmenion advised that if he were in Alexander's place, he would accept the favourable terms. Alexander famously replied that he would accept the terms 'were I Parmenion', but he could not since he was Alexander.[50] Alexander rejected Darius' offers and brazenly stated in his response message that

> he needed no money from Dareius [*sic*], nor to receive a part of the country in place of the whole; for all the country and all the treasures were already his; if he chose to marry Dareius' daughter, he would marry her, even if Dareius did not give her.

Alexander gave the Persian ruler an ultimatum that he either surrender to him or be prepared to fight for his kingdom. He attributed his victory at Issus to the favour of the gods and now referred to himself as the ruler of Asia. This declaration was a precursor to Alexander later taking the title 'King of Asia'. The king was openly presenting himself as a rival of Darius for the throne of Asia.[51]

Many have speculated that Alexander's father Philip would have been content with the western half of the empire and agreed to the terms. Accepting the terms would have had its advantages for Alexander. The treaty would have prevented Alexander's empire from becoming overextended and leave him to focus his attention on building an empire in the eastern Mediterranean region. He could have then proceeded with his colonial efforts, building numerous Greek cities in the conquered lands. The region of northern Syria would prove uniquely suitable for development, something Alexander's successors Antigonus and Seleucus would exploit. The end result would have been a smaller and more stable Macedonian empire.[52]

On the other hand, while seemingly logical, accepting the treaty presented some danger. Alexander would have had to leave the core of the Persian Empire intact. As they subsequently proved, the Persians could still raise a massive army and still posed a significant threat. Agreeing to the terms would have been based on trust in Darius' good faith; something Alexander could not ensure. Other than wanting his family back, the Persian ruler may simply have been employing delaying tactics until he was ready for another round of fighting.

If we examine the situation from the Persian perspective, Darius had every reason to still believe in victory. He had massive resources to call upon, while Alexander would become bogged down for months taking coastal cities like Tyre and Gaza. Darius had no reason to panic or hastily sign over his daughter and half his empire. The ancients may have exaggerated the offers by Darius to present a Persian king in desperation before the mighty Alexander.[53]

Phoenicia and Egypt

While Darius amassed a new army in Mesopotamia, Alexander now focused on capturing the coastal city-states of Phoenicia. Some have criticized Alexander for not pursuing Darius directly and allowing the Persians to regroup, but the king had strategic reasons for his actions.[54] Alexander wanted to eliminate the Persian navy by seizing its bases of support and resupply. To defeat the Persian navy would mean bringing the Phoenician and Cypriot cities under his control. The Phoenicians and Cypriots provided the bulk of Persian naval forces. If the Persian naval bases fell, Alexander could protect Greece from a naval invasion the likes of which Memnon had been planning. Alexander's fears for Greece were particularly relevant now as the Spartans were planning war against Macedonia and hoped for Persian aid.

In the wake of Alexander's advance, all the major Phoenician cities surrendered to him except for the island city of Tyre. The king of Tyre, Azemilcus, felt secure behind his formidable defences. Darius is likely to have encouraged Tyre's resistance to stall Alexander's advance. The citizens of the city hoped that Darius would reward them for their efforts. As Diodorus notes, they 'cheerfully faced the prospect of a siege. They wanted to gratify Dareius [*sic*] and keep unimpaired their loyalty to him, and thought also that they would receive great gifts from the king in return for such a favour.' Azemilcus was also perhaps expecting aid from his sister city of Carthage in North Africa. The Tyrians declared that they would not let either the Persians or the Macedonians into their city. Alexander would not tolerate even this neutral stance and wanted the city's submission. Miletus had also attempted to adopt neutrality only to be stormed by Alexander.[55]

Alexander could have bypassed the city by marching onward to Egypt, but felt that the conquest of Tyre would have strategic benefits. Alexander viewed Tyre as the key to controlling the region. If Alexander could conquer Tyre, his hold on Phoenicia would be complete and the kings of Cyprus would submit. Alexander could then advance to Egypt without fear of troubles in his rear. Curtius points out that Alexander could not allow Tyre to remain untaken as it would damage his reputation. If Tyre could successfully ward off the Macedonians, other cities may have felt they could do the same.[56]

The king asked to gain entrance to the city under the excuse that he wished to pray at Tyre's shrine to the deity Heracles (originally Melqart). The Tyrians, sticking to their neutrality, declined Alexander access to the city. Alexander's ploy was not entirely unique, as Philip had employed a similar strategy against the Scythians. Philip declared his intention to raise a statue to Heracles on the Danube. The Scythian king offered to set the statue up, but refused to allow Philip and his army to enter the area. If Philip were to put the statue up by force, the Scythians threatened to demolish it. Thus, in part, Philip used the disagreement over Heracles to justify his war with the Scythians.[57]

Tyre, with its natural position, presented a difficult obstacle for Alexander's army. The king began to construct a mole reaching out to the island fortress. The siege would be time-consuming, dragging on for some six to seven months from the winter of 333 to the summer of 332 BC. The fleets of Alexander's new Phoenician and Cypriot allies would prove decisive in the final victory of the Tyrians. The city of Tyre paid a heavy price for resisting Alexander, with 6,000 to 8,000 citizens killed in the fighting, 2,000 crucified and another 30,000 sold into slavery. As at Thebes, Alexander was sending a message to those who resisted his rule. The Macedonian ruler topped off the affair by offering his long-awaited sacrifice to Heracles.[58]

With Tyre subdued, Alexander intended to add Egypt to his ever-growing empire. The main obstacle in his path was the Persian garrison at Gaza. The Gazan defenders were commanded by the eunuch Batis. As per Curtius, Batis 'was a man of exceptional loyalty to the (Persian) king'. He had readied the city to resist Alexander, bringing in supplies and hiring local Arab mercenaries. The Persians had prepared for a siege, having gathered the necessary supplies. Like Tyre, Gaza delayed

Alexander's advance further and gave Darius more time to assemble an army. In the autumn of 332, Alexander took Gaza by siege and executed its eunuch commander.[59]

After the garrison at Gaza gave up, Alexander resumed his advance on Egypt. Egypt had recently undergone a period of turmoil. The Egyptian satrap had been killed at Issus, likely along with much of his satrapal contingent, weakening Egypt's defences. The leadership of the province reverted to the new satrap Mazakes. Mazakes was challenged for power in Egypt by a group of Greek mercenaries led by Amyntas. Amyntas was the same man who had offered Darius advice before Issus. He had survived the battle and set out for Egypt with his fellow mercenaries. It is possible that Darius actually sent these mercenaries to secure Egypt and prevent its surrender to Alexander. In any case, Amyntas fought and defeated Mazakes in a battle, only to be killed shortly after that. Mazakes' defeat combined with the death of Amyntas left Egypt in a poor position to mount any defence against Alexander and his army.[60]

Mazakes surrendered Egypt to Alexander without a fight, and the king occupied Memphis. Alexander's time in Egypt was particularly eventful. He took the title of pharaoh and paid homage to the Egyptian gods. He then undertook a mission into the desert to the Siwa oasis and became the 'son of Ammon'. Additionally, Alexander is said to have laid the foundations for the great commercial metropolis of Alexandria.[61]

When Darius learned of Alexander's capture of Egypt, he briefly contemplated leaving Mesopotamia for the depths of his empire. The Persian grip on their outlying provinces, particularly those on the border of India, was likely starting to weaken. By moving into the interior of Persia, he could draw upon more men for the war by personally pressuring the satraps. However, for whatever reason, Darius ultimately declined to retreat and continued assembling his army in Mesopotamia for a showdown with Alexander.[62] Following his Egyptian escapades, Alexander set off to bring Darius to battle.

Attempted Persian Reconquest of Asia Minor

After their defeat at Granicus, the Persian forces in Asia Minor regrouped in the north-eastern part of the region. The Persians still had Paphlagonia, Pontus and at least part of Cappadocia under their sway. After Issus, numerous soldiers had fled the battlefield north, swelling Persian numbers in the region. The Persian administration continued to function, coins were minted at Sinope and ambassadors were still sent to the Great King. Gathering what forces they had at their disposal, the Persians attempted to retake Asia Minor, moving against Antigonus in Phrygia. Antigonus defeated the Persians in a series of battles, maintaining Alexander's hold on the critical region. Had the Persians proved successful, it surely would have derailed Alexander's entire campaign.[63]

The Spartan War

In Greece, King Agis III of Sparta, encouraged by the Persians, made open war against Macedonia. According to Diodorus, Darius gave him both ships and money for the effort. The Spartan king also recruited some 8,000 Greek mercenaries who had fought with Darius at Issus. With these forces, Agis was able to conquer Crete and instal garrisons on the island. In the opening stages of the conflict, King Agis fought a battle against the Macedonian commander Corrhagus in the region. The Macedonians suffered a critical defeat in the engagement. Corrhagus fell in the combat, along with much of his force.[64]

Antipater, Alexander's regent in Macedonia, marched to the Peloponnese with an army against the Spartans. The Spartans suffered a defeat at Megalopolis in the ensuing campaign and King Agis fell in the battle. The loss and death of Agis brought an end to the Spartan threat; Antipater had demonstrated his competence as regent in the king's absence. Alexander famously dismissed the conflict between Antipater and the Spartans as a 'battle of mice' compared to his war in Persia.[65]

The Battle of Gaugamela

The coming Battle of Gaugamela was to be the decisive engagement of the war between Alexander and Darius. In the autumn of 331, Alexander marched into Mesopotamia at the head of some 47,000 soldiers to face the Persian Great King. Darius was waiting for him with a mighty host with contingents drawn from throughout his eastern empire. By our lowest estimate, the Persian army numbered some 40,000 cavalry and

200,000 infantry.[66] As stated previously, Greco-Roman accounts almost universally inflate Persian numbers and Darius' army, in reality, would have been significantly smaller. Nonetheless, the Persians would still have outnumbered the Macedonians considerably.

Darius had put maximum effort into building up manpower and supplies for the campaign. For use at the battle, the Persian king had assembled a special force of 200 scythed chariots. These chariots were, in effect, Darius' secret weapon which he indeed hoped would have a decisive impact on the battlefield. According to Diodorus, Darius 'drilled his troops daily and made them well disciplined by continued training and practice'. According to Curtius, Darius even went so far as to have spikes driven into the ground in preparation for Alexander's cavalry. Darius made camp on the plain of Gaugamela near the town of Arbela. The terrain advantages of the site were evident as the open plain held great benefits for his large army. Darius would not allow his army to fight on poor terrain for a second time. To summarize, the Persians were very well prepared and had chosen their ground on which to fight. The challenge awaiting Alexander was the greatest of his military career.[67]

As Alexander approached, Darius tasked his trusted general Mazaeus with delaying the Macedonian advance along the Euphrates and Tigris rivers. The Persian king additionally ordered Mazaeus to devastate the surrounding territory in a scorched earth campaign. It seems that the Persians were finally taking Memnon's advice to try to weaken Alexander indirectly. Despite Mazaeus' efforts, Alexander managed to push across both rivers. The Macedonian advance was so swift that Mazaeus proved unable to destroy the local food supplies. The Persian general limped back to Darius' camp, having done his best to delay the Macedonians. Alexander arrived on Mazaeus' heels and encamped opposite the Persian army.[68]

On the night before the engagement, Parmenion had recommended to Alexander that the Macedonian army launch a night attack. Parmenion's plan of action had the advantage of taking the larger Persian army by surprise in its camp. Alexander considered such an attack too risky and voiced a wish to fight the Persians fairly. The Macedonian ruler was ever mindful of his reputation and did not want men to say that he stole victory. The Persians looked to have expected such a ploy as they deployed all night, robbing themselves of sleep.[69]

The next day Alexander deployed his army in a formation resembling a box with a double line of infantry and cavalry on the wings. The amassed Persians far overlapped Alexander's army in length. Alexander opened the battle by moving to his right in an attempt to shift his army on to rougher terrain. Darius could not allow Alexander to redeploy as it would negate his terrain advantage. The Persian king moved to block Alexander and envelop the Macedonian army.[70]

The battle then commenced between the two armies. Both the kings encouraged their men to battle: Alexander atop his horse and Darius in his royal chariot. On the wing opposite Alexander and Darius, Parmenion faced off against Mazaeus. Early in the battle, Darius unleashed his scythed chariots on Alexander's right wing. The damage proved to be minimal as the soldiers parted ranks, allowing the vehicles to go past harmlessly. The battle's turning-point came when Alexander took advantage of a gap that had formed in the Persian lines. He charged through with his elite cavalry, supported by part of the phalanx. As Arrian recounts, Alexander 'led them on at the double, and, with a loud battle cry straight at Dareius [sic].'[71]

It was a replay of Issus, with Darius' comrades dying around him while attempting to resist Alexander's charge. As the Macedonians drew closer, Darius' chariot-driver was hit by a spear. Darius' comrades believed him to be killed for a time, throwing them into grief and certainly damaging morale at a key moment. As the engagement turned in Alexander's favour he again moved towards the Persian king. Darius at first contemplated resisting, briefly drawing his sword, but chose instead to escape the battlefield. Plutarch dramatically recounts how the Great King's chariot became 'entangled and stuck amidst all the corpses' and had to abandon it for a horse. His retreat did not go unnoticed, as the royal chariot was visible to many in the melee. The Persian army soon began to disintegrate and follow its king in flight.[72]

Alexander began pursuing Darius, only to halt when a messenger arrived from Parmenion. Alexander now turned away from chasing Darius back to assist his comrades. Parmenion was under heavy attack by Mazaeus on the opposite wing and was in danger of being overrun. The Persians had even managed to penetrate into Alexander's camp. As per our ancient sources, Alexander was irritated by the message as it prevented him from catching the Persian king. How a messenger could make it through the carnage and dust to deliver the message has been questioned. The ancients may have been simply making up a story to explain Alexander's failure to catch Darius. Regardless, Alexander proceeded to Parmenion's wing, where he fought a sharp cavalry engagement as the Persians retreated.[73]

Meanwhile, Darius and his kinsmen had crossed the River Lycus to relative safety. Darius contemplated destroying the bridge across the river before the Macedonians arrived. Burning the bridge would have made Darius' escape all the more probable, but would leave thousands of his soldiers stranded. Darius declared that 'he preferred to give a passage to his pursuers rather than take one away from those who were in flight.' From the battlefield, the Persian king proceeded to Media with hopes of gathering yet another army. Alexander marched on Babylon and received the surrender of the city.[74]

The Battle of Gaugamela was nothing short of a disaster for the Persian Empire. The Persian losses for the battle numbered perhaps 40,000 in total. Alexander's army sustained some 500 dead and a greater number wounded, including several prominent commanders. The two consecutive defeats shook the confidence of the Persian elite in Darius' military ability. For Alexander, the victory at Gaugamela was a decisive turning-point. As Justin notes, 'By this battle he (Alexander) gained the dominion over Asia.' Following the battle, Alexander officially assumed the title of 'King of Asia'. Here he was making a statement: he was no longer an invading monarch but the rightful ruler of Asia.[75]

Alexander's accomplishments from the time he threw his spear ashore to Gaugamela were astounding. The king had bested the Persian satrapal army at Granicus and seized control of Asia Minor. He smashed the army of King Darius at Issus and claimed Phoenicia, Cyprus and Egypt for his empire. With the final decisive victory at Gaugamela, Alexander, in effect, destroyed the Persian Empire. By the end of 331, Alexander could truthfully boast that he had taken Asia as a 'spear-won prize'.

The defeat of the Persian army at the hands of the Macedonians left a lasting impression. Greeks and Romans had a low opinion of the fighting ability of Eastern soldiers. Lucian illustrates this developed bias well in his fictitious satire *Dialogues of the Dead*. In the text, Lucian has Alexander's father Philip mock his accomplishments, remarking, 'Whom did you ever conquer that was worth conquering? Your adversaries were ever timid creatures...gold-laced womanish Medes and Persians and

Chaldaeans... ran away before they were within bow-shot.' Contrary to Lucian's remarks, the Persians had proven themselves time and again to be able opponents. The Persian army, particularly its cavalry and Darius' elite guardsmen, put up heavy resistance against the Macedonians. The Persians, in several instances, pushed their Macedonian foes close to their limit. Had Alexander been slain or Granicus or Parmenion's wing broken at Issus or Gaugamela, the results of the war would have been very different.

In addition to the Persian soldiery, the Great King Darius does not deserve his reputation as an incompetent coward. Darius took a personal role in directing Persian war efforts and demonstrated himself to be an innovative commander. He was willing to adopt tactical and strategic changes in an attempt to regain the initiative. After the defeat at Issus, the Persian ruler raised a new army, focusing on the issues of supply and training. The terrain he chose at Gaugamela was well suited for the battle at hand. On the strategic front, Darius bogged Alexander down in siege warfare at Tyre and Gaza while operating against his rear in Asia Minor and supporting the Spartans in Greece. The king did everything he could to make Persian victory a possibility. The failure of Persian efforts is a tribute to Alexander's excellent generalship, the competency of his top lieutenants and the skill of the Macedonian soldiery.

Chapter Six

Winning Hearts and Minds

In the previous chapter, we addressed how Alexander achieved victory over King Darius and claimed the kingship of Asia. We will now turn to Alexander's efforts at the local level in the newly-conquered territories. In his efforts to claim the throne of Asia, Alexander followed in the footsteps of the Achaemenid kings while, at the local level, he tried to contrast himself with them. Alexander sought to win the hearts and minds of the local populace. His strategy was to present himself as a benevolent ruler who had come to liberate them from the cruel Persians and other local tyrants. Alexander adapted himself to the unique cultural and religious practices found in the territories he conquered. In this way he made himself acceptable to the local ruling elite and assimilated himself into native political structures. The king's astute local policies and attempts to win over the local elite proved on the whole successful in Asia Minor, Phoenicia, Egypt and Babylonia.

Asia Minor

Alexander had proclaimed that 'freedom of the Greeks was the object for which he had taken upon himself the war against Persia.' To Alexander's disappointment, his arrival in Asia did not initiate a native Greek uprising against Persia. The Greek population chose to wait and see how events played out. In recent years, they had endured too much back and forth with Parmenion and Memnon warring across their lands. Their decision to stay quiet was likely further influenced by the fact that many Greeks of Asia Minor were currently in Persian service. The Greek cities were also occupied by Persian garrisons and ruled by Persian-backed officials. Greeks who joined Alexander could potentially have faced retribution from the Persians.[1]

It was not until Alexander's victory at the Granicus River that 'the greater part of Asia (Minor) came over to his side.' With this military triumph, Alexander moved to capture popular support. When he arrived in Asia, Alexander gave his men strict orders against pillaging. This measure had the dual goal of establishing good relations with the populace and not destroying what would soon be Macedonian property. As Diodorus states, Alexander succeeded in 'winning over the (Greek) cities by kind treatment'. The 'barbarian' non-Greek population of the mountains also came down, pledging loyalty to Alexander.[2]

Alexander proved to be lenient towards the cities that supported the Persians. Sardis fell captured without violence. The town of Zeleia, which had hosted the Persian war council, was spared from destruction by Alexander as he deemed it under duress at the time.[3] At Ephesus, Alexander had to balance between different political factions in the city. Previously, the city had been pro-Macedonian and raised a statue to Philip. Memnon had punished the city by having the statue torn down and installing a pro-Persian oligarchy. Alexander, in turn, disbanded the oligarchy, made Ephesus a democracy and allowed pro-Macedonian exiles to return to the city. The populace turned on those who supported Memnon and murdered several men. Alexander stepped in and stopped any further vengeance killings. This act likely gained him some support among the former loyalists of Memnon and the Persians.[4]

Additionally, during his stay at Ephesus, Alexander thought to honour the Temple of Artemis. The Macedonian king had a connection to the temple because of the fire that had occurred at his birth. Memnon had also looted it previously, and Alexander wanted to show his goodwill. He decreed that Ephesus would pay the same tribute to Artemis as they did to the Persians. A brief dispute did arise over the temple between Alexander and the Ephesians. Alexander wanted to inscribe the Temple of Artemis himself and, in exchange, offered them generous monetary compensation. The Ephesians viewed the idea of a mortal dedicating the temple as sacrilegious. However, they knew they could not refuse Alexander bluntly and did so in a way that flattered the king. They remarked that it was 'inappropriate for a god to dedicate offerings to gods'. This flattery seems to have been enough to please Alexander and he did not force the issue.[5]

When he advanced into Caria, Alexander found another essential ally in Queen Ada of Caria. She had been the wife of the Carian King Idrieus, the same man who subdued Cyprus for King Ochus. Following

Idrieus' death, Ada attempted to reign as a sole monarch, but her brother Pixodarus interceded and assumed the throne. Pixodarus was the same prince whose daughter Alexander and his brother competed over to marry.

By 334, however, Pixodarus had also died, and the rule of Caria had passed to his son-in-law Orontobates. Queen Ada contested Orontobates' authority over the kingdom. Decisively, Orontobates had the support of the Persian satraps and established his rule in the capital of Halicarnassus. Ada meanwhile controlled the critical fortress of Alinda, which Arrian described as being 'one of the strongest positions in Caria'. When Alexander arrived in the region, Ada approached him, offering an alliance which the king enthusiastically accepted. A coalition with Ada had many strategic benefits for Alexander. First and foremost, the Macedonian ruler would gain both a local ally and a strategic fortress without a fight.[6]

Ultimately Alexander would place the whole of Caria under Ada's rule. Ada would adopt Alexander as her 'son' to formalize the arrangement, a step Alexander did not discourage. Ada was also apparently popular with the people, and Alexander, by restoring her throne, 'won the loyal support of the Carians by the favour that he bestowed on this woman' and 'all the cities sent missions and presented the king with golden crowns and promised to co-operate with him in everything.' Ada and Alexander would remain on close terms even after his departure from Caria. According to Plutarch, she would send him 'delicacies and sweetmeats every day, and finally offered him bakers and cooks who were supposed to be the most skilled in the country'. Alexander's kind treatment of Ada would mirror his relationship with other female royals.[7]

In contrast to his warm friendship with Ada, Alexander's relationship with the tyrant Dionysius, ruler of Heraclea Pontica, was fraught with difficulties. Dionysius had taken advantage of Alexander's victory at Granicus and the collapse of Persian power to expand his influence in the region. He was a tight-fisted ruler who had banished those who had opposed him from the city. These exiles appealed to Alexander to capture the city and establish a democracy. It seems Alexander had gained himself a reputation as someone supportive of democracy against oligarchies and tyrannies. Dionysius, distressed by the thought of Alexander intervening, took steps to increase favour among his people. He also successfully appealed to Alexander's sister Cleopatra for help in deterring the king.

The tyrant's efforts were enough, and Alexander allowed him to remain in power. When Alexander died, Dionysius was said to have been relieved and put up a statue to the god of joy to commemorate the occasion.[8]

The cities of Lycia proved to be amenable towards the conqueror. The citizens of Phaselis sent Alexander a golden crown. Alexander, flattered, came to Phaselis in person while sending his comrades to accept the surrender of the other Lycian cities. The citizens of the city requested Alexander's support against the Pisidians. The Pisidians had established a fort near the city and used it to raid the countryside. Alexander agreed to assist his new friends and captured the hostile fort. The Pisidians would prove to be a continued issue and harassed Alexander's army as it advanced through its territory.[9]

Alexander attempted to repeat his success at Phaselis with the city of Aspendos on the Eurymedon River. Initially, Alexander and the Aspendians were able to come to amicable terms. The king would not put a garrison in the city in exchange for a tribute of money and horses. However, when Alexander marched away, the city reneged on its agreement with the king. The leaders of Aspendos did not believe Alexander would bother returning in person. To their surprise, Alexander returned promptly and Aspendos submitted again, this time on far harsher terms.[10]

Gordion in Phrygia was perhaps the most symbolic city Alexander visited in Asia. Gordion was the city of King Midas, the legendary ruler of Phrygia. According to the legend, King Midas had lived in Macedonia during his youth only to be expelled by Alexander's ancestor King Karanos. This history between Macedonia and Midas would have presented an obvious attraction for Alexander. Midas' standing as a model for kingship as well would not have been ignored by Alexander. King Midas held similar significance from the Persian point of view.[11]

Gordion was also home to the so-called 'Gordian knot'. According to legend, whoever undid the knot was destined to be the ruler of Asia. This prophecy was a challenge that Alexander had to accept. The king famously undid the knot either by pulling its pin or cutting it in half. Alexander did this before a crowd of his comrades and local Phrygians for maximum propaganda value. By undoing the knot, Alexander was claiming the kingship of Midas. The fact that Midas' legacy pre-dated the Persians by centuries had an added benefit for Alexander.[12]

When he marched off to fight Darius, Alexander had left Asia Minor only partially secured. Alexander's satraps had the task of subduing the region. In the king's absence, Calas, satrap of Hellespontine Phrygia, attempted to conquer Bithynia on behalf of Alexander. The Bithynian King Bas proved a challenging foe, and he repulsed Calas' 'well-equipped' force. Balakros, Alexander's satrap of Cilicia, ran into similar local resistance and was killed fighting the Pisidians.[13]

Cappadocia looks to have presented the greatest danger to Macedonia. Alexander had appointed a governor for the territory, but he does not look to have assumed control for whatever reason. The Cappadocian King Ariarathes build up significant amounts of wealth and raised an army. According to Diodorus, the Cappadocians could field some 30,000 infantry and 15,000 cavalry. After Alexander's death, Ariarathes went to war with his Macedonian successors. The Cappadocian king was ultimately defeated and executed. Even with this victory, the region seems to have only partially come under Macedonian rule and maintained its own dynasty.[14]

Phoenicia and Cyprus

With Darius' defeat at Issus, Phoenicia and Cyprus were ripe for the taking. Petty kings subject to the Persians ruled over the cities of this region. These cities had a rich history of merchant ventures and provided the essential elements of the Persian navy. The region itself provided the main support base for the Persian navy, with Asia Minor now largely under Alexander's control. Winning over these kings would be a critical element in the final victory for Alexander.

Alexander first entered into negotiations within the coastal island city of Arados. King Gerostratus of Arados was away from his city, commanding a section of the Persian fleet. In the king's absence, his son Straton ruled Arados on his behalf. When Alexander arrived, Prince Straton, likely with his father's permission, surrendered Arados and its adjoining mainland city of Marathos. Numerous other Phoenician leaders joined Arados in surrendering; according to Justin, several kings came before Alexander wearing filets. Alexander also attended a banquet with the kings of Cyprus and although Alexander attended, the kings paid the expenses.[15]

Establishing Macedonian rule over the Phoenician city of Sidon was critical for Alexander. Along with Tyre, Sidon was the most significant urban centre in the region. During the reign of Ochus, Sidon had allied itself with the breakaway state of Egypt against Persian rule. When Ochus' army arrived to attack the city, the Sidonese king Tennes had second thoughts about his Egyptian alliance. Tennes betrayed his city to the Persians by gathering hundreds of the leading citizens of Sidon and marching them out of the city to the enemy camp. Ochus had the Sidonese nobles executed and then stormed the undefended city, massacring the populace. With the city's capture complete, Tennes had outlived his usefulness and Ochus had him executed. With these recent memories of Persian brutality, it's unsurprising that public opinion in the city favoured Alexander.[16]

At the time of Alexander's arrival, King Strato ruled over Sidon. Strato was not a popular ruler but rather a puppet well known for his 'friendship' with the Persians. The Sidonese people took the opportunity of Alexander's arrival to depose him 'out of hatred for Persia and Darius'. The citizens of Sidon then asked Alexander to name the new king for them. Alexander entrusted the task of choosing a new king to his closest companion, Hephaestion.[17]

Sidon's leading citizens were gathering individual support in an attempt to get themselves elected king. If Hephaestion made the wrong choice, factional violence in the city looked like a real possibility. Hephaestion at first favoured a wealthy man with whom he had struck up a friendship and offered him the throne. The man declined, but did recommend to Hephaestion another man named Abdalonymus. He was a distant relative of the Sidonese royal family but at present living as a commoner. Taking his friend's advice, Hephaestion informed Alexander of his choice. The Macedonian ruler had Abdalonymus abandon his 'rags', dressing him in royal garb before bringing him to the city's central marketplace to announce his kingship. By this public announcement, Alexander wanted it known that the new king had his complete approval. Abdalonymus proved a good choice as it defused the situation. He was not a political figure and thus did not offend any of the Sidonese elite. Abdalonymus likely remained a loyal supporter of Alexander, and the famed Alexander Sarcophagus found near Sidon is sometimes attributed to him.[18]

During the siege of Tyre, Alexander called upon his new Phoenician and Cypriot allies to assist him. Alexander's new allies sent their fleets to assist the Macedonians in the capture of Tyre. King Gerostratus of Arados and King Abdalonymus of Sidon personally led their city's contingents during the siege. In addition to the ships, 'a good many engineers had collected from Cyprus and the whole of Phoenicia.' These allied forces proved critical in Alexander's capture of the island fortress. During the sacking of Tyre, the Sidonians rescued many Tyrian citizens when they entered the city, viewing the people as kin.[19]

For their efforts at Tyre, Alexander rewarded his new allied kings. The Phoenician and Cypriot fleets then assisted Alexander's move down the coast against Gaza and Egypt. Following the conclusion of this campaign, Alexander sent his allied fleet to Greece. They put up a blockade around Sparta, preventing further Persian assistance, and operated against Spartan-Persian garrisons on Crete. Alexander also had the ships conduct anti-piracy operations to clear the sea lanes of his new empire.[20]

Leaving Egypt and arriving back in the Levant, Alexander faced a revolt centred on the city of Samaria. The populace of Samaria had murdered the local Macedonian commander Andromachus, burning him alive. This act by the Samaritans could not be left unpunished, and Alexander advanced upon the city. The king quickly subdued the rebels, and those who murdered Andromachus surrendered to him.[21]

During his return to this region, Alexander also made a reform of the empire's finances. When he conquered Asia Minor, he had put a man named Koiranos of Beroia in charge of collecting tribute. In Phoenicia he had done a similar thing, appointing a certain Philoxenos. Alexander disbanded the independent offices of Koiranos and Philoxenos and instead established a centralized system. He put his friend Harpalus in charge of all funds as the official treasurer of the campaign. The treasurer followed the army all the way to Ecbatana in Media, securing the treasury of that city. He was later dispatched back to Babylon while Alexander departed for India.[22]

Egypt

Arriving at the Egyptian border town of Pelusium, large crowds emerged to acclaim Alexander. The Egyptians greeted Alexander as a liberator from the Persians and happily accepted Macedonian rule. If we take our Greco-Roman sources as fact, the Persians 'governed harshly' over Egypt, and their government was 'avaricious and arrogant'. The Persians committed numerous acts of terror upon the Egyptians. Cambyses and Xerxes were known to have been particularly harsh towards the Egyptian people. As noted, Ochus also had demolished the walls of the most prominent Egyptian cities and looted their temples of treasure. Bagoas is even said to have carried off the sacred Egyptian religious texts for ransom.[23]

Alexander marched into the Egyptian capital at Memphis. There the conqueror participated in a religious ceremony with the ruling elite. The Egyptians expected Alexander to follow their unique system of traditions and spiritual practices. Egyptian pharaohs, though having great power, were bound by an imperial protocol that regulated their actions. Alexander would have abided by these traditions to gain the Egyptians' approval. If one follows Diodorus' description of standard Egyptian procedures, Alexander would have taken up position beside the Egyptian high priest. The common people would have gathered around and prayed for the king's long life and happiness. The priest would give a speech about the king's positive attributes, and then the king would recall his errors and be forgiven.[24]

When Alexander sacrificed to the gods, he singled out the holy calf representing the Egyptian god Apis. As per Egyptian custom, the calf deserved special care and was not even allowed near the unclean water of the Nile. Herodotus reports how the Persian king Cambyses slaughtered the holy calf. Cambyses' actions, if true, were a great insult to the Egyptians. Alexander wanted to demonstrate how different he was from the Persians. Paying tribute to Apis proved an effective way for him to show his goodwill.[25]

The less reliable *Alexander Romance* presents other interesting details about Alexander's time in Egypt. According to the *Romance*, at Memphis the priests recognized Alexander as the pharaoh of Egypt. The text further informs us that Alexander sought to connect himself with Egypt's last native leader, Pharaoh Nectanebo II. Alexander embraced a statue of the former pharaoh and proclaimed himself as Nectanebo's son. A similar story can be found in Herodotus when the Egyptians alleged Cambyses was of Egyptian ancestry as the son of Cyrus and the daughter of an

Egyptian pharaoh. It seems the Egyptians were more receptive to being ruled by someone of their royal bloodline, and Alexander was happy to conform to their expectations.[26]

During his time in Egypt, Alexander settled administrative matters in the kingdom. He would authorize the recruitment of 6,000 Egyptian youths as royal pages. One can speculate that they would have the same function as the Macedonian page system of training future Egyptian military and political figures. According to Curtius, Alexander set out 'administrative matters without tampering with Egyptian traditions'. Alexander maintained the Egyptian administrative system of 'nomes', appointing two nomarchs in Egypt named Petisis and Doloaspis. The ethnic background of these individuals is unclear: Petisis may have been a Persian and Doloaspis an Egyptian.[27]

The two officials split the province between themselves, with Petisis getting the north or Lower Egypt and Doloaspis the south or Upper Egypt. This division reflected the historical division of Egypt. Alexander likely did not want Egypt controlled by a single powerful satrap in case of rebellion. The recent Persian experience of constant Egyptian revolts must have been on the king's mind. The nomarchs actually possessed significant power and should not be seen as mere puppets of the Macedonians. By giving the Egyptians a role in the administration and not altering their historic governing structure, Alexander took an essential step towards solidifying native support.[28]

Alexander additionally appointed half a dozen other lesser officials. The most prominent of these was Cleomenes, a Greek from the city of Naucratis on the Nile. According to Arrian, Alexander assigned Cleomenes rule over 'Arabia about Hermopolis' on Egypt's western frontier. Cleomenes was 'to permit the district governors to govern their own districts as had been their way all along, but that he was to exact from them the tributes, while they were ordered to pay these to him'. After Alexander left the province, Cleomenes would consolidate Egypt under his leadership, becoming the sole satrap. Petisis reportedly resigned soon after assuming office and Doloaspis fades from history. Any plan Alexander had for divided rule in Egypt thus fell by the wayside.[29]

Cleomenes would gain a reputation for cruelty among the Egyptians. Arrian refers to him as 'an evil man who had done many grievous wrongs in Egypt'. Sometimes Cleomenes' rule is used to claim that Alexander neglected the administration of his empire. According to Arrian, Alexander, towards the end of his reign, became aware of Cleomenes' wrongdoings but chose to ignore them in exchange for him constructing tributes to Hephaestion. Alexander's friend had just died and wanted him honoured in Egypt.[30]

There is an opposing argument to be made for Cleomenes' effectiveness as ruler of Egypt. He proved to be an active administrator. His tactics for gathering funds may have been heavy-handed, but he collected a considerable sum of gold for the empire. He also oversaw the construction of Alexandria and population transfers to the new city. Perhaps Alexander could simply not afford to remove such an able lieutenant. In the aftermath of Alexander's death, Ptolemy seized power in Egypt and murdered Cleomenes. Ptolemy's success in establishing his Egyptian dynasty is partly due to the groundwork laid by Cleomenes.[31]

Siwa and Cyrene

The most controversial episode of Alexander's time in Egypt was his venturing to the oracle of the Egyptian god Ammon at Siwa in the Egyptian desert. According to the ancients, Alexander's chief motivation for visiting the site was to learn of his divine origins. The Macedonian ruler was not the first to make a venture to the oracle of Ammon. The heroes Heracles and Perseus had made the journey. The Persian King Cambyses lost an army attempting to reach Siwa. By travelling to the desert oracle, Alexander was equalling Heracles and Perseus while outdoing the Persians.

The coastal city of Cyrene, in present-day Libya, heard that Alexander intended to journey into the desert. They sent Alexander numerous gifts including horses and chariots. The citizens of the city invited Alexander to come and visit them. Unsurprisingly, Alexander did not venture to Cyrene as it would have been a journey far out of the way. The king did establish a treaty of friendship with Cyrene, but he did not incorporate the city into his empire.[32] Later the Ptolemaic dynasty would add Cyrene to its Egyptian empire.

When the king arrived at Siwa after a perilous journey, the priests hailed him as the son of Zeus-Ammon. According to Justin, Alexander had actually sent word to the oracle priests ahead of time to facilitate the desired response: '(Alexander) instructed the priests, by messengers whom he sent before him, what answers he wished to receive.' Returning to Memphis from his excursion, Alexander sacrificed to his new father, Zeus-Ammon. He then had his army parade through the city and held festivities to celebrate.[33]

Visiting the oracle at Siwa had significant political implications in Egypt. Making a pilgrimage to the Egyptian holy site and being declared the son of Ammon, Alexander raised his stature among the Egyptians. The oracle served to confirm Alexander's status as pharaoh and successor to the native dynasties. Ammon was a god also known to the Greek world. Herodotus, for example, mentions Ammon in connection with the oracle at Dodona in Epirus. By gaining the acknowledgement of the oracle, Alexander could link Egypt and Greece's religious traditions together through the worship of Ammon. The visit to Siwa is comparable to Alexander's actions at Gordion, where he attempted to embrace the native Phrygian tradition and link it with his Macedonian heritage.[34]

Babylonia

Ancient Babylon with its 'beauty and antiquity…drew to it the eyes, not only of the king, but also of all, and deservedly'. Alexander's triumphant entrance into the city is one of the king's more ironic moments, the scene famously captured by French painter Charles Le Brun. As per our sources, the Egyptians, the Babylonians viewed Alexander as a liberator. The Babylonians had lined the road leading to the city with flowers, reminiscent of Cyrus the Great's triumphant entrance into the same venue. Babylon's wealth was put on full display for Alexander with altars of silver, perfumes and exotic animals including lions and leopards. The Macedonian soldiers and Babylonians celebrated with a grand feast.[35]

The leading citizens and priests assembled to greet Alexander on his arrival. According to Curtius, the Babylonians acknowledged Alexander as their 'new king'. Whether Alexander actually became 'King of Babylon' is somewhat complicated as Darius the Great had officially abolished the title. However, to the Babylonians, Alexander was to be their de facto ruler as he had been pharaoh to the Egyptians. Alexander went to the royal palace to great propaganda effect and 'made an inspection of Darius' furniture and all his treasure'.[36]

According to Greek sources, the Babylonians, like the Egyptians, had suffered under Persian rule. Babylonia staged uprisings during the crisis period that followed Cambyses' death and again at the time of Xerxes' ascension. Diodorus reports that the Persians had 'carried off' spoils from the city. Herodotus tells us how Xerxes stole a sacred Babylonian statue and murdered the priests. Xerxes is also said to have destroyed the temple of the Babylonian god Marduk-Bel.[37]

The alleged Persian repression of Babylon has been challenged by recent scholarship. Our Greek sources are quick to demonize Persian rule and contrast it with Alexander. However, Babylon was an extremely important centre for the Achaemenid Empire. The Persian kings undoubtedly worked to cultivate a relationship with the local elite. This support base built by the Persians would not have disappeared merely with Alexander's victory over Darius. It is possible that the Persians were not entirely detested by the population when Alexander entered the city.[38]

As in the case of Egypt, Alexander encouraged local religious practices. The two main religious groups mentioned in our sources are the Magi priests and the Chaldean astrologers. The Magi now sang the praises of Alexander and the Chaldeans advised him on universal matters. As reported by Arrian, Alexander abided by the advice of these religious leaders and sacrificed to the chief Babylonian deity Marduk 'in the manner they prescribed'. Alexander also ordered the rebuilding of the temples to Marduk. According to Strabo, the task of reconstructing the large pyramid was monumental; merely clearing the rubble would have taken 10,000 men two months.[39]

Babylon would take on particular importance to Alexander. The city would serve as the de facto capital of his Asian empire and the location of his imperial treasury. According to Xenophon, Cyrus the Great had also made Babylon the principal capital of his empire. To oversee the treasury, Alexander appointed his old friend Harpalus. The king thought Harpalus would be able to manage monetary matters while he was off campaigning effectively. This turned out to be an error on Alexander's part when Harpalus abused his office.

On his return to Babylon in the spring of 323, Alexander entered into a dispute with the Chaldeans. The latter spoke of bad omens for him entering the city. Alexander, however, suspected that the Chaldeans' motivation was financial. Work on the ruined Babylonian temples had not been conducted 'with any zeal' in the king's absence. The Chaldeans were gaining revenue from donations which Alexander thought they did not want to spend on rebuilding the temple. Ignoring the omens, Alexander would enter the city, taking up quarters in the Babylonian palace of King Nebuchadnezzar II, where he would spend his final days. Regardless of their motives, ignoring the astrology of the Chaldeans would incidentally cost Alexander his life as in Babylon he came down with a fatal fever.[40]

Alexander's victory over the Persians was not only military but also political. He waged a parallel political campaign to win hearts and minds at a local level. In Asia Minor, Alexander won over the major cities of the coast. By honouring local customs and religious traditions, Alexander secured a support base among the population in Egypt and Babylonia. The king's alliances with local dynasties such as Queen Ada, King Gerostratus and King Abdalonymus proved to be an important factor in his military victory over the Persians. As a whole, Alexander's local policies were thoroughly successful. The only mark against the king is that he did not fully subdue Asia Minor and continued to encounter native resistance in some corners.

Chapter Seven

Alexander the Accursed

Alexander's time in the Persian homeland of Persis was a critical episode for the king. During this period, Alexander did the most to earn his Iranian nickname of 'the Accursed'. His measures in Persis differed from his usual policy of appeasing the conquered. The 'destruction' of Persepolis, Alexander's failure to crown himself Persian king and his alleged persecution of Persian religion are some of the most controversial episodes in his reign.

The Battle of the Persian Gate

In the winter of 331/330, Alexander, the newly-proclaimed 'King of Asia', marched out from Susa eastward towards the Persian homeland. On the march, Alexander confronted the Ouxioi, a warrior hill tribe. The Ouxioi would not let Alexander pass unless he paid the same tribute to them as they had demanded from the Persian kings. Alexander unsurprisingly had no interest in agreeing to such a deal. He undertook a short expedition and subdued the rough tribesmen. The Persian satrap of the Ouxioi, Madates, appealed to Sisygambis for aid and she convinced Alexander to be lenient with the tribesmen.[1]

With the Ouxioi defeated, Alexander advanced into Persis itself. The satrapy was an enclosed region situated within two mountain ranges with plains in between. Owing to its terrain, Persis was difficult to access from the outside. The territory was known for its fertile land, an abundance of cattle and a plentiful supply of water. As Curtius states, 'No region in all Asia is regarded as more health-giving.' In Alexander's time, numerous villages dotted the fertile region. As Diodorus writes, 'In density of population, too, this country far surpassed the other satrapies.' The residents of Persis were some of the most warlike in Asia, with 'every man being a bowman and a slinger'.[2]

The satrap of Persis, Ariobarzanes, was determined to resist Alexander's advance by all means. He assembled some 7,000 cavalry and 40,000 infantry. The satrap took up a position to block Alexander's passage through the mountains to Persepolis. Ariobarzanes was making a last stand for the Persian people, reminiscent of the Spartans at Thermopylae.[3]

Arriving before the Persians, Alexander attempted to force the pass. This effort failed, presenting Alexander with one of his rare reverses. The king showed himself to be undeterred and now sought a way to flank the Persian position. Alexander began to interrogate prisoners to see if they had any knowledge of the terrain. Among the prisoners was a shepherd named Pharnuches who was familiar with the territory. Pharnuches' father was Lycian and his mother Persian, thus he could communicate with both Greeks and Persians. Putting great trust in this man, Alexander had him lead the Macedonian flank march forward through the mountains. This flank attack made in conjunction with a renewed frontal assault drove the Persians from their positions. Pharnuches would be handsomely rewarded by Alexander for his assistance.[4]

Escaping the battlefield, Ariobarzanes fled to the capital of Persepolis. The garrison of the city chose to close the city gates to the retreating Persians. Apparently the soldiers within Persepolis thought the Persian cause to be lost. Left with few options, Ariobarzanes renewed the struggle with Alexander and was killed soon after. Following the battle Alexander, deviating from his usual behaviour, massacred Persian soldiers and inhabitants alike. As Plutarch recounts, 'there was a great slaughter of the prisoners taken; for Alexander himself writes that he gave orders to have the inhabitants butchered, thinking that this would be to his advantage.' This brutal act was the first sign that Alexander's stay in Persis would be bloody.[5]

The Sack of Persepolis

Persepolis was undoubtedly the most beautiful city of the Persian Empire, well-known for the 'richness of its buildings'. Construction had begun under the reign of Darius and rapidly expanded under Xerxes. Artisans were brought from throughout the empire to work on the project, including Ionian Greeks. It was here that Xerxes constructed his great palace and housed the royal treasure. Stamped in the nearby mountainside were the tombs of the Persian kings. To the Persians, the city was surely an object of pride, but to the Greeks it was the city that spawned the invasions of their homeland. As Curtius states, '(Persepolis) capital of the entire Orient, from which so many nations previously sought justification, the birthplace of so many kings, once the special terror of Greece.'[6]

Having eliminated Ariobarzanes, Alexander advanced upon Persepolis. It was the city that he referred to as 'the most hateful' in Asia. Before entering Persepolis, Alexander declared his intention to destroy the city to please his ancestors. Alexander had returned to his propaganda image as a Pan-Hellenic avenger. The king looked determined to exact revenge from the city and its populace. These cruel measures were largely contrary to Alexander's behaviour in Asia thus far. Usually only cities that resisted Alexander suffered his wrath, such as Thebes and Tyre.[7]

The march to the city was prompt as Alexander sought to capture the treasury before the Persians could disperse it. Alexander opened negotiations with Persepolis' governor Tiridates who offered to betray the city to the king. It is not surprising that the garrison would be willing to surrender as they had already locked out Ariobarzanes. Capturing Persepolis without a fight was a great coup for Alexander as the city's defences were formidable with a triple-walled citadel.[8]

Allegedly on the road to Persepolis, Alexander met 800 Greek captives who the Persians had mutilated. Where these mutilated Greeks came from and how they ended up as prisoners is a mystery. The prisoners were all older men, so one imagines they had been prisoners for some time. Alexander was emotionally affected by the encounter and promised to avenge them. He then rewarded the survivors handsomely. Similar to Darius' supposed mutilation of prisoners before Issus, this episode might merely be a literary invention to show Persian cruelty. If the story is true, it certainly provides a greater explanation for Alexander's subsequent destructive actions. The king perhaps thought himself justified in taking revenge on the city for the prisoners' sake.[9]

Much of the populace had fled Persepolis in the wake of the Macedonian advance. Those people who chose to remain in the city would suffer for it. Some Persian citizens committed suicide rather than face the wrath of the Macedonians. Alexander turned Persepolis over to his men for plunder. The city, filled with riches from all over the known world, was a grand prize for Alexander's soldiers. The plundering lasted for an entire day as the Macedonians pillaged the palaces of the Persian kings. Alexander largely allowed the violence to proceed, though in keeping with his chivalrous image he did step in, ordering his men to stop brutalizing women.[10]

Alexander captured the Persepolis treasury in its entirety. It had accumulated since the days of Cyrus, numbering some 120,000 talents. Alexander rewarded his close companions from the loot for their labours in Asia thus far. Alexander decided that he did not want the money to stay in Persepolis as he felt the populace was untrustworthy. He chose to move the treasure to Susa and called up a great many pack animals for the task. At Susa, the treasure would be secure and kept under strict guard. It's worth noting that Alexander was also holding Darius' mother and children at Susa. It seems that the king was trying to concentrate his valuables, both gold and hostages, at a single location.[11]

Alexander allowed Tiridates to remain governor of Persepolis and established a garrison in the city. The Macedonian ruler then set off to subdue the surrounding countryside of Persis. Alexander departed the city with only light forces, leaving his baggage behind to speed his movements. The winter weather proved to be terrible, with snow, ice and freezing temperatures. The terrain was also difficult, with Alexander at one point having to dismount from his horse and continue on foot. He took to devastating the area and captured several villages. He made contact with the local Mardian people and learned of their unique customs. However, the weather proved too horrible, and after thirteen days a surely frustrated Alexander was forced back to Persepolis.[12]

The 'Destruction' of Persepolis

The looting of Persepolis was not the most controversial episode of Alexander's stay in the city. Following Alexander's return from his winter foray, Persepolis was 'destroyed' in a fire started by the king. The 'destruction' of Persepolis is perhaps the single most explosive episode in the king's life. What sparked Alexander to commit this act and the extent of the damage inflicted is a matter of some dispute.

Arrian presents Alexander's choice to 'destroy' Persepolis as a matter of strategy. In his account, the king, before acting, discusses with Parmenion whether to burn the city or not. Parmenion advises Alexander not to burn Persepolis, arguing

> ...that it was not seemly to destroy what was now his own property, and that the Asians would not be induced to join him, if he seemed determined not to hold fast the sovereignty of Asia, but merely to pass through it in triumph.

Parmenion's thoughts employed the same logic Alexander himself showed in Asia Minor when he ordered his soldiers not to loot the countryside, which would soon belong to them anyway. However, despite Parmenion's best efforts, Alexander remained unconvinced and still had the urge to punish the city. As Arrian records,

> (Alexander) replied that he proposed to punish the Persians in recompense for what they had done in their invasion of Greece; for their wrecking of Athens, their burning of the temples, and for all the other cruel things they had done to the Greeks; for these, he said, he took vengeance.[13]

Our other ancient sources present a very different picture. In these versions, Alexander hosted games and a banquet in honour of the capture of Persepolis. These gatherings were common among the Macedonians and included heavy drinking. Present at the event was an Athenian woman named Thais, a mistress of Ptolemy. Thais, affected by drink, began to make extremely flattering remarks to the king and Alexander, under the influence of wine, fell under her spell.[14]

Thais, a native Athenian, possessed a great hatred of the Persian kings. She began to talk of burning Xerxes' palace and even began to set it on fire herself. Then, playing upon Alexander's manhood, she encouraged the king not to let herself, a woman, take the glory of burning the palace. Thais also reminded Alexander that he would gain the gratitude of the Greeks for such an act. Alexander's companions were of little help as they then joined in pleading with the King of Asia to burn the palace.[15]

Perhaps too drunk to comprehend his actions, Alexander put Xerxes' palace to the flame and all his comrades joined in on the act. The army quickly took notice and soon arrived to put out the fire. The men were surprised to see Alexander taking part and felt obliged to join in on the burning. The portions of the palace made of cedar quickly burned and the fire spread. The beautiful gardens of the Persian kings perished in the blaze. The ancients were eager to present the irony of an Athenian woman destroying Xerxes' palace.[16]

It is uncertain whether we should take Arrian's or the divergent accounts to be factual. It may be that Arrian is trying to cover up the debauchery of his hero and rationalize the crime. It's worth noting that one of Arrian's primary sources was Ptolemy's lost history, who would not be keen to discuss the role of his mistress in the destruction. Also the question remains whether Alexander's actions were thought out or done on a whim. Plutarch states that he is unsure if Alexander's actions were 'premeditated'. On the other hand, Alexander did declare his intention to destroy Persepolis before arriving at the city and his actions are therefore hardly surprising.[17]

Another question is the extent of the damage inflicted on the city. Curtius reports that Persepolis was wiped off the map almost without a trace. Diodorus, in contrast, mentions how years later, during the Successor Wars, Persepolis still served as the capital of Persis and its satrap Peucestas hosted a grand feast at the city. If Diodorus is correct, the city was clearly not 'destroyed' but only partially burned. In a similar example, Artaxerxes III Ochus 'destroyed' Sidon, yet the city was still functioning when Alexander arrived. Archaeological evidence also points to the limited nature of the destruction, limiting it to the section of the city containing Xerxes' palace. Overall, we can conclude that Alexander's destructive actions at Persepolis, while devastating, were far less severe than what he did at Thebes.[18]

Alexander's decision to 'destroy' Persepolis spurred mixed opinions among the ancients. Arrian disapproved of the act of punishing Persians for their ancestors' crimes. The Macedonian soldiers were ashamed at the destruction and the possible drunkenness of their king. At the same time, they may have taken heart, thinking that this episode marked the end of the Pan-Hellenic War and that they would soon be going home. However, these hopes would not come to fulfilment as Alexander still intended to push onward to claim the rest of the Persian Empire.[19] Alexander himself later expressed regret for the destruction he inflicted on the city. Curtius adds that Alexander came to believe that the Persians would have been humiliated even more had he ruled his empire from Xerxes' palace and sat on the Persian throne.[20]

It is important that we take a moment to examine the sacking from the Persian perspective and what it meant to them. To the Persians, the sacking of their ceremonial capital and the burning of Xerxes' palace must have been devastating to their psyche. Persepolis was not only a political centre but also a major religious site that held yearly Zoroastrian festivals. Perhaps Alexander's actions at Persepolis could be interpreted as part of a strategy of crushing the Persian will to continue fighting. With Darius having suffered two defeats and all their major political centres in Macedonian hands, one imagines Persian morale was at an all-time low. On the other hand, as Parmenion pointed out, the events showed Alexander with the image of a plunderer who wanted to destroy and move on.[21]

Alexander at Pasargadae

After entering Persepolis, Alexander also received the surrender of nearby Pasargadae. Pasargadae was the capital of Cyrus' empire and the site of his great victory over the Medes. The governor of Pasargadae, Gobares, gave up without a fight and handed over the 6,000 talents of the city's treasure. Nothing else, however, is stated about Alexander's actions at the city until years later, after his return from India. The fact that Alexander ignored Pasargadae is peculiar considering the city's importance as a political centre and its connection to Cyrus.[22]

Pasargadae, as the first capital of the Achaemenid state, held an important ceremonial function. Traditionally, Persian rulers went to Pasargadae for their official coronation ceremony. They would have to obtain the blessing of the Magi and the gods for their rule. They also had to undertake a series of established rituals. For example, Artaxerxes II, on the death of his father Darius II, travelled to the city of Cyrus for such a coronation ceremony as Plutarch describes in his life of the king:

A little while after the death of Dareius [sic], the new king made an expedition to Pasargadae, that he might receive the royal initiation at the hands of the Persian priests. Here there is a sanctuary of a warlike goddess whom one might conjecture to be Athena. Into this sanctuary the candidate for initiation must pass, and after laying aside his own proper robe, must put on that which Cyrus the Elder used to wear before he became king; then he must eat of a cake of figs, chew some turpentine-wood, and drink a cup of sour milk. Whatever else is done besides this is unknown to outsiders.[23]

During his time in Cyrus' city, Alexander did not attempt to undergo such a ritual and claim the Persian throne as the new Great King or King of Kings. He did not meet with the Magi or get a blessing from the gods for his rule. Plutarch confirms this when he states 'King Alexander never refused to bestow the royal title upon other hands, nor did he proclaim himself King of Kings, although many kings received their position and title from him.'[24] How can we account for Alexander's declining of the Persian kingship when he accepted rule over Egypt and Babylonia?

Perhaps he was content with the greater title 'King of Asia' and did not feel it necessary to claim the Persian throne. Maybe he thought it would undermine his Pan-Hellenic agenda and hurt his support with the Greeks. A more obvious explanation could be that Alexander did not believe Persians would support such a move. Had Alexander taken the step of having himself crowned, it likely would have been a hollow move without the support of the Persian elite or the Magi. It would have been especially problematic as Darius still lived at this point.

Traditionally in order to become Great King, one had to be of the Achaemenid line and a direct ancestor of Cyrus. As Herodotus writes of the tribes in Persis, 'the chief tribe is that of the Pasargadae; to them belongs the clan of the Achaemenidae, the royal house of Persia.' The kingship of Persia was limited to the Pasargadae and, in particular, to the Achaemenid clan. The Persians were even sensitive about princes being born prior to a Great King's accession. For an example, we can look to the conflict between Artaxerxes II and Cyrus the Younger. Artaxerxes was born before his father's rule, while his younger brother Cyrus was born during his father's reign. Cyrus used this to his advantage and attempted to claim legitimacy over his older brother.[25]

Nonetheless, if Alexander truly wanted to be the Great King, he could certainly have forced the issue. Centuries later, the Seleucid King Antiochus III did just that, taking on the title of Great King. Apparently, Antiochus believed the title would help him win over people in the East, regardless of any controversy it caused. It is curious that Antiochus, who modelled himself heavily on Alexander, took the title but that Alexander did not think it wise. Whether Alexander should have taken the Persian throne and why he did not will remain a subject of debate.[26]

Alleged Suppression of Iranian Religion

According to Iranian traditions, Alexander destroyed Persian religious works at Persepolis. The most egregious allegation against Alexander is that he burned the Zoroastrian *Avesta*. If true, this would have been a truly devastating blow to followers of Zoroaster's faith. However, the evidence against Alexander should be treated with some caution as it stems from traditions written centuries later under the Sassanid dynasty. None of our Greco-Roman historians mention Alexander committing such a crime. Also it is important to note that historians are sceptical if a written version of the *Avesta* even existed in this period for Alexander to burn.[27]

Even if we let Alexander off the hook for burning the *Avesta*, the king did commit other acts of suppression against Iranian religious traditions. As previously stated, Persepolis was a centre for Zoroastrian festivals and Alexander must have inflicted a great deal of spiritual damage. Later, when he entered the city of Ecbatana in Media, he looted the temple to the water goddess Anahita of its treasures. This particular temple would find itself repeatedly robbed by Alexander's successors.[28]

On a separate occasion, Alexander again disrespected Anahita. This time he violated a shrine to the goddess. In this case, the king's actions may have been those of ignorance. As per Iranian custom, corpses were either embalmed or left to be devoured by dogs and birds. Alexander stumbled upon the latter at a sanctuary to Anahita. The king had the bodies taken away and disposed of as per Macedonian custom. Alexander may simply have been doing what he thought was decent, but the local Iranians certainly would not have seen it that way. It is also noteworthy that the Persian coronation ceremony was associated closely with Anahita and Alexander had not undergone this ritual. From the evidence, it seems clear that Alexander did not honour Persian and Iranian traditions with the same level of respect as he did those of the Egyptians or Babylonians.[29]

Putting aside these specific instances, Alexander does not appear to have intended to conduct a great persecution of Iranian religious traditions. On several occasions in his reign, Alexander abided by traditional Persian customs. He allowed Darius' mother to bury any fallen warriors in Persian fashion after Issus. When the wife of Darius died, he had her buried according to Persian customs. When hosting a reconciliation banquet at Opis towards the end of his reign, Persian Magi were present and participated in the proceedings. Alexander looks to have even inherited, from his Achaemenid predecessors, influence over affairs in the Zoroastrian faith. When Hephaestion died, Alexander ordered the Zoroastrians to put out their sacred fires in mourning as they had done when a Persian king died.[30]

Alexander's time in Persis remains a divisive episode. His actions in Persis stand apart from his benevolent acts in Egypt and Babylonia. The events at Persepolis confirm the fact that Alexander, for all his chivalry, could be equally cruel. It's hard to completely ascertain his rationale for burning Persepolis; whether it was part of a war strategy, revenge or simple drunkenness. The destruction itself seems to have been exaggerated by the ancients, and modern evidence points to Alexander's actions being more limited in scale. Nonetheless, it must have been shocking for the Persians to have their royal city looted and Xerxes' palace burned. Why Alexander did not accept the Persian throne is another mystery. The king's lack of Achaemenid blood and his soldiers' sympathies undoubtedly played a role. The allegations that Alexander oppressed Zoroastrian religion and Iranian traditions are complex. At times the king committed acts of disregard to the native practices, while on other occasions he proved tolerant of them.

Chapter Eight

Alexander Against Bessus

King Darius' murder by his kinsman Bessus proved to be a turning-point in Alexander's conquest of Asia. The Great King was now dead and with him whatever remained of the Persian Empire. Bessus' actions presented both a danger and an opportunity for Alexander. By murdering King Darius and assuming the throne, he had become a grave threat to Alexander. If Bessus could rally renewed support, he could threaten Alexander's hold on Asia. From another point of view, Bessus' murder of Darius was a lucky break for Alexander. The King of Asia could now unite the Persian elite on a mission to avenge Darius by punishing the usurper. Alexander's eventual capture and savage punishment of Bessus has sparked diverging viewpoints. Was it meaningless cruelty, or did it serve a greater purpose?

Death of Darius

Following his defeat at Gaugamela, Darius had fled to Media. In Media he hoped to raise yet another army with which to combat Alexander. The Persian king predicted that Alexander would focus on capturing the Persian royal capitals, giving him some breathing space. As Arrian points out, 'Dareius was not mistaken' in his assessment as Alexander did not pursue him directly but instead occupied Babylon, Susa and Persepolis. It was not until spring of 330, following his winter stay at Persepolis, that Alexander again took up the hunt for Darius.[1]

Alexander, informed of Darius' whereabouts, resolved to move quickly into Media to catch the Persian king. Darius' hopes for assembling a new army had faltered, and he now decided to retreat further into the depths of his empire. The route to Media was unsuitable for a large army, giving Darius' small party a chance to escape and prevent any quick pursuit.[2]

Outside his personal entourage and a few thousand remaining Greek mercenaries, Darius' most powerful remaining contingent was the

Bactrian cavalry under their satrap Bessus. Bessus was a relative of Darius and had commanded the left wing of the Persian army at Gaugamela. After the disaster, he had fled with the king to Media. Bessus' former loyalty to the king had begun to waver while his personal ambitions grew. The prominence of Bessus and his Bactrians among the remaining soldiers would ultimately lead to the Persian king's undoing.[3]

Alexander marched into Media, occupying the capital of Ecbatana. The fall of Ecbatana added to Babylon, Susa and Persepolis gave Alexander control of all the major Persian capitals and residences of the Persian kings. Parmenion would be left to hold Ecbatana with a garrison securing the city's treasury. Alexander also appointed a Persian nobleman Oxydates as satrap over Media. Oxydates was known to be an enemy of Darius, having been previously imprisoned by the king. Alexander likely felt confident that this Persian would serve him loyally due to his past. This arrangement served best to secure Alexander's line of supply by putting in place a trusted commander and an enemy of Darius.[4]

Departing Media, Alexander began a close pursuit of Darius, driving the Persian king into the neighbouring province of Parthia. Darius' support began to falter along the march as men deserted the king. A conspiracy began to develop against Darius within his inner circle. These men believed Darius had failed as a leader and should be removed. The plot included Nabarzanes, Darius' *hazarapatis* (grand vizier), Barsaentes, satrap of Arachosia and Zarangiane, Satibarzanes, satrap of Areía, and most importantly, Bessus, satrap of Bactria.[5]

Faced with growing opposition, Darius had attempted to rally his remaining followers with a speech declaring that he would not become a Mithrenes or a Mazaeus. Applause followed from the king's remaining followers, but Nabarzanes was unmoved by the speech. The vizier recommended that Darius 'hand over the auspices and the rule for a time to another, who shall be called king no longer than until the enemy shall withdraw from Asia; then he will return the sovereignty to you when he has won victory.' Nabarzanes added that the army should move to Bactria and that Bessus, as satrap of Bactria, should be made king.[6]

Nabarzanes' plan was, in theory, a compromise solution in which Darius would still retain his titles while another, in whom the men had more confidence, would lead the army. Giving Bessus command once the army arrived in Bactria did make a great deal of sense as he would have greater knowledge of his satrapy than Darius. However, it's hard to imagine that Bessus would have simply resigned and given power back to Darius if he defeated Alexander. It is more likely that Bessus and his followers would simply have murdered Darius at a later date. Darius recognized the true intentions of Nabarzanes. The Persian king reached for his sword, but quickly found himself surrounded by Bessus' Bactrians and disarmed.[7]

Now effectively a prisoner, Darius fell into a state of depression about his circumstances. Meanwhile, Bessus began a campaign to win over the remaining soldiery with tales of Bactria's wealth and fertility. The remaining Persian soldiers looked to have been won over by Bessus. In contrast, the Greek mercenaries remained loyal to the Great King and offered to assist Darius in escaping. Darius refused to leave with the Greeks as he felt it would mean abandoning his countrymen for foreigners. Bessus now had an urge to kill Darius and seize absolute power at once. However, Bessus suppressed such urges as he thought Darius could still be a useful bargaining chip.[8]

The arrest of Darius and the assumption of command by Bessus were reported to Alexander by a Babylonian named Bagistanes and Antibelos, son of Mazaeus. This is interesting to note as it shows that both the Babylonians and Mazaeus continued to assist Alexander's military efforts. Subsequently, Alexander closed the distance in his pursuit, arriving at a campsite Bessus had only recently used. From a prisoner captured at the camp, Alexander learned that Darius was now being led around in a carriage. The Persian king being cart-bound would slow his escape considerably, and Alexander pressed on with great force, seeing an opportunity to capture his rival.[9]

Bessus hoped to reach Bactria before Alexander could catch him. Alexander, however, proved too fast and caught up to Bessus' column. Bessus and his conspirators demanded that Darius flee with them on horseback. The Persian king bluntly refused, perhaps at this stage wishing to retain his dignity and surrender to Alexander. As per Curtius, Darius took Alexander's arrival as a divine message that the king would protect him. Unable to get Darius to flee, the conspirators mortally wounded the Persian king. The Persian ruler was left on the roadside, barely alive. Bessus and his allies expected the dying Darius to delay Alexander and expedite their flight from the scene.[10]

Bessus now headed for his satrapy of Bactria, leaving behind many of his followers at the mercy of Alexander. When Alexander arrived, he had no trouble in defeating Bessus' men, taking many captives. The captives are said to have far outnumbered the small Macedonian vanguard sent against them. Following the brief engagement, Alexander's men began to search for Darius through Bessus' baggage train. A Macedonian Polystratos came upon the dying Darius at a watering hole.[11]

All our accounts concerning Darius' death are highly fictionalized and written to make it seem as if Darius accepted Alexander as his successor. Allegedly, Polystratos gave the Persian king some water and a translator came forward. As per our sources, Darius lamented his fate and now thought Alexander's actions 'to be those of a prince, not of a foe' and hoped the empire would fall to his hands. He spoke of the cruel irony that Alexander had spared his family while his relative Bessus had murdered him. The Persian king wished for a 'decent rather than a magnificent' funeral and mused about someone avenging his death. Darius, the last Great King of the Achaemenid house, then expired. The dynasty of Cyrus had finally come to an end. According to Justin, Darius died near the Parthian village of Thara. The historian eagerly points out the irony that the Parthian Empire would one day arise from this territory and come to rule Persia.[12]

Alexander arrived on the scene too late as Darius had already died. The event greatly 'distressed' him, and he even wept at the sight of the murdered king. As Plutarch records,

> When he saw Darius pierced through by javelins, he did not offer sacrifice nor raise the paean to indicate that the long war had come to an end; but he took off his own cloak and threw it over the corpse as though to conceal the divine retribution that waits upon the lot of kings.

Alexander may have indeed been disturbed by Darius' demise. He always considered kings above the mortal man and would have been dismayed to witness any king die at the hands of his own men.[13]

Alexander gave Darius' body to his mother Sisygambis and sent it back to Persepolis for an honourable burial in the Persian royal tombs. In sending the body back to Persis, Alexander was fulfilling royal precedent. He had previously buried Darius' wife with honours. In both cases, Alexander sent an important message to the family of Darius and the Persian nobility. However, something suspicious is that we have not found a tomb for Darius among the royals at Persepolis. Perhaps the king's body never underwent an official internment alongside his relatives.[14]

The death of Darius ruined any potential plans by Alexander to force the Persian king's submission along with the Persian Empire's elite. Alexander would have to find a new way to gain the support of Asians and Bessus presented the perfect target. Alexander would now seek to demonize Bessus as Darius' murderer and present himself as Darius' chosen avenger. The Persian and Asian nobles, instead of fighting the Macedonian invaders, would now be more focused on the villainous Bessus.

Artaxerxes V

Bessus had proceeded to his satrapy of Bactria and prepared to resist Alexander. In Bactria, Bessus took the dramatic step of assuming the Persian kingship under the name Artaxerxes V. He began to wear the marks of Persian royalty reserved for the Achaemenid kings. Bessus' assumption of the Persian kingship was a significant event. These actions by Bessus presented a direct challenge to Alexander's rule as 'King of Asia'. Bessus was now not merely a rebel, but a usurper of the Persian throne.[15]

Bessus appears to have presented himself as a freedom-fighter against Alexander. He tried to rally the populace for something akin to a patriotic war. Following his assumption of the throne, Bessus made significant efforts to prepare for Alexander's arrival. Diodorus describes how he 'set to work enrolling soldiers, manufacturing an adequate stock of weapons, and busily making everything ready for the approaching time of need'.[16]

Bessus allied himself with nomadic Scythian tribes to the north on the Jaxartes River. The Scythian peoples were the skilled horsemen who had killed Cyrus the Great. A contingent of them had fought against Alexander at Gaugamela and proved themselves to be tough opponents. The support of these nomads was essential for Bessus if he had any hope of resisting Alexander.[17]

Additionally, Bessus attempted to disrupt the territories already under Alexander's control. By this strategy, he could delay the king and give himself more time to prepare. Bessus gave his support to Satibarzanes, a renegade satrap in Areía who had revolted against Alexander. The usurper also appointed his own satrap in Parthia and sent him off to start a rebellion in that satrapy. These actions demonstrate the critical danger Bessus presented to Alexander. The Macedonians were depleted in strength, leaving many soldiers behind for garrison duties and marching on strained logistics.[18]

Bessus' Banquet

Fortunately for Alexander, Bessus was never able to fully win the support of the Persian elite. One can perhaps attribute this to how Bessus assumed his position. The murder of Darius was undoubtedly controversial, as was Bessus assuming the kingship on his own accord. In theory, the Persian throne now belonged to Ochus, the young son of Darius, who was held prisoner by Alexander.[19] Bessus, however, did not make any attempt to recognize Ochus as heir. By all measures, Bessus was a usurper who had murdered the legitimate ruler and assumed the throne without right. Lacking the legitimacy of his predecessor, Bessus felt a need to justify his actions to his comrades outwardly.

On one occasion Bessus, in conference with his generals, attempted to explain his removal of Darius. Bessus presented Darius as incompetent and unfit to rule the empire. Bessus used the example of how Darius had chosen to engage Alexander in the confined area of Issus over the advice of his advisors, leading to an unnecessary disaster. Bessus claimed that the Macedonians were not a powerful foe, only that they had gained easy victories due to Darius' poor generalship. As Curtius writes, 'Bessus, in insolent language and so proud of a sovereignty gained by murder as hardly to be in his right mind.'[20]

One of Bessus' followers, a Mede named Cobares, was bold enough to criticize the self-proclaimed monarch. Cobares said that Bessus, instead of bombastic speeches, should look to planning for the campaign. Even more boldly, Cobares questioned Bessus' right to rule, remarking 'you sustain a great burden on your head, a kingly crown' and further 'the kingdom you hold is another's, which makes it easier for you to part with it.' Bessus, in drunken anger, attempted to then kill Cobares but was restrained by his men. This mirrors Darius' attempt to kill Nabarzanes, only to be held back.[21]

Fearing for his life, Cobares left that night and defected to Alexander. Alexander did not punish him for his role in Bessus' usurpation. In fact, 'his safe reception and the gifts promised by Alexander attracted Bessus' leading generals.' Alexander's favourable reception of Cobares undoubtedly played on the minds of Bessus' commanders as things grew more and more desperate for their cause.[22]

Alexander's Speech

In the Macedonian camp, Alexander faced his own wave of dissatisfaction in the ranks. The king felt that at this moment he stood at 'the very threshold of victory' with 'a few runaways and slayers, murderers of their master' the only thing left in his way. All he now needed to do was eliminate Bessus and his followers to secure his victory in Asia. In contrast to their king, the soldiers were tired of war and, with the death of Darius, wanted to head for home. Determined to reinvigorate his army, Alexander turned to his famed oratory to deliver the results.[23]

In a speech before his assembled army, Alexander explained that Bessus would have no trouble seizing a 'vacant kingdom' and the need to continue the war in Asia. Alexander wanted to secure the fruits of his victory, reminding his men that 'our empire is new and, if we are prepared to admit the truth, insecure'. He believed that it was a great danger to let Bessus roam free and the murder of Darius to go unpunished, stating 'often to ignore a tiny spark has roused a great conflagration'. In Alexander's opinion, the Persians could then, in the future, again rise to pose a danger to the Greek world, 'but by Heaven! If presently it shall have been announced that the same wretch (Bessus) is laying waste to the Hellespont?' Alexander asked his men to follow him in destroying Bessus before he could consolidate his rule. Alexander's speech had the intended effect and rallied the Macedonians for the campaign against Bessus.[24]

Significantly, Alexander did not forget his Persian audience when making the speech. Alexander made sure to highlight the crime Bessus had committed by killing Darius and that he would have Bessus 'nailed to a cross'. The king reiterated how he would have 'spared' Darius and 'saved' him from Bessus. These statements say much about Alexander's intentions at this stage in the campaign. His goal was to gain legitimacy through winning the support of the Persian nobles. Alexander hoped to paint himself as an honourable man who only intended to take Darius' empire, not murder the Persian ruler. Meanwhile, the usurper Bessus was an evil traitor who was deserving of punishment. In this way, Alexander hoped he could convince the Persian elite to recognize him as the legitimate ruler of Asia and support him against Bessus. Alexander's propaganda efforts following Darius' death appear to have worked as Darius' brother Oxyathres and some 200 Asian noblemen came over to his side.[25]

The Campaign Against Bessus

It was not until the spring of 329 that Alexander was able to take up the pursuit of Bessus and march into Bactria. The Macedonians had been distracted, reducing a rebellion in Areía by the satrap Satibarzanes. Bessus' position proved to be weaker than was perhaps expected. The usurper adopted scorched earth tactics in an attempt to stall the Macedonians. Alexander marched into the satrapal capital of Bactra and Bessus fled across the Oxus River.[26]

The Oxus proved no significant obstacle to Alexander. After crossing the river, the Macedonians pursued Bessus. Bessus' lack of strength was apparent as he did not attempt to contest Alexander's crossing. The only thing holding Alexander back was the harsh terrain that wore out his horses. The king confiscated replacements from the local Sogdian people. The latter seem to have remained largely neutral in the war between Alexander and Bessus. However, Alexander's advance into their territory must have irritated them as they would stage a great uprising later that year.[27]

Bessus' cause now looked hopeless and his comrades began to lose faith in him. The nobleman Spitamenes, a close confidant of Bessus, hatched a conspiracy against the usurper. He gathered a group of Darius' former friends around himself. Together they plotted to gain Alexander's favour by betraying Bessus and 'avenging' Darius. Spitamenes used his closeness to Bessus to dismiss his guards from outside his tent before entering with his co-conspirators. Bessus was tied up, stripped of his royal garb, and word sent to Alexander for him to come and collect his prize. Alexander, pleased, rewarded Spitamenes and his comrades with 'fine gifts'.[28]

The Punishment of Bessus

Alexander's capture of Bessus proved to be another turning-point for the king. Bessus' usurpation had presented a great danger to Alexander and the possibility of renewed Persian resistance. With Bessus' capture, Alexander could now breathe a sigh of relief. The King of Asia intended to use Bessus' capture for maximum propaganda effect. He knew the Persians wanted revenge for the murder of Darius and he would give it to them. The capture of Bessus was a golden opportunity for Alexander to prove himself as the true legitimate heir to Darius.

According to Arrian, Alexander sent his loyal comrade Ptolemy to swiftly take custody of Bessus. Spitamenes handed over the chained prisoner to the Macedonian general. The Persian noble was pleased to do so, 'avenging both you and Darius my kings, I have brought you the slayer of his lord.' Alexander gave Ptolemy specific instructions regarding his royal captive. He ordered Bessus to be brought 'bound, naked, and wearing a wooden collar, and thus conduct him, stationing him on the right of the road by which he and his army were about to pass.' Alexander designed this scenario to humiliate Bessus in the greatest of ways. Alexander wanted the punishment of Bessus and his avenging of Darius to be seen by all.

The Persian-Asian elite applauded Alexander's punishment of Bessus. According to Curtius, Bessus in chains was 'a sight as pleasing to the barbarians as to the Macedonians'. Spitamenes expressed his pleasure at the punishment of Bessus, wishing 'Darius might open his eyes to behold the spectacle'. Alexander subsequently arrived in person to make an even greater propaganda show out of Bessus. As Arrian records, Alexander used the occasion to demonstrate his new stature as 'King of Asia', riding to the scene in Darius' royal chariot.[29]

Alexander, dismounting from the vehicle, proceeded to publicly berate Bessus. This display was clearly for the ears of the gathered Asian and Persian nobles. Alexander questioned Bessus as to why he had first seized Darius, who had been his king, his relative and his benefactor, then led him about in chains and murdered him. Bessus defended his actions, claiming that he had acted on his own but with the consent of Darius' leading officials. This claim by Bessus is partly valid as he had the support of Darius' grand vizier and several satraps. However, Bessus' justifications did little to appease Alexander, who had Bessus whipped and his offences read out.[30]

The punishment of Bessus was to be a lengthy process. Alexander handed over the usurper to Darius' brother Oxyathres who was eager for revenge. Oxyathres had Bessus taken back to Bactria and tried before an assembly for his betrayal of Darius. He was then sent to Ecbatana and tried before another even higher assembly of Medes and Persians before finally being executed. All the accounts agree that they inflicted horrible punishments upon Bessus before he died. The worst of it comes from Plutarch, who has Bessus being lashed between two trees and ripped apart.[31]

Diodorus recounts that Bessus, after his eventual demise, was not given a royal burial. The usurper's remains were instead scattered. This act was in keeping with the traditional Persian treatment of traitors. Alexander would have read about such a practice in the *Anabasis*. Orontas, a man who had betrayed Cyrus the Younger, was put on trial and then executed. Due to his betrayal, Orontas was not honoured with a burial or a gravesite. Alexander surely thought Bessus deserved a similar fate to Orontas.[32]

Alexander's savage treatment of Bessus paints the king in an awful light. Even Arrian, one of Alexander's great admirers, could not approve of Bessus' punishment. The historian viewed the act as barbaric based on Persian customs. In Alexander's mind, however, the torture of Bessus was necessary to 'avenge' Darius and win over the Persian elite. As noted earlier, the Persian nobles very much enjoyed seeing Bessus bound. Oxyathres wanted vengeance for his brother, and that is just what Alexander gave him.[33]

Chapter Nine

Imitator of the Persians

With his assumption of the Asian throne, Alexander began to take on Persian and Asian attributes. The ancients were quick to point out how Alexander moved away from his traditional Macedonian habits to those of the Easterners. In the words of the satirist Lucian, Alexander 'took to aping the manners of your conquered Medes' in his habits. Arrian notes how 'Alexander was carried away to the extent both of copying Medic and Persian splendour.' When confronted by dissenting Macedonians, upset by the king's Eastern turn, Alexander remarked, 'I am accused of transferring the customs of the vanquished to the Macedonians! True, for I see many things we should not blush to imitate; and so great an empire cannot fitly be ruled without contributing some things to the vanquished and learning from them.' Alexander's imitation of the Persian kings included adopting Asian dress, the employment of Persian bodyguards, eunuchs, ushers at court, the use of Darius' royal chariot, great Eastern-style hunts, extravagant banquets and the introduction of the proskynesis ritual.[1]

Eastern-Style Dress

The Persian Great King and his subjects wore a specific dress to signify their rank. Curtius provides a description of Darius' attire before the Battle of Issus:

> The attire of the king was noteworthy beyond all else in luxury; a purple-edged tunic woven about a white centre, a cloak of cloth of gold, ornamented with golden hawks, which seemed to attack each other with their beaks; from a golden belt, with which he was girt woman-fashion, he had hung a scimitar, the scabbard of which was a single gem. The Persians called the king's head-dress cidaris; was bound with a blue filet variegated with white.[2]

The most important part of the Persian king's dress was the tiara. According to Xenophon, wearing a tiara as a symbol of royalty went back to the time of Cyrus. As the historian notes in the *Cyropaedia*, 'Cyrus himself upon a chariot appeared in the gates wearing his tiara upright.' It's important to note that the Persian kings wore the kitaris (an upright tiara). The other Persians wore a different kind of tiara as illustrated by Herodotus: 'Persians were equipped in this way: they wore on their heads loose caps called tiaras.' Plutarch concurs with the upright tiara being associated with kingship. He provides an example that when Xerxes was 'performing the functions of a king' he wore the tiara upright, but when he went to greet his brother, pressed 'down the crest'.[3]

In 330, during his time in Parthia, Alexander took the dramatic step of adopting Persian or Median dress.[4] Controversy exists as to exactly what Eastern attire Alexander began wearing. Our sources provide slightly differing accounts on the subject:

Arrian: 'Nor do I at all commend his taking to Median garb instead of the traditional Macedonian dress, especially since he was a descendant of Heracles. Moreover, he did not blush to exchange the head-dress he had long worn as a conqueror for the tiara of the conquered Persians.'[5]

Curtius: 'he encircled his brow with a purple diadem variegated with white such as Darius had worn, and assumed Persian garb, not even fearing the omen of changing from the insignia of the victor to the dress of the conquered.'[6]

Diodorus: 'he put on the Persian diadem and dressed himself in the white robe and the Persian sash and everything else except the trousers and the long-sleeved upper garment.'[7]

Justin: 'Alexander assumed the attire of the Persian monarchs, as well as the diadem, which was unknown to the kings of Macedonia, as if he gave himself up to the customs of those whom he had conquered.'[8]

Plutarch: 'he first put on the barbaric dress...however he did not so far as to adopt the Median costume, which was altogether barbaric and outlandish, and he wore neither trousers, nor a sleeved vest, nor a tiara. Instead he adopted a style which was a compromise between

Persian and Median custom, more modest than the first, and more stately than the second.'[9]

Lucian: 'abandoned the Macedonian cloak in favour of the candys, assumed the upright tiara.'[10]

To summarize, all our main sources concur on the point that Alexander and his comrades adopted some form of 'Median' dress. Arrian and Plutarch's accounts, however, differ regarding the extent. According to Arrian, along with Lucian, Alexander took on the full Persian dress, including the kitaris headdress. In contrast to Arrian, Plutarch presents Alexander wearing a more conservative dress without the full Median attire or the kitaris. Also some dispute exists over whether Alexander traded in his Macedonian cloak for the Persian kandys 'long-sleeved upper garment'. Diodorus denies that Alexander wore the garment, while Lucian mentions its use.[11]

If Arrian and Lucian are correct and Alexander did indeed adopt the kitaris, it is exceptionally significant. The kitaris signified kingship to the Persians as Xenophon writes, 'the King alone may wear upright the tiara that is upon the head.'[12] Bessus had also adopted the upright tiara when he declared his rule over the Persians. If Alexander indeed adopted the kitaris and the kandys, it sent a clear message to the Persian elite. The Macedonian ruler had taken on the imagery of the Achaemenid kings.

Despite the doubts of Plutarch, it makes perfect sense for Alexander to wear the kitaris. Alexander's goal was to make the Persian elite accept him and make the transition to his rule as painless as possible. The Macedonian ruler could not afford to deny wearing the ceremonial kitaris. It is almost unthinkable that Alexander would have allowed Bessus to wear the upright tiara while he did not. We can also look to coinage, which shows Alexander sporting the upright tiara as a further indication.[13]

Alexander probably used the kitaris only for select occasions. The king's primary headgear was the more modest diadem. Curtius accounts for Alexander's items at the time of his death. The historian notes the presence of the king's diadem, but not the kitaris.[14]

As mentioned above, Alexander wanted his companions to share in his adoption of Persian ways. The Macedonians adopted the wearing of 'gold and purple' robes. According to Curtius, the Macedonians found the outfits distasteful and were 'forced' to wear them by the king. In Justin's opinion, Alexander made his friends wear the attire because he thought 'such innovations should be viewed with dislike, if adopted by himself alone'. Alexander probably had other reasons for making his companions share his new attire. Cyrus the Great had his comrades adopt Median clothing after his conquest of the Median Empire and Alexander may have been following Cyrus' example. The giving of valuable clothing was a tradition among the Persians. Herodotus notes that Darius the Great planned to award one of his comrades and his descendants after that an annual gift of Median clothing.[15]

Our ancient sources provide explanations for Alexander taking on Eastern dress. According to Arrian, Alexander wanted to give the Persians the impression of not being 'wholly removed from them' and their customs. As per Plutarch, Alexander may have changed his dress out of 'a desire to adapt himself to local habits'. Alexander understood that 'sharing of race and of customs is a great step towards softening men's hearts.' Plutarch, in his *Moralia*, further adds that Alexander 'as sovereign of both nations and benevolent king he strove to acquire the goodwill of the conquered by showing respect for their apparel.' Alexander felt that by adopting their ways, the Persians 'might not feel hate toward them as enemies'. Plutarch further compares Alexander to a hunter who wears animal skins to mollify his prey.[16]

Persian-Macedonian Court

The Macedonian court would undergo a remodelling after Alexander ascended to the Asian throne. Alexander, when hosting court, wanted to present himself in a way befitting his new title of 'King of Asia'. According to Athenaeus, Alexander began to make use of Darius' royal tent which he had captured during the war. The tent was said to have been massive in size and luxurious, containing 100 couches and with 50 golden pillars supporting it. Within the tent itself was a 'golden chair, on which Alexander used to sit and transact business, his body-guards standing all around'.[17]

Significantly, Alexander began to wear Darius' ring and make use of the Achaemenid royal seal. According to Curtius, Alexander used Darius' ring when conducting policy in Asia and his Macedonian ring for affairs in Europe. Nothing outlines the dual Persian-Macedonian nature of the new kingdom better than Alexander's use of these two rings. He wanted it to appear as if he was issuing orders just as the Achaemenids had before him. In the same way at Tarsus, he began issuing coins in the Achaemenid fashion. It is important to note that he did not use Darius' ring when conducting business with the Greek world. Likely the Greeks would not have been pleased by receiving decrees marked by the Persian seal. However, as Plutarch notes, Alexander's letters to Greece had begun to take on a more authoritative tone as he dropped his usually friendly greetings.[18]

Alexander kept the Persian royal ushers at their posts. The ushers were men drawn from the 'Asiatic races' and assigned to assist the court's procedures. According to Plutarch, Chares of Mytilene, who wrote a lost history of Alexander, was a member or even the head of the royal ushers. Chares was known to have been familiar with stories 'often told by the barbarians who dwell in Asia'. The position of ushers must have required a person like Chares, who was familiar with both Greek and Persian ways.[19]

The royal harem of Darius also continued to be maintained at Alexander's court. The harem included 365 concubines, one for every day of the year. The women were said to have been of 'outstanding beauty' and drawn from throughout Asia. Every night they were paraded before the Persian king so he could select a partner. Darius would take his entire entourage with him on campaign, including his concubines. Alexander made use of the harem only 'sparingly' as he did not wish to offend the Macedonians. Nonetheless, it is significant that Alexander maintained the harem, not wanting to part from the Persian custom.[20]

The court was attended by 'distinguished persons' drawn from the Persian and Asian elite. The most prominent of these was Oxyathres, the brother of Darius. He had supported Alexander against Bessus and oversaw the usurper's punishment. Oxyathres became part of Alexander's inner circle and a member of his group of bodyguards. For Alexander, what could have been better than Darius' brother's support to lure Eastern noblemen to the king's court? As Curtius reports, when Alexander was pursuing Bessus, some 200 nobles joined his efforts.[21]

According to descriptions of the king's court, Alexander employed numerous bodyguards. He had 500 Macedonian guards and 500 melophori (apple-bearers), the most elite unit of the Persians, on command within his royal tent. Outside on guard were 1,000 elite Macedonians, 500 Susians, and 10,000 Persians representing the infamous Immortals. Alexander additionally had some 1,000 archers posted around the perimeter. All the Eastern guards were lavishly dressed in multi-coloured clothing. Elephants are said to have also been present around Alexander's tent. Darius had used elephants at Gaugamela and the king had captured these. In India, Alexander would also have had the opportunity to acquire the beasts for his court. It is worth drawing attention to the fact that the guards did not form mixed racial units. The Macedonians and Asians each maintained their own separate configurations.[22]

According to Aelian, no one dared to approach Alexander in his tent 'without good reason, as he aroused great fear; his pride and good fortune had raised him to the position of a tyrant.' Curtius provides an anecdote in which a soldier, delirious from exhaustion and the cold, stumbled into Alexander's tent. Alexander sat the sick man down on his throne by an open fire. The soldier did not notice at first that it was the king or his throne. Eventually, he came to his senses and was startled, fearing punishment. Alexander calmed him, saying, 'Soldier, do you realize how much better a lot you Macedonians enjoy under a king than the Persians do? For them sitting on a king's throne would have meant death: for you it means life.'[23]

Darius' tent, like the upright tiara, was perhaps only used sparingly by Alexander. Alexander liked to move swiftly and a lengthy baggage train carrying such a tent would have slowed things down considerably. Whenever Alexander did use the tent, it would have made for a grand display of his new power to the Persian and Asian elite. As Polyaenus notes, 'Among the Macedonians and among the Greeks, Alexander's court of justice was plain and simple; but among the barbarians, in order to strike them with the greater awe, it was most splendid and imperial.' Alexander obviously wanted to influence the Asians by seeming as powerful as possible.[24]

Recruitment of Asian Soldiers

When Alexander arrived in the upper satrapies, he began the process of recruiting Asian soldiers. This recruitment drive started with the cavalry, which the king opened up to Asian recruits. Arrian mentions a newly-formed unit of javelin men dating to the summer of 330. The historian fails to specify whether they were made up of Asians or not, but it's a possibility. More precisely, in the autumn of 328, Arrian tells us that Alexander began to enlist cavalrymen armed with javelins from Bactria and Sogdiana. These Asian horsemen would be helpful to Alexander when campaigning on the steppe.[25] Several factors spurred Alexander to turn towards the provinces of Asia for recruits.

Following the defeat of Darius and the Pan-Hellenic War, Alexander had begun to release from service soldiers of the Greek city-states. The most prominent group that went home was the Thessalian cavalry that had served Alexander so ably at his great battles. The Macedonians had also sustained significant losses in cavalry since the onset of the campaign and could no longer expect significant mounted reinforcements from Macedonia. To fill the void left by these departing soldiers and the growing casualty figures, Alexander began to recruit men from his new Asian empire. As Diodorus explains, Alexander's strategy for recruiting Asians was to 'secure replacements from the Persians equal to the number of these soldiers whom he had released'.[26]

Great Eastern Hunts

Since his youth Alexander was known to have been an avid hunter, and his love for the sport continued unabated during his Asian campaigns. He would hunt to get his mind off the great challenges he faced or, as Plutarch puts it, 'for diversion'. After assuming the Asian throne, Alexander's hunts began to change, becoming far larger than those held in Macedonia. The largest of such hunts occurred in the forest of Bazaira in Central Asia. Alexander and his companions brought down some 4,000 animals and had a giant feast with the army.[27]

The hunts themselves began to take on a more symbolic role for Alexander. The king modified his hunting style to fulfil new Eastern expectations for him as 'King of Asia'. Great royal hunts were a pastime for rulers of the Near East, particularly lion hunts. The Persian kings had employed the image of a king slaying a lion in their imperial symbolism. Macedonian kings may have hunted lions prior to Alexander's reign as some were native to northern Greece, but undoubtedly on a far more limited scale to the East. Alexander, in imitation of the Persian and other

Eastern monarchs, would adopt these symbolic lion hunts. These hunts allowed Alexander to embrace the imagery of Near Eastern kingship.[28]

Alexander was eager to show his prowess as king by slaying Asian lions, and he is said to have often worn lion skins as Heracles had done; a demonstration of martial prowess and his ancestry. Plutarch reports how Alexander fought and killed a lion in the presence of a Spartan ambassador. The ambassador was impressed and remarked, 'Nobly, indeed, Alexander, hast thou struggled with the lion to see which should be king.' Alexander, in this instance, was plainly showing off his ability for an ambassador to a country that was hostile to Macedonia.[29]

The combat hunts could prove dangerous for both Alexander and his companions. When Alexander was hunting in Syria, a lion of enormous size attempted to leap to kill the king. Fortunately for the king, the beast was intercepted by his comrade Lysimachus. Alexander's comrade Peucestas was bitten by a bear and nearly died during a hunt. On another occasion, one of Alexander's officers, Perdiccas, accidentally wounded another named Craterus while striking at an animal. Both these incidents greatly distressed Alexander, who worried for their recovery. Regardless of the dangers, these hunts were essential for Alexander's image and he would not tolerate anyone upstaging him in these hunts. Alexander was angry at Lysimachus for saving him in Syria, claiming he could have killed the lion himself. In another instance, Alexander raged at and flogged one of his pages for killing a boar which he had marked out for himself.[30]

The Persian kings, during their hunts, had a right to the first kill. On one occasion, the Great King Artaxerxes II was out hunting with his general Megabyzus. During the excursion, a ferocious lion leaped at the king. Megabyzus reacted quickly to protect his sovereign, hitting the beast with a javelin. Instead of being praised for his actions, Artaxerxes berated Megabyzus. In Artaxerxes' mind, his general had violated his rights as king by taking his kill. The king ordered Megabyzus beheaded for the insult but soon after relented, letting his general live. This event illustrates just how symbolic the hunting was for reigning monarchs. Alexander's fury at those who took his select kill or upstaged him was due to the same royal protocol practised by the Achaemenid kings.[31]

Lysimachus was known on another occasion to have engaged a lion in single combat. According to some sources, Alexander himself maliciously trapped Lysimachus with the beast. Lysimachus only survived by wrapping his hand in a cloak and pulling out the lion's tongue. Nonetheless, the Macedonian warrior suffered severe lacerations. Like Alexander, Lysimachus came to recognize that the conquest of great beasts was important for royal imagery. Lysimachus used lions on his coinage in commemoration of his victorious single combat.[32]

The Royal Chariot

While in Asia, Alexander used a chariot on several occasions. It has been speculated that this chariot was, in fact, the royal chariot of Darius. Alexander captured Darius' chariot in the aftermath of the Battle of Issus when the Great King abandoned it. After capturing Gaza, Alexander dragged the city's eunuch commander behind his chariot, mirroring Achilles' dragging of Hector's corpse. At Babylon, Alexander entered the city on a chariot to much fanfare. The use of the vehicle at Babylon is crucial as it came right after his official declaration of Asian kingship. Alexander wanted to demonstrate his new royal status to the Babylonians.[33]

The most significant use of the royal chariot was during the capture of Bessus. As noted previously, Alexander rode up to the usurper in the chariot.[34] His arrival occurred in full view of Spitamenes, Oxyathres and other members of the Eastern elite. Alexander was attempting to influence them by the display. Curtius provides a detailed description of the royal chariot that Darius used and the awe-inspiring image it would have presented to the viewer:

> The king's chariot, in which he rode was outstanding from the rest. Both sides of the chariot were adorned with images of the gods, embossed in gold and silver; the yoke was ornamented with sparkling gems, and on it rose two golden images a cubit high of the king's ancestors, one of Ninus and the other of Belus. Between these they had consecrated a golden eagle, represented with outstretched wings.[35]

The chariot looks to have become Alexander's means of luxury convenience on the march. As Plutarch writes, 'If he were making a march which was not very urgent, he would practise, as he went along, either archery or mounting and dismounting from a chariot that was under way.'[36]

Alexander reportedly hunted from atop his chariot. The king employed both bows and javelins while in pursuit of his prey. The use of bows and javelins while mounted on a chariot were well-known symbols of Persian kings and Alexander employed them for this reason.

According to Athenaeus, Alexander would conduct these hunts dressed as the goddess Artemis. Athenaeus, however, is likely confusing Alexander's Persian dress with that of Artemis. Our ancient sources viewed Persian attire as akin to womanly dress. Curtius at Issus referred to Darius wearing 'woman-fashion'. The chariot, hunting and Persian dress combined fully demonstrate Alexander's commitment to imitating the Persian kings.[37]

Splendid Banquets and Parties

After the Battle of Issus, Alexander first began to abandon his modest ways and host extravagant banquets. According to Justin, Alexander 'contemplated the wealth and display of Darius, he was seized with admiration of such magnificence. Hence it was that he first began to indulge in luxurious and splendid banquets.'[38] Though symposiums were common in Macedonian society, Alexander's took on a different flavour in the East. The king's banquets were yet another mark of Alexander's beginning to imitate and adopt the habits of the Persian kings.

Persian royal banquets were long-lasting lavish affairs. The preparations alone are said to have taken half the day. Servants were required first to bathe and then put on white clothing before attending the king. Concubines would entertain the guests with their singing. The food included the rarest delicacies such as ostriches. Also recorded is the presence of the 'king's pillow' worth 5,000 talents of gold and the 'king's footstool' of 3,000 talents, demonstrating the Persian monarchy's immense wealth.[39]

Alexander's banquets developed on lines similar to their Persian predecessors. Alexander embraced all the pleasures that court life had to offer: 'There was a general slipping into foreign habits.' Alexander's close friend took on the position of 'eater' or taste-tester found at Persian courts. According to Curtius, Alexander's banquets began early and went on throughout the night. In imitation of the Persian king's concubine recitals, 'captive women were bidden to sing after their manner of a song of discordant and hateful to the ears.' Notably, Alexander's drinking started to play a more significant role in his affairs. Arrian reports how Alexander's 'drinking was prolonged' and that the king 'had already taken to barbaric ways in drinking as well'. Arrian's statement is interesting as the Macedonians were known for heavy drinking at banquets, but Alexander now took things even further.[40]

The banquets were not always about pleasure and could serve an important role in Alexander's diplomacy. As Curtius recounts, on one occasion, Alexander received the surrender of two prominent tribes when he was campaigning in India. He then invited their ambassadors and tribal leaders to a banquet to improve relations with the conquered. He set out to impress these leaders with a great feast and lavish decorations. The guests took their seats on golden couches. According to Curtius, Alexander 'put on show all the decadence that had long existed among the soft-living Persians'.[41]

Athenaeus reports to us that Alexander would host even more elaborate parties. Alexander would play-act as different gods wearing the 'horns of Ammon' and 'sandals of Mercury' at these events. There is also some question as to whether Alexander would dress in female attire. The king would allegedly imitate Diana 'whose dress he often wore'. Athenaeus is undoubtedly making a point about Alexander's claimed divinity by referencing Ammon. The allegation that Alexander dressed like Diana, as with the clothing of Artemis, could be mistaken for his Persian attire.[42]

When Alexander was in Carmania, after returning from India, he submitted utterly to excess. Though Arrian doubts the story, Alexander supposedly held a 'Dionysus' celebration. Alexander wore 'festive dress' and held great banquets with plenty of drinking. Dionysus, according to legend, had travelled through Asia, reaching India, and Alexander was now paying homage to the god.[43]

Alexander 'decided to imitate the god's procession'. The king ordered the local villages 'strewed with flowers and garlands' and then had his army march drunk for seven days. The march turned out to be very reckless as the area had yet to be entirely subdued. Curtius believed that it wouldn't have taken much for the natives to have captured Alexander and his comrades in this state.[44] Alexander seemed unaware of the dangers and rode in royal style, as Plutarch describes:

He himself was conveyed slowly along by eight horses, while he feasted day and night continuously with his companions on a dais built upon a lofty and conspicuous scaffolding of oblong shape; and waggons without number followed, some with purple and embroidered canopies, others protected from the sun by boughs of trees which were kept fresh and green, conveying the rest of his friends and commanders, who were all garlanded and drinking.[45]

Eunuchs

Eunuchs had played an important role at the Persian royal court since the time of Cyrus. According to Xenophon, Cyrus the Great viewed eunuchs to be 'superior to all others in fidelity to his master'. They have a reputation as evil schemers, but that should not obscure the critical part played by eunuchs in imperial administration. We can look to the reign of King Ochus, where the eunuch Bagoas wielded great power and became grand vizier. Bagoas' accomplishments were not limited to a courtly role as he led soldiers in Egypt and administered the upper satrapies. Bagoas, until his death at the hands of King Darius, was the most influential figure in the empire and its kingmaker. In Darius III's reign, we see the eunuch Batis serving the Persian king loyally by holding Gaza against Alexander.[46]

At Alexander's Asian court, eunuchs also had a significant role. According to Curtius, Alexander had numerous eunuchs in his service. Arrian confirms the presence of eunuchs at Alexander's court in a story set shortly before Alexander's death. Arrian reports how a criminal brazenly walked into the palace and sat down on Alexander's throne. The eunuchs were stunned by the episode but felt they could not interfere, 'owing to some Persian custom...but rending their garments began to beat themselves on their breasts and faces as if some terrible disaster had happened.' The incident came to Alexander's attention, and he had the criminal executed.[47]

Alexander may have employed eunuchs in diplomatic roles. A man named Euxenippus escorted a departing delegation of Sacae tribesmen on behalf of Alexander. According to Curtius, Euxenippus was 'a favourite of the king because of his youthful beauty'. His looks rivalled even those of Hephaestion, but he was reportedly too effeminate and lacked the latter's charms. While not officially confirmed, Euxenippus fits the description given of other eunuchs.[48]

The most famous of Alexander's court eunuchs was Bagoas. He was not related to the former Bagoas of Ochus' reign, and it's likely that the most important eunuch of the Persian court traditionally took on this name. This Bagoas was known to have been close to King Darius and, according to Curtius, was the Persian king's lover. At some point, after the war broke out, he became assigned to Nabarzanes, Darius' grand vizier, and the same man who joined with Bessus to betray the Persian king.[49]

After the death of Darius, Nabarzanes chose to surrender to Alexander, taking Bagoas along with him. Alexander, at first, was not of a mind to accept Nabarzanes' pleas for a pardon. To Alexander, Nabarzanes had betrayed his king and was no better than Bessus. Nabarzanes' numerous gifts proved insufficient to win over the Macedonian king. It was only the pleas of Bagoas that changed Alexander's mind on the issue.[50]

Alexander took Bagoas into his service and the two became lovers. Curtius writes that Bagoas 'had won the regard of Alexander through prostitution'. Plutarch recorded one occasion when Alexander kissed Bagoas in front of his men after the eunuch won a prize for singing and dancing. Alexander, according to Aelian, once went to Bagoas' house for a meal and a drink. Alexander had now again taken the place of Darius, this time by inheriting his favourite eunuch.[51]

Bagoas would establish for himself some level of influence at the court of Alexander. He proved instrumental in the removal of Orsines, satrap of Persis. Bagoas also may have even received a military command during the Indian campaign. A person called Bagoas, son of Pharnuches, is reported to have been one of the fleet commanders travelling down the Indus. Some historians have connected Pharnuches with the Lycian herdsman who led Alexander's men at the Persian Gate. If these two figures were of the same family, it would further explain Alexander's and Bagoas' close relationship.[52]

The Proskynesis Ritual

The most divisive of Alexander's Persian-centric policies was his introduction of the proskynesis ritual in the winter of 328/327. Proskynesis was a submission ritual performed at the Persian court between the

Persian Great King and his subjects. The ceremony may have been in use since the founding of the Persian Empire. As Xenophon notes, Cyrus the Great would 'exchange greetings' or perform the ritual when meeting other nobles. Alexander had experienced this ritual first-hand following the victory at Issus when he met Darius' mother Sisygambis. As per Persian custom, Sisygambis bowed down before Hephaestion (thinking he was Alexander) to signify her submission to someone of higher status.[53] Herodotus provides us with the best description of how proskynesis occurred among the Persians:

> When Persians happened upon each other on the street, one can tell whether or not they are equals simply by watching them. For instead of declaring greeting to each other, they kiss each other on their mouths; and then, if one is inferior to the other, they kiss each other on their cheeks; but if one of them is of a much lower status, he falls to the ground and prostrates himself before the other.[54]

Alexander introduced the proskynesis ritual at one of his regularly held banquets. According to Curtius, Alexander 'ordered the Macedonians to pay their respects to him in the Persian fashion and to salute him by prostrating themselves on the ground'. As per Justin's account, Alexander 'ordered people to do obeisance before him instead of saluting him'[55] Present for the ritual were Alexander's comrades and members of the Asian elite. Plutarch describes the proceedings:

> Alexander, after drinking, handed the cup to one of his friends, and he, on receiving it, rose up so as to face the household shrine, and when he had drunk, first made obeisance to Alexander, then kissed him, and then resumed his place upon the couch.[56]

Alexander's introduction of proskynesis did not meet with approval in all corners. Callisthenes, the great-nephew of Aristotle and Alexander's official court historian, was critical of the undertaking. Callisthenes, like Aristotle, held negative views towards 'barbarian' Persian ways. He criticized those flatterers who praised Alexander excessively: 'You should rather have remembered that you are not attending nor advising some Cambyses or Xerxes, but a son of Philip.'[57]

When the cup came around to Callisthenes, he drank from it but skipped the ritual bow. The historian then approached Alexander for a kiss as if nothing was amiss. Alexander was in conversation at the time and at first didn't notice that Callisthenes had not bowed. When informed, Alexander refused to kiss Callisthenes. As Callisthenes was departing the ceremony he mocked Alexander, reciting multiple times the Homeric line, 'Patroclus too died, a man far better than you!' Callisthenes' message to Alexander was simple: Patroclus was not a god, and neither are you.[58]

The disagreement between Alexander and Greeks like Callisthenes over the ritual is rooted in the Greeks' misconceptions of Persian practices. The Persians viewed proskynesis merely as a protocol for submitting to a superior and did not consider it a demeaning activity. In submitting even to full prostration, the Persians did not view themselves as bowing to a divine being. Despite the common belief, the Persian Great King was not considered a living god by his people. The king had a special connection to the Ahura Mazda, but he was not worshipped.[59]

The Macedonians and Greeks, in contrast, saw proskynesis in a far different light. They viewed the ritual as something far more malicious than court protocol. They inaccurately surmised that the Persian kings believed themselves to be gods and their subjects to be mere slaves. Our ancient sources fall into this same trap of labelling the Persians as divine kings. This inaccurate viewpoint has coloured their interpretations of Alexander's actions. Aelian and Cornelius Nepos provide descriptions of occasions when Greeks had previously been asked to perform proskynesis.

Aelian tells us of an occasion when the Persians asked a group of Greek ambassadors to submit before the Great King. The Persian grand vizier noticed the Greeks' displeasure at the thought and found a middle ground to appease them. The Greeks avoided performing the act by dropping a ring and making it look as if they bowed when they were really picking it up. This play-acting satisfied the Great King without them having to, in their eyes, debase themselves.[60]

Cornelius Nepos describes another time when the Athenian general Conon wished to speak to the Great King. The Persians gave Conon the choice of sending a letter or meeting the Persian ruler in person. However, the Persians warned Conon that he would have to perform proskynesis to the king if he came in person. Conon himself was not against submitting before the king, but knew that his countrymen would be ashamed of his actions. The Athenian thus chose to instead submit a letter, avoiding any controversy.[61]

Curtius' and Arrian's descriptions of the ritual further demonstrate Greco-Roman mischaracterization of proskynesis. Curtius states that Alexander undertook the ritual so that 'he might usurp divine honours'. Arrian concurs that Alexander 'desired people to bow to the earth before him, from the idea that Amnion was his father rather than Philip'. Both Curtius and Arrian are again simply misinterpreting normal Persian court protocol as something wicked. In keeping with his pro-Persian policies, Alexander was more focused on winning over his new Persian and Asian subjects rather than his own divinity.[62]

On a personal level, Alexander does not appear to have taken his divinity seriously. On one occasion, when bleeding from an arrow wound, Alexander remarked, 'This, my friends, that flows here, is blood, and not ichor, such as flows from the veins of the blessed gods.' This line comes from the *Iliad* where Diomedes cut Aphrodite and divine ichor flowed from the wound. By quoting the *Iliad*, Alexander was alluding to the fact that he would bleed ichor if he were a god.[63]

Arrian is more accurate when he states that Alexander's intention was to adopt 'characteristic(s) of Persian royalty' and emulate 'the ways of the Persians and Medes'. Alexander understood that proskynesis would be controversial among Macedonians and Greeks. However, the Persian nobles and officials of Alexander's court likely expected the new King of Asia to continue the rituals of the Persian kings. In Alexander's mind, if the proskynesis could assist in subduing the Asian elite, there was no reason not to perform the ceremony. As Arrian notes, Alexander only undertook the proskynesis after consulting 'the most illustrious of the Persians and Medes at his court'.[64]

Alexander's sensitivity to his new Persian companions is clear from his rage towards Macedonians who mocked the ritual. One time, a Persian slipped while making his submission to Alexander. Alexander's comrade Polyperchon proceeded to humiliate the Persian. Alexander took this mockery as a personal offence to him. The king dragged Polyperchon from the couch on which he was seated and threw him onto the ground. On another occasion in Babylon Cassander, the son of Antipater, laughed at Persians submitting to Alexander. Alexander again lashed out, grabbing Cassander by the hair and smashing him up against a nearby wall. These events illustrate how seriously Alexander took the ritual and that any mockery of his Persian allies was a personal affront to him.[65]

Opposition to Alexander's Persian Policies

The proskynesis ritual was not the only time Alexander faced opposition from his comrades. Philotas, the son of Parmenion and commander of the elite Companion cavalry, had been unhappy with Alexander's leadership since the army's stay in Egypt. He was frustrated that he had not received enough of a share of the credit for the recent victories and mocked Alexander's claim to be the son of Ammon. Alexander at first chose to ignore such rumours due to his previous friendship with Philotas. The king also still needed Parmenion's support for the coming battle at Gaugamela. After the great victory, the relationship between Philotas and Alexander seems to have deteriorated further.

Diodorus records an anecdote that illustrates Alexander's and Philotas' diverging viewpoints. Alexander was sitting on the throne of King Darius, but the seat proved too long for the king and his feet dangled below it. One of Alexander's pages brought over a nearby table on which the king could rest his feet. A eunuch burst into tears at the sight of Alexander using the table of Darius as a foot-rest. Alexander was perplexed and asked why the eunuch was crying. The king felt 'he had committed an act of arrogance quite the reverse of his gentleness to the captives.' Alexander then called upon the page to come and remove the table. Philotas objected to its removal, deeming it spoils given to him by 'providence'. This story fully displays Alexander's tendency to be more benevolent towards the Persians and the opposite to his Macedonian comrades like Philotas.[66]

Sometime in the autumn of 330, Philotas became part of a plot to murder Alexander. Parmenion's absence in Media likely compounded issues between the former friends. It is unknown whether Philotas was actively involved in planning the king's death or merely knew about the plot and failed to report it to the king. Ultimately Philotas was tortured, tried before a tribunal and executed.[67]

Now the question turned to what to do with Parmenion. At that moment, the veteran general was managing Alexander's line of supply. He was also a beloved figure within the army and could present a significant danger. Alexander had no way of knowing how Parmenion would react to his son's death. Alexander decided that his second-in-command could no longer be allowed to live. The king dispatched assassins who swiftly killed the unsuspecting Parmenion. The move can be viewed as a turning-point for Alexander as he rid himself of Philip's greatest commander.[68] This plot against Alexander would not be the last as the Macedonian veterans became increasingly frustrated with the king.

Anger over Alexander's actions even filtered down to the level of the average soldier. The Macedonians were said to have 'been distressed' by the death of Parmenion. Soldiers began to make statements against the king and write letters home criticizing him. Alexander moved to crush such acts of defiance within the army. Through someone the king was able to learn about those in the camp who spoke ill of him and even read their mail going home. These soldiers Alexander cordoned off into a separate formation called the 'disciplinary unit', the idea being that the dissenters would not be able to influence any other soldiers. The fate of this unit was likely to be settled as colonists in the rebellious upper satrapies.[69]

As Alexander expanded his pro-Persian policies, inevitably opposition grew. Disgruntled forces came not only from enlightened Greeks such as Callisthenes but also from the Macedonian veterans. According to Curtius, 'in the whole camp the feeling and talk of all was the same' and the Macedonian soldiers 'openly detested' Alexander's actions. They felt that Alexander 'had changed from a ruler of Macedonia to a satrap of Darius'. Alexander was aware of his Macedonians' disapproval but likely felt that gaining Persian support was of greater importance. He attempted to justify his adoption of Persian dress as 'wearing Persian spoils' taken by the conquest. He also tried to appease his soldiers with 'generous gifts', but the men rejected them as 'distasteful'.[70]

These tensions between Alexander and the Macedonian veterans boiled over explosively with the murder of Cleitus in the autumn of 328. Alexander had stabbed his friend to death after a vicious drunken argument. The murder of Cleitus happened in the context of Alexander assuming new Persian attributes and the abandonment of his previous habits. According to Arrian, Cleitus was disturbed by 'Alexander's change towards the more barbaric style and the expressions of his flatterers'. One of Cleitus' complaints was that his Persian guards had denied him access to Alexander. As Plutarch records, 'we think those already dead are the lucky ones for not living to see Macedonians flogged with Median rods and pleading for a chance to see our king.' Arrian's account of the argument makes allusions to the betrayal of Darius by Bessus and how Alexander feared being abandoned by his followers. At one point during the altercation with Cleitus, Alexander sought his Macedonian guards, but they froze in place. Cleitus implied that Alexander, like Darius, was becoming a 'king in name only' without any support.[71]

Another plot would emerge against the king in the spring of 327, known as the 'pages' conspiracy'. The spark for the conspiracy was Alexander's harsh punishment of his page Hermolaus for a minor offence. Hermolaus found other comrades willing to take action against Alexander, and they pledged to kill the king while he slept. However, the plot went awry after Alexander was warned and did not return to his chambers, instead spending the night drinking with his comrades. The following day the plot was uncovered by Ptolemy and the conspirators seized.[72]

Alexander brought the conspirators to trial before a Macedonian assembly. Hermolaus boldly declared to Alexander that they plotted to kill him because 'you have begun not to rule us as free men, but to lord over us as if we were slaves.' The disgruntled page further accused Alexander of being a deserter of the Macedonian cause for his adoption of Persian ways. After the declaration, Hermolaus' own father drew his sword and attempted to kill him. Alexander personally intervened, restraining the father and letting Hermolaus continue. Perhaps the king thought an open airing of grievances would lessen tensions within the army. Alexander responded to Hermolaus' speech in kind, refuting the accusation of tyranny and reminding the soldiers of their spoils from the conquest. In the end, Alexander had Hermolaus and his co-conspirators executed for their crime.[73]

Alexander used the opportunity of the conspiracy to also eliminate Callisthenes, who was known to have been a friend and mentor of Hermolaus. The historian was innocent of involvement in the plot, but his criticism of the king played a role in sparking it. The exact manner of his death is unclear from the sources; either he died of disease while imprisoned or Alexander had him hung. The break between Alexander and his old teacher Aristotle was now complete.[74]

As King of Asia, Alexander embraced Persian ways to solidify his rule. He began to employ the royal items associated with the Achaemenids, such as the upright headdress, royal chariot, the royal tent, the seal of Darius and great royal hunts. The royal court took on an Eastern flavour as Alexander incorporated the harem, eunuchs, ushers, melophori and the proskynesis ritual. Opposition to Alexander's policies developed from Greeks and Macedonians who disapproved of his Eastern turn, and these dissenters were often dealt with brutally by Alexander.

Chapter Ten

Consolidating Asia

With the death of Darius, Alexander sought to consolidate his rule over Asia. The usurper Bessus was not the only major foe with whom Alexander had to contend. The satrapies of Areía, Bactria and Sogdiana proved to be areas of constant disorder. Rebels waged determined resistance against the king. Alexander only crushed these insurgents after great military effort. The king also undertook colonial and urban enterprises to stamp his rule in the East. Allegedly, he brought 'civilization' and 'Hellenization' to change the natives' habits.

Alexander was not content with ruling only a portion of the Persian Empire. He wanted to claim the entirety of his prize. To accomplish this goal, he had to campaign north into Central Asia to the Jaxartes River and in the east to the Indus River in India. Only after subduing these outlying regions could Alexander claim dominion over the Persian state. All those within the claimed boundaries of Alexander's new empire who resisted his rule were viewed as rebels against the legitimate king.

Rebellion of Satibarzanes

Satibarzanes earned distinction as the first of Alexander's appointed Asian satraps to betray the king and revolt against him. Satibarzanes held the satrapy of Areía under Darius III and fought at Gaugamela with the Great King. The satrap was distinguished for his 'generalship and for personal bravery'. Satibarzanes had joined Bessus in overthrowing Darius. According to Arrian, Satibarzanes was one of the men who fatally wounded Darius when he refused to flee Alexander's advance. Satibarzanes chose not to stay with Bessus and instead surrendered to Alexander. Astonishingly, Alexander did not punish Satibarzanes for the murder of Darius and even reappointed him as satrap of Areía. His appointment may be a testament to the satrap's influence in the province.

The move was a critical error on Alexander's part as Satibarzanes would prove himself disloyal.[1]

In the summer of 330, when Alexander was positioning himself to crush Bessus, Satibarzanes led his province in revolt. The renegade satrap murdered the Macedonian officer Alexander had left behind and raised an army. When word reached Alexander, he delayed his march against Bessus and turned back to deal with the rebel. Alexander is said to have marched at breathtaking speed to reach Areía. Satibarzanes was surprised by Alexander's arrival and not yet prepared to resist the Macedonians. Most of Satibarzanes' men scattered and the satrap fled for his life. Alexander restored order and appointed another Persian named Arsakes as satrap.[2]

In the winter of 330/329, after his inglorious flight, Satibarzanes regrouped his forces and prepared to re-engage the Macedonians. He contacted Bessus and received cavalry from the usurper, who was more than happy to spur rebellion in Alexander's rear. Alexander detached forces from the campaign against Bessus to crush the rebel. The Macedonian officer Erigyius led the expedition supported by the Persian lords Artabazos and Phratapherenes, who had joined Alexander. Together the coalition would engage Satibarzanes' army in battle and kill the rebel. The revolt in Areía collapsed again with its leader's death. The people of Areía surrendered 'not unmindful of the merits of Alexander'.[3]

Rebellion of Spitamenes

The most significant rebellion against Alexander's rule broke out in Sogdiana. Arrian attributes the uprising to fear of Alexander's wrath. The king had summoned the governors of the region to a meeting which 'seemingly portended nothing good for them' so they chose not to attend and instead revolt. Perhaps the rebellion can also partly be attributed to Alexander's requisitioning of Sogdian horses during his campaign against Bessus. While not the direct spark, it may have increased the Sogdians' distaste for the Macedonians.[4]

The Sogdian revolt would be a long-running affair, lasting a year from the autumn of 329 to the autumn of 328. The campaign would be bloody, as Diodorus states, 'Alexander defeated the Sogdiani who had revolted and slew more than one hundred and twenty thousand of them.'[5] To

Alexander, the Sogdians were rebelling against their legitimate ruler and had to be dealt with harshly. Alexander had no intention of allowing any of his 'spear-won land' to slip away from his grasp.

The Sogdians were led in their rebellion by Spitamenes. Spitamenes had previously been instrumental in the fall of Bessus by arresting the usurper. He had even viewed Alexander's punishment of Bessus as fitting revenge for Darius. Alexander rewarded Spitamenes and his comrades for their actions against Bessus. It is unknown exactly why Spitamenes turned against Alexander. The betrayal looks to have taken Alexander entirely by surprise. He even asked Spitamenes for help, not knowing he was leading the rebellion![6]

The Sogdian rebellion soon spread into neighbouring Bactria. Spitamenes knew that he would need the support of the Bactrians if he was to have a fighting chance against Alexander. He turned to the former Bactrian soldiers of Bessus for support against the Macedonians. Some 7,000 Bactrian cavalrymen had surrendered to Alexander after the defeat of Bessus. Spitamenes chose to employ trickery to gain the allegiance of these men. The rebel leader claimed that Alexander had ordered them executed for supporting Bessus. Judging by Alexander's recent treatment of Bessus, it must have seemed believable enough. Spitamenes had little issue in winning the Bactrians over for his cause.[7]

Alexander moved rapidly to crush Spitamenes' revolt. He attacked the major centres of rebellion, sacking several cities, the most prominent being Gaza and Cyropolis. According to Arrian, Alexander ordered his soldiers to kill all the men in the settlements. Spitamenes turned to the Scythians for aid, and the rebel leader was able to recruit some 600 of their number. He used his improved forces to besiege the Macedonian citadel of Markanda. When a Macedonian relief column arrived, Spitamenes ambushed them, massacring some 2,000 infantry and 300 cavalry.[8]

Spitamenes' victory was a critical event for Alexander as it temporarily shattered the Macedonian aura of invincibility. Alexander needed to reassert himself and save face after the defeat. He sped with all haste to the site of the disaster but arrived too late to catch Spitamenes, who had slipped away with his men. The king reclaimed some of his honour by burying the dead soldiers. Alexander, in anger, then proceeded to ransack the countryside and kill those who had assisted in the attack.[9]

Alexander was critically concerned about news of the defeat spreading. It could demoralize the Macedonians or spur more natives to revolt against his rule. The king ordered the few survivors of Spitamenes' massacre not to tell anyone of the defeat. Alexander even threatened the men with execution if they disobeyed his orders.[10] This incident proves again that Alexander took matters of morale extremely seriously. The campaign was at a critical stage, and Alexander needed to keep his beleaguered army motivated.

After wintering, Alexander continued the pursuit of Spitamenes into Sogdiana. Alexander dispersed his forces into five columns. The columns advanced, attacking Spitamenes' forts and rounding up the populace. Alexander's comrade Hephaestion resettled the dispersed Sogdians in new locations. By this strategy, Alexander and his men slowly reduced the rebel territory in Sogdiana.[11]

With Sogdiana locked down by Alexander, Spitamenes shifted the war into Bactria. With greater Scythian support, Spitamenes and his followers raided widely. He again achieved success, overrunning a Macedonian fort, killing the garrison and taking its commander prisoner. An attempt by the Macedonians to sally against him ended in another defeat.[12]

This engagement would prove to be Spitamenes' last triumph. The Macedonians flooded Bactria with soldiers, and soon Spitamenes found 'every place occupied by Macedonian garrisons and no likelihood of escape anywhere'. His Scythian raiders were slowly cornered and suffered a defeat. Spitamenes, in desperate straits, opted for a final great attack upon the Macedonians. In the ensuing battle, the Macedonians emerged victorious over Spitamenes' rebels.[13]

The defeat spelled the end for Spitamenes; his supporters among the Bactrians and even his Sogdians began to desert him. Frustrated by the defeat and lack of booty, the Scythians raided Spitamenes' baggage before fleeing. To compound his issues, Alexander now marched against him in person. In the most likely account, Spitamenes, in the end, was betrayed and murdered by his comrades. The rebels then sent his head to Alexander in the hope of appeasing the Macedonian ruler.[14]

Curtius and the *Metz Epitome* provide yet another alternative version of Spitamenes' death. It's worth elaborating upon as it again focuses on Alexander's chivalrous image. In this version, Spitamenes' beautiful wife murders him. The wife then came before Alexander to claim credit for the act with hopes of a reward. According to Curtius, Alexander was in two minds and unsure how to proceed. On the one hand she had killed his great foe, but on the other she had murdered her own husband, the father of her children. Spitamenes is said to have been a tender husband, and she had no reason to betray him other than personal gain. Ultimately, the king decided that her cruelty made her unworthy of a reward. Alexander additionally may have refused her because he did not want people to believe that a woman's beauty could influence him.[15]

Great Civilizer of Asia?

Our ancient historians were eager to present Alexander as a great Hellenic civilizer. The king purportedly founded some seventy cities throughout his empire. However, most of these 'cities' amounted to no more than garrison towns. In Plutarch's words, Alexander, through his civilizing efforts, 'sowed all Asia with Grecian magistracies' and 'overcame its uncivilized and brutish manner of living'. Plutarch credits Alexander with establishing laws that continued to govern the East into his time. In Plutarch's opinion, the people of Asia under Alexander's rule 'are happier than those who escaped his hand; for these had no one to put an end to the wretchedness of their existence, while the victor compelled those others to lead a happy life.'[16]

Alexander also allegedly 'changed the savage natures of countless tribes'. Plutarch attributes countless reforms to the king. Alexander allegedly 'educated' the Hyrcanians and introduced agriculture to the Archosians. The peoples of Persia, Susa and Gedrosia learned to read Homer and memorized the tragedies of Sophocles and Euripides. The Bactrians paid homage to the Greek gods and began to bury their dead rather than leave the bodies exposed. The Sogdians were taught not to kill their parents and the Persians not to take their mothers as wives.[17]

Perhaps the king's actual most enduring contribution to 'civilization' was the construction of Alexandria in Egypt. Alexander allegedly marked out the borders of the city himself using barley since no chalk was available. The king then ordered the surrounding region to send citizens for the city's settlement. After Alexander's death, Alexandria would flourish, becoming the great commercial hub of Ptolemaic Egypt.[18]

Alexander's Colonists

Bactria and Sogdiana were important regions for Alexander's 'civilizing' efforts. As per Strabo, Alexander had razed the cities that proved rebellious and founded eight new cities in the region. The building of these cities went hand in hand with the settling of Greek colonies in the newly-conquered territories. As Curtius explains, Alexander believed 'Asia could be held by an army of moderate size, because he had distributed garrisons in many places and had filled the newly founded cities with colonists.' While this may have been a sensible way for Alexander to secure the territory as per our sources, the Greeks were largely unhappy with being colonists in a land not their own. Many of the colonists 'sorely missed the Greek culture and way of life, cast away as they were in the furthest corners of the realm' and were 'dissatisfied with living amongst the barbarians'.[19]

In 326 BC, a revolt broke out among the colonies near Bactra, the capital of Bactria. According to the ancients, the cause of this revolt is normally linked with the colonists' homesickness for Greece. However, modern scholars have challenged this claim of homesickness. The vast majority of the colonists were Greek mercenaries. These men had desired to fight in the East of their own accord; it's therefore unlikely that missing Greek customs would have sparked a revolt. More likely, the mercenaries were unhappy with their new station as colonists. The mercenaries perhaps expected a greater role for themselves than mere colonists. If they revolted and marched home, they could expect to be hired by other Greek states.[20]

The rebellion spread through the province, 'not so much through hostility to Alexander, as from fear of punishment'. The rebels organized themselves under a man named Athenodoros, who then went so far as to assume the title of king and begin a campaign against Macedonian rule in the province. Local Bactrians also joined the Greeks in their uprising. The rebels seized the fortified citadel of Bactra after its garrison was caught unprepared. The fall of Bactra marked a significant blow to Macedonian rule in the region.[21]

The rebellion soon after its great success began to devour itself. Infighting soon broke out among the rebels. A Greek named Biton and a Bactrian called Boxos colluded to murder Athenodoros at a banquet. The Greek rebels then seized the two conspirators, executing Boxos and exiling Biton. Biton left the colonies for Greece with the remainder of his followers. This episode in Bactria illustrates the difficulties faced by Alexander's colonial enterprises in Asia.[22]

The Greek colonists in Asia presented Alexander's immediate successor Perdiccas with a major issue with which to contend. With Alexander dead, the colonists broke out into full-scale revolt and wished to return home. The colonists organized themselves and raised an army of some 20,000 infantry and 3,000 cavalry. Perdiccas sent his general Peithon to deal with the rebels and ordered him supported by the satraps of the region. Many of these satrapal forces assisting Peithon were likely to have been Asian cavalry.[23]

As Peithon marched against them, Perdiccas began to grow nervous. He feared Peithon would join forces with the Greeks and then betray him. Peithon, in fact, looks to have intended to do just this. Perdiccas insightfully gave the Macedonians orders to kill the rebels, regardless of Peithon's opinion. Peithon moved to engage the Greeks in battle. He was able to win over one of their commanders along with 3,000 men. With the help of this turncoat, Peithon emerged victorious over the Greeks. He then came to an agreement with the colonists, and the bulk of them laid down their arms. The Macedonians, however, remembered Perdiccas' orders and broke the agreement, massacring the Greeks.[24]

Euergetae, Nysa, Branchidae and Cossaeans

When considering the treatment of conquered peoples, Alexander judged them based on their history and character. In Alexander's words, 'The clemency of kings and leaders depends not only on their own dispositions, but also upon those of their subjects.'[25] The king throughout his reign demonstrated that he could be very kind or extremely harsh depending on the circumstances. This is visible in his treatment of the Euergetae, Nysaians, Branchidae and Cossaean peoples. A chivalrous Alexander met the Euergetae and Nysaians, while the Branchidae and Cossaeans suffered from a tyrant.

The Euergetae (Helpers) were a people who inhabited the satrapy of Zarangiane. Alexander came into contact with them during his march against Bessus in the autumn of 330. They had been formerly called the Arispians but had taken on this new name after assisting Cyrus the

Great. According to our sources, the Euergetae had given Cyrus shelter when his army suffered from the cold and was short of food. They then assisted Cyrus in his doomed campaign against the Scythians. Due to their support of Cyrus, Alexander offered his praise to the Euergetae and granted them freedom within his empire. He further rewarded them with money and expanded their territory. Before departing, Alexander assigned them a former secretary of Darius as their governor. This man's appointment further indicates that Alexander re-employed the Persian administrative officials to run his empire.[26]

The people of Nysa, who Alexander encountered during his Indian venture, received favourable treatment from the king similar to the Euergetae. Initially, Alexander actually attacked the Nysaians, who promptly sued for peace. They sent a delegation of their citizens led by a man named Akouphis to Alexander and explained to him the supposed origins of their city. The Nysaians claimed their city's founder was Dionysus, who named the city after his nurse. Alexander was won over by the legend and decided to spare the city. He then made Akouphis its governor and granted the citizens autonomy. The Nysaians even managed to talk Alexander out of demanding the usual noble hostages.[27]

Alexander's treatment of the Branchidae stands far apart from that of the Euergetae and Nysaians. The city's ultimate destruction is a further example of the king's policy towards 'traitorous' Greeks. The Branchidae were descendants of Greeks from the area around Miletus. During the time of Xerxes, they had agreed to co-operate with the Persians, handing over the temple treasures of Didyma. They then left Miletus and were resettled in the upper satrapies of the Persian Empire. The natives could still speak some Greek and, when Alexander arrived, they welcomed the king with open arms.[28]

Alexander was initially unsure what action to take. He called together the men from Miletus in his army and asked for their opinion. The Milesians were conflicted themselves as some hated the Branchidae for their treachery but others were willing to forgive their countrymen. Alexander, without a clear resolution from his men, contemplated their fate for himself. In the end, the King of Asia decided on the Branchidaes' annihilation.[29]

Alexander rode through the open gates while his soldiers surrounded the city. The Branchidae held out olive branches to Alexander, but this did not lessen the king's wrath. The Macedonians killed the citizens and eradicated the city. Alexander even had the city's groves ripped up, leaving the territory devastated. This destruction was yet another message from Alexander to those who chose to betray their fellow Greeks. Notably, this incident occurred after the apparent end of the Pan-Hellenic war at Persepolis. The events with the Branchidae confirm that the king still employed the theme of Greek unity even in his latter campaigns.[30]

In the winter of 324/323, Alexander embarked on an expedition against the Cossaeans, who were a mountainous people known for their skill as fierce warriors. They had failed to acknowledge Alexander as 'King of Asia'. Having resisted the Persians in the past, the Cossaeans did not fear the Macedonians. The tribesmen had a habit of raiding for plunder and then retreating to the mountains for protection. Alexander could not allow these acts to continue and was determined to subdue the brigands. His winter expedition against the Cossaeans took some forty days. The Cossaeans were taken by surprise, thinking that the terrain and weather would have deterred the Macedonians.[31]

According to Plutarch, Alexander slaughtered all the inhabitants from the boys to the old men. In some accounts, Alexander is even accused of wiping out the Cossaeans completely. However, as happened at Persepolis and Sidon, the Cossaeans appear again in the Diadochi period, still harassing armies crossing their lands. According to Arrian, Alexander attempted to change the Cossaeans' habits and 'founded cities there to end their nomadic way of life and make them ploughmen and tillers of the soil. Thus they would have possessions, and fear of losing them would end their mutual aggression.' Again here we are given an image of Alexander as a 'civilizer' who tamed the supposed barbaric ways of the Asians.[32]

Securing the Northern Frontier

Prior to the rebellion in Sogdiana, Alexander had embarked on a mission to secure his northern frontier. He pushed up to the Jaxartes River, the historic boundary of the Persian Empire. The Persians had marked the border with the city of Cyropolis along the Jaxartes. As Strabo writes, 'Cyra [Cyropolis] being the last city founded by Cyrus and being situated on the Jaxartes River, which was the boundary of the Persian Empire'.

Alexander, having razed Cyropolis during the rebellion of Spitamenes, now founded the new city of Alexandria Eschate (Alexandria the Furthest) in its place.[33]

The establishment of Alexandria Eschate was swift, only taking seven days by Curtius' account. Alexander merely had his men construct walls around an established camp. The foundation of this city was a bold declaration, as Cyrus had made with his founding of Cyropolis, of Macedonian dominance in the region. Alexandria Eschate would be garrisoned and settled with colonists to help control the territory. With the building of this city, Alexander established a clear boundary for the borders of his new empire. Polybius notes how 'on its borders [the Alexandrian Empire] a ring of Greek cities was founded by Alexander to protect it from the neighbouring barbarians.' The town would mark the division between Alexander's empire and the Scythians. In a larger sense, the river line divided what the Greeks considered Asia and 'Europe', where the European Scythians lived.[34]

Alexander did not want continued Scythian interference within his empire and their support of rebel elements. The Alexandria Eschate served to separate the population of his kingdom from contact with the Scythian tribes to the north. The Macedonian king also perhaps viewed the city as a staging point should an invasion of Scythia prove necessary. As Arrian outlines, the city's location had strategic advantages 'in an excellent position for his invasion of Scythia, should that ever take place, and for an outpost of the country against the raids of the tribesmen dwelling on the other side of the river'.[35]

While the rebellion of Spitamenes persisted, Alexander did, in fact, face an invasion by the Scythian tribes. The Scythians, proud of their warrior prowess, boldly claimed that Alexander 'would not dare to attack the Scythians or that he would learn the difference between Scythians and the natives of Asia'. Alexander remembered that the Scythians had killed Cyrus, and Darius had failed in his fight against them. The king nonetheless accepted the challenge, moving his army to the Jaxartes River.[36]

Alexander intended to cross the Jaxartes and take the fight to the tribes. The omens for a crossing, however, were unfavourable. Nonetheless, Alexander was determined to cross whatever the resistance, stating that 'it was better to go to any extremity of danger than, after subduing almost all Asia, to be a laughing stock to Scythians.' Alexander was always very conscious of his image as king and refused to show any weakness. Macedonian rule would not be entirely secure if he backed down now. Failure to act could perhaps encourage rebellion and further Scythian intrusion into his empire.[37]

To give cover to the river crossing, Alexander employed bolt-throwers to drive off the Scythians. The nomads, unaccustomed to the barrage, retreated and allowed the Macedonians access to the other bank. Having got his army across, Alexander engaged the Scythians in battle and carried the day. The Scythians retreated, and Alexander may have caught them if not for a sudden illness. The escape of the Scythians and the king's momentary debilitation presented an opening for peace negotiations. A message from the Scythian king arrived, blaming the conflict on a rogue group of Scythians outside his control. The Scythian king now proposed peace and promised to obey Alexander.[38]

This olive branch proved enough for Alexander, who ended hostilities. Battling against the Scythians would have been an unnecessary distraction from his true objectives in Asia. If Alexander were to push further north, it would take him away from established borders into the unknown. The king's operation against the Scythians had been punitive in nature and can be compared to his campaign against the Getae north of the Danube.[39]

The Scythians would later send another envoy to Alexander. The Scythian king had since died and his brother had assumed the throne. The new king pledged to renew his support for Alexander and offered to pay homage before Alexander in person. He also offered his daughter in marriage to the Macedonian king and Scythian noble daughters for marriage to Alexander's companions. This offer was a tempting arrangement and could have proved a convenient way for Alexander to secure his border. A precedent existed as King Philip may have taken a Scythian wife after his war against them. Nonetheless, Alexander, for whatever reason, chose to decline the match.[40]

Alexander also formed another alliance with the neighbouring Khorasmians. The Khorasmian king agreed to ally with Alexander and support his future military venture against the Indians. Additionally, Curtius reports an envoy from the Sacae arrived to join with Alexander. The king graciously had one of his male servants Euxenippus escort them on their homeward journey. These alliances served to further strengthen Alexander's position along his northern border.[41]

Securing the Eastern Frontier

In the summer of 327, Alexander set out to invade India. According to Arrian, Alexander 'by subduing India would then have all Asia'. This campaign, similar to his actions on the Danube and Jaxartes, was not Alexander striking into the dark. The invasion aligned with his aim of subduing the entire Persian Empire. Alexander's probable objective was to extend his empire to the Indus River. By reaching the Indus, Alexander would have roughly reached the border of Darius the Great's empire.[42]

Indians from the territories 'dwelling west of the Indus' were known to have fought at Gaugamela under Darius. However, Persian rule over the Indians west of the Indus had collapsed with Alexander's conquest, if not before that. Petty Indian kings now dominated the region. Looming larger was the Indian Nanda Empire that ruled the north of the Indian subcontinent. The Nanda Empire, according to our ancient sources, had a massive army including numerous elephants.[43]

The army Alexander assembled for the expedition against the Indians was perhaps the largest he ever fielded. Curtius records that 'there were 120,000 armed men who followed the king to that war.' Plutarch reports Alexander's army at the campaign's end numbered 120,000 infantry and 15,000 cavalry. One must be sceptical as to whether Alexander could gather this many men for the effort. The logistical problems of supplying such an army would be immense.[44]

If the numbers are accurate, it must be due to Alexander's recruitment of Asian soldiers. Arrian and Curtius report the presence of 'Bactrians and Sogdians' and 'Scythians and Dahae' in the campaign. The involvement of these horsemen provides evidence that, at least among the cavalry, Alexander took Asian soldiers to India. In theory, he had almost the entire Persian Empire from which to draw manpower for the campaign. If the Persian kings could field such a force, why not Alexander? So perhaps we cannot completely disregard the numbers of Curtius and Plutarch.[45]

Alexander conducted the India campaign in brutal fashion reminiscent of his actions in Sogdiana. His forces committed regular massacres of civilians during the campaign. Additionally, Alexander ordered tens of thousands of Indian captives enslaved. His campaigns had certainly taken on a crueller nature since the conflict with Spitamenes. The king was likely growing frustrated at continued resistance within his empire.[46]

In India, Alexander employed his usual diplomatic strategy of forming alliances with local rulers. In the opening stages of the campaign, Alexander fought a war with the Assacani people. The Assacani leader engaged the invading Macedonians but died soon after. Rule of the Assacani then fell to his mother, Queen Cleophis. Cleophis held the fortified settlement of Massaga. Alexander began operations against Massaga, but was wounded in the leg while riding near the town's stone walls. The Macedonians proceeded to encircle Massaga, bringing up heavy siege equipment.[47]

Cleophis found herself in a similar situation to Ada of Caria in that she controlled a fortified city that Alexander would probably rather not have to take by storm. Under the circumstances, the queen decided to sue for peace. The surrender, however, was complicated by a group of mercenaries under Cleophis' command. The mercenaries refused to surrender the city to Alexander and became rebellious. Cleophis opened secret negotiations with Alexander so as not to arouse the mercenaries. However, they learned of the queen's messages and contacted Alexander themselves. They offered a compromise in which they would leave the city in exchange for safe passage. Alexander agreed to the deal, but when the mercenaries left the city, he massacred them anyway. It was not one of Alexander's finer moments.[48]

After the city's surrender, Cleophis came out of her settlement along with her noble ladies to meet the king. Alexander allowed Cleophis to maintain her throne as his vassal. Curtius alleges that it may have been the queen's beauty that won Alexander over. Rumours spread that Alexander subsequently had an affair with Cleophis, which produced a son named Alexander. The alliance with Cleophis gave Alexander another local ally to support his advance and delivered him a key fortress.[49]

Later in the campaign, Alexander formed an alliance with King Mophis of Taxiles. He had sent word to Alexander promising his support before the onset of the campaign. When Alexander arrived in his territory, Mophis assembled his forces to assist Alexander. Marching on, Alexander received an important prisoner, Barsaentes, a close ally of Bessus. The rebel had fled eastward and allied with a local Indian ruler. Barsaentes and his Indian partner now fell captive to the Macedonians and were brought before Alexander in chains. Alexander, still playing the role of the avenger, sentenced Barsaentes to death for his betrayal of

Darius. Barsaentes' ally had some thirty elephants which the king gifted to Alexander's new ally King Mophis.[50]

Alexander next turned his attention upon the two rival Indian kingdoms of kings Abisares and Porus. Alexander attempted to get their submission by 'spreading fame of his name'; i.e. to intimidate the Indians. Abisares yielded to pressure and surrendered, but Porus preferred to meet Alexander in battle. The campaign against Porus would climax at the Battle of the Hydaspes River. The battle was a hard-fought affair, the most significant since Gaugamela. Alexander defeated Porus, but also recognized his bravery and usefulness. As with his plans for Darius, Alexander acknowledged that Porus could be more valuable alive than dead.[51]

Alexander first sent the brother of King Mophis to speak with Porus. Porus, however, met the attempted parley with violence, killing the brother. Alexander then more wisely employed a friend of Porus who gained the Indian ruler's surrender. Alexander famously addressed the Indian king, asking him what treatment he desired. As the story goes, Porus answered, 'Treat me, Alexander, like a king.' Alexander would confirm Porus' 'sovereignty over the Indians of his realm' and 'from then on found him in all things faithful'.[52]

Making this strong Indian ruler a friend did much to shore up Alexander's eastern border. Porus would hold the territory for him and provide a greater buffer kingdom at the edge of his empire. He proceeded to award more territory to Porus, enlarging his lands. In this way, Alexander no longer had to rule the lands directly and could let Porus administer the territory. Alexander had a far greater strategic reason to spare Porus and it was not merely his valour on the battlefield. Following his victory at Hydaspes, Alexander founded the dual cities of Nikaia-Boukephala similar to Alexandria Eschate; they served the function of marking the empire's new borders.[53]

Alexander's army ultimately came to a halt on the Hyphasis [Beas] River. The king appeared to be preparing for a further advance to the Ganges River. The Nanda Empire, in response, had assembled an overwhelming force to block the Macedonian advance. Alexander's soldiers, knowing they would be in for a bitter fight, decided to finally mutiny. Some historians have speculated that Alexander may have had a hand in encouraging the mutiny. He may have felt that his objectives had been satisfied as he had reached the borders of the old Persian Empire. Any further advance would have had great risk attached to it. It was better to halt now and turn back, leaving Porus in place to guard the border. Legitimate evidence exists to support the theory that Alexander always intended to turn back. For example, prior to this point, Alexander ordered a fleet built on the Indus River in his rear. It's unclear why he would do this unless he intended to return and utilize it as he subsequently would.[54]

The 'mutiny' did not end Alexander's operations in India. The king took his army down the Indus, conquering the tribes along the river. The greatest resistance to his advance came from the Malloi. Alexander besieged their capital and personally stormed into the city with only a few men. The king fell, wounded by an arrow that almost cost him his life. The Malloi were massacred without mercy by the furious Macedonians. Having reduced the tribes along the Indus, Alexander resolved to depart India and return to the core of his Asian empire.[55]

In consolidating his rule over Asia, Alexander faced numerous challenges. The rebellions of Satibarzanes and Spitamenes were costly affairs only suppressed with great effort. Alexander's reputation as a 'civilizer' and 'Hellenizer' are greatly exaggerated. The king achieved what he set out to do regarding the borders of his new state. He brought the Scythians to heel through a combination of military action and negotiation. The establishment of Alexandria Eschate, along with other garrison towns, helped seal up the border. In India, Alexander established his rule in the Indus region with his victory at Hydaspes and an alliance with King Porus. By the autumn of 225, Alexander could justifiably claim to have consolidated his rule over the vast majority of the former Persian Empire.

Chapter Eleven

Alexander and the Women of Asia

O ur ancient sources are eager to present Alexander as a gallant figure who treated women with the utmost respect. In Curtius' words, Alexander 'felt respect for a woman of royal stock who had suffered a reversal of fortune'. The king was known to have given orders to stop the abuse of women at Persepolis. Once, Alexander punished a soldier for rape by throwing him to wild beasts.[1]

A famous example of Alexander's chivalry occurred during the siege of Thebes. Timoclea, sister of a prominent Theban general killed at Chaeronea, was attacked by Alexander's rampaging soldiers. She retaliated by murdering the man who assaulted her in turn, and was placed under arrest. The matter came to the attention of Alexander and he intervened, setting her free after learning that she was the sister of a general.[2]

On another occasion at his Asian court, Alexander noticed an 'exceptionally beautiful' Persian woman visibly upset. She was not singing or taking part in the festivities like the other Persian women present. Something about her bearing told Alexander she was of the noble class. The king discovered that the woman was the granddaughter of Artaxerxes Ochus and the wife of Darius' kinsman Hystaspes. Alexander set the woman free, returning her possessions, and ordered her husband found so they could be reunited.[3]

Alexander's 'Mother' Sisygambis

Following the Battle of Issus, the Macedonians seized the camp of Persian King Darius. Reading accounts of the Macedonian entrance into Darius camp leaves one with a graphic image. In the words of Curtius, 'no form of evil was lacking' as the soldiers ransacked the camp for valuables. They showed little respect for the Persian noblewomen, robbing them of their jewels and clothing. Some women tried to flee, but were rounded up and brutally dragged back to the camp by their captors.[4]

The abuse of Darius' courtly women must have been particularly humiliating. According to Plutarch, the Persians kept a 'jealous watchfulness of their women'. Alexander's soldiers' poor treatment of these women violated the Persians' 'dearest and proudest' possessions. Women who had lived their whole lives in luxury were subject to the worst abuses. The fall of Darius' camp, in many ways, symbolizes the collapse of Persian power.[5]

It must have been even more distressing for the Persians as Darius' family was present in the royal encampment, including his mother, sister-wife, two daughters and young son. Darius' mother Sisygambis was a proud woman who had lived through the worst violence of Ochus' reign. Stateira I was Darius' sister-wife, described by our sources as the greatest beauty in Asia. Darius' daughters Stateira II and Drypetis were in their teenage years and still young enough to sit on their grandmother's lap. Darius' son and heir Ochus was still in his childhood. These royal captives were now at the mercy of the Macedonians.[6]

After returning from his post-battle pursuit of Darius, Alexander went to the captured Persian camp. He entered Darius' tent and the remaining servants of the Great King greeted him. They had prepared for Alexander's arrival by putting out the most extravagant trappings. It was said to have been an Eastern custom to 'welcome the conqueror in the tent of the conquered king'. Alexander took the reception 'as an omen for his conquest of the empire of all Asia'. Following a bath, as he was sitting down for a meal, Alexander heard the cries of Darius' family.[7]

A Persian eunuch had spotted the cloak of Darius, which he had thrown off during the pursuit, among the captured loot and reported it to the royal family. Darius' family wept, believing the Persian ruler to be dead. Alexander, unnerved by the wailing, wished someone to go and tell them that Darius still lived. He sent one of his companions named Leonnatus to speak with the women.[8]

As Leonnatus approached Darius' family, they spotted his weapons and believed this to be the end for them. They did not send anyone to go and greet Leonnatus but kept him waiting for some time. He eventually entered the tent of his own accord, and the women begged Leonnatus to be allowed to bury Darius. Leonnatus informed them that Darius was alive and assured them that they would not suffer mistreatment. Leonnatus further communicated to the women that Alexander had no ill will towards Darius but was fighting what he considered a 'lawful' war. Darius' women rose, gave thanks to Alexander and ceased their crying.[9]

The next day Alexander and his companion Hephaestion came to visit the Persian royals. The two friends dressed alike, which caused a bit of confusion. When they approached Sisygambis, she prostrated herself at the feet of Hephaestion due to his slightly taller and more handsome appearance than Alexander. Sisygambis, informed by attendants of her error, soon made amends. Alexander shrugged off the incident, remarking 'Never mind Mother, for he too is Alexander.' Alexander would refer to Sisygambis as his 'second mother' in a similar vein to Ada of Caria from this point onward.[10]

According to our sources, Alexander decided to show how generous he could be to Sisygambis. The king promised that she would 'experience nothing inconsistent with her former happiness'. He covered her in jewellery and allowed her to bury any of her friends killed at Issus in the Persian style. Alexander made a further pledge to Sisygambis that Darius' daughters would be married 'even more generously than Darius had promised', that he would care for Darius' son as his own and that Darius' wife's 'dignity' would be maintained. Alexander's generosity clearly moved Sisygambis, and she remained faithful to the king from this point onward.[11]

Sisygambis would later appear in the historical narrative at Gaugamela. When the Persians attacked the Macedonian camp, they came close to the Persian royal family. The Macedonian guards fled, and many of the prisoners were rebelling. Sisygambis, despite the urging of her servants, did not take the opportunity to escape. She may have decided to stay in place out of respect for Alexander or perhaps out of fear of punishment. Curtius notes how she did not want to celebrate prematurely. Sisygambis' actions proved correct as she surely would have been recaptured by Alexander.[12]

Following Alexander's victory at Gaugamela, the royal family ventured to Susa. They began to take lessons in the Greek language. Curtius reports that Alexander sent Sisygambis a gift of purple cloth from which to make clothes. The present, however, backfired as, according to Persian customs, it was beneath noblewomen to work with wool. Learning this, Alexander came in person to apologize, pleading ignorance of their ways. Alexander honestly stated that his sisters and mother enjoyed making clothing for him. The king, rather than insulting the Persian women, attempted to treat them as if members of his own family.[13]

Sisygambis would later serve as an intermediary between Alexander and a Persian commander named Medates. Medates was attempting to get a ceasefire with Alexander but to no avail. In desperation, he sent a message to Sisygambis, who was a relative of his. The Persian general had heard how Sisygambis was now called 'mother' by Alexander. Sisygambis initially hesitated to assist Medates, believing that she might 'take too great advantage of the victor's [Alexander's] indulgence'. Eventually, she did send a letter to Alexander asking him to spare Medates and his followers. Alexander responded favourably to Sisygambis' message. The king ordered that Medates be pardoned. In Curtius' opinion, 'if Darius had been victor, his mother could not have obtained more from him.'[14]

The ancient sources all praise Alexander's treatment of Sisygambis' and Darius' family. According to Diodorus, Alexander 'won universal recognition throughout his own army for his exceeding propriety of conduct' and he further adds his viewpoint that 'of (the) many good deeds done by Alexander there is none that is greater or more worthy of record and mention in history than this.'[15] Alexander clearly did treat Sisygambis well, but he likely had political motivations for his kindness. The king knew that gaining the support of Sisygambis would go a long way towards building legitimacy in the eyes of the Persian elite. Let us not forget that Alexander, for all his generosity, still kept Darius' family as prisoners and hostages. Sisygambis and her family had few options open to them other than to support Alexander.

Queen Stateira I, Wife of Darius

Queen Stateira was said to have been the most beautiful woman in Asia. Our sources are adamant that Alexander did not abuse her during the queen's time in captivity. Curtius notes that Alexander 'far from violating...took the greatest care that no one should make shameful sport of her person while prisoner.' Arrian says similarly that despite Stateira's beauty, Alexander 'felt no love, or mastered himself'. As per Plutarch, Alexander only had relations with Barsine before his marriage and never 'laid hands upon these women'. Justin recounts that Alexander had only visited her on one occasion when meeting Sisygambis. The king's words echo our sources' descriptions: Alexander called the Persian women 'torments to the eyes' and would not allow people to speak of Stateira's beauty in his presence.[16]

These accounts are very similar to the story of Panthea, the wife of the Susian king in Xenophon's *Cyropaedia*. Cyrus treated her with respect and refused to look upon her. In Xenophon's account, Cyrus used Panthea to get her husband to surrender. Alexander may have wished to copy Cyrus by using Darius' wife to get the Persian king to submit. However, the untimely death of Stateira robbed Alexander of any chance of repeating Cyrus' success.[17]

Roughly eighteen months after her capture by Alexander, Queen Stateira died. Sources differ regarding the cause of her death. Curtius reports exhaustion, while in Justin and Plutarch's accounts, she died during childbirth. Alexander was visibly upset by the event and cried at the sight of her body. Justin states how Alexander 'mourned for her death, and attended her funeral; acting, in that respect, not from love, but merely from kindness of feeling'. He magnanimously gave her a funeral in the Persian style. Granting her a proper Persian funeral was a meaningful gesture on the part of the king.[18]

As per our sources, the queen's death was reported to Darius by a eunuch who had escaped from Macedonian captivity. Darius lamented that he had been unable to prevent Alexander from murdering his wife. The eunuch, if our sources are to be believed, vouched for Alexander's honour and told Darius that no mistreatment occurred. Darius now viewed Alexander as an even more noble individual. Darius prayed to the gods that in the event of his defeat, 'grant that no other man may sit upon the throne of Cyrus but Alexander.' Again our sources are attempting to demonstrate Alexander as Darius' legitimate successor.[19]

However, historians are sceptical of the events that transpired around Stateira's death. If the queen did die in childbirth, that raises many questions. The father could not have been Darius due to the large time gap. It seems unlikely that anyone would have had access to the queen during her captivity without the knowledge of Alexander. Some have accused Alexander of taking advantage of his captive, resulting in her subsequent death from childbirth. It would certainly explain why the king was so mournful at her death.[20]

Alexander had already been intimate with the captive Barsine. He himself once spoke of how Achilles 'from whom he traced his ancestry, had united with a captive maiden'. Even if Stateira merely died of exhaustion from the journey, this would not speak favourably of Alexander's care. Darius may not have had as favourable a view of his family's imprisonment as the sources allege. Curtius hints at this during Darius' speech at Gaugamela, where the king laments that Alexander kept the royal family as if 'criminals' and in his prison.[21]

Roxane, Wife of Alexander

At the onset of spring 327, Alexander advanced upon the mountainous outcrop known as the 'Sogdian Rock'. The locals deemed the Rock impregnable due to its terrain, and it served as a rallying point for rebels fleeing Alexander. Local nobles kept their wives and children on the Rock for protection. The daunting nature of the terrain presented a significant challenge for the Macedonians. Undeterred, Alexander's men scaled the heights and forced the Rock's submission. This victory brought Alexander possession of the wives and children of his enemies; in effect a repeat of Issus and Damascus. Among the prisoners was the family of the powerful Bactrian lord Oxyartes. Oxyartes' daughter Roxane ('Little Star') would become Alexander's most legendary lover.[22]

At a banquet, following the victory, Alexander first laid eyes on Roxane while she was taking part in a dance. Roxane was said to have been second only to Darius' wife in beauty and it appears that Alexander fell in love with her at first sight. Unexpectedly, he decided to take the Asian princess as his wife rather than simply keep her as a concubine like Barsine. The marriage must have taken his comrades by surprise as Alexander had previously refused the idea of marrying an Asian when asked by the Scythian king. Interestingly, Alexander also persuaded a number of his comrades to take other local noblewomen as wives. The king stated how 'it was important for establishing his empire that Persians and Macedonians be joined in wedlock; that only in that way could shame be taken from the conquered and haughtiness from the victors.'[23]

Even if it was sincerely a love match, Alexander likely had political and military motivations for marrying Roxane. As Plutarch assures us, the marriage 'was a love affair' but also notes that the union 'harmonizes well with the matters which he (Alexander) had in hand'. Alexander fundamentally did not want 'her people to think they were being done any wrong'. Alexander may have thought that the marriage to Roxane would help bring peace to the region. Rebels in Bactria and Sogdiana continued to be a nuisance, requiring a significant manpower commitment. At this time Alexander was planning his Indian expedition and undoubtedly did not want an insurrection arising in his rear. His efforts appear to have had the desired effect as the populace 'were encouraged by the partnership… they were beyond measure fond of Alexander'. Alexander's marriage to Roxane was very much out of his father's playbook of marrying a local woman to maintain peace.[24]

The marriage to Roxane had the added bonus of winning over her father, the powerful nobleman Oxyartes who, when he heard the news of Alexander's proposal, was delighted. The Bactrian lord from this point onward served Alexander. Two of Oxyartes' sons would become part of Alexander's retinue and later his elite cavalry. Alexander, in return, is said to have treated Oxyartes well and restored his territory to him. Oxyartes would later assist Alexander in his subsequent campaign against another rebellious outcrop, the 'Rock of Khorienes'.[25]

Roxane accompanied Alexander during his invasion of India. According to the *Metz Epitome*, in India Roxane would have a child by the king, but it did not live for long. At the time of Alexander's death in the summer of 323, Roxane would be pregnant with another child, the future Alexander IV. Roxane 'was held in honour among the Macedonians' due to her pregnancy by the king. The Asian queen allied herself with Alexander's immediate successor Perdiccas. Perdiccas understood that winning Roxane's support would strengthen his hand. The *Metz Epitome* preserves a tradition that Alexander actually asked Perdiccas to marry Roxane before his death. It is perhaps telling of her status that Perdiccas did not attempt to marry her. Perdiccas had no interest in marrying a 'barbarian' and instead sought to win a Macedonian bride for himself.[26]

Together Perdiccas and Roxane sought to eliminate those who could rival them. The two plotters fulfilled Sisygambis' fears by turning upon the two daughters of Darius. If Darius' daughter Stateira claimed to be pregnant by Alexander, it could present a serious danger. Perdiccas likely also felt it prudent to eliminate the remainder of Darius' line. Roxane tricked Stateira with a fake letter into coming to a set location. She then had the Achaemenid princess and her sister murdered, hiding the bodies in a well. Perdiccas is said to have been 'privy to the deed and a partner in it'. After the murder of Perdiccas and the outbreak of the Successor Wars Roxane and Alexander IV would find themselves as pawns at the mercy of Alexander's former generals. In 310, Cassander, the son of Antipater, had Roxane and her son murdered.[27]

Our ancient accounts of Alexander's relationship with Sisygambis, Stateira and Roxane present the king as a noble prince. Granted, Alexander proved himself on many an occasion to be of noble character. He treated Sisygambis with honour and she became his 'mother'. Roxane he honourably married instead of treating her as a mere concubine. Stateira, if you believe the ancients, was treated with complete respect by the king. Yet despite Alexander's kindness towards these women, we cannot ignore the political implications of his actions. Alexander wanted Sisygambis' support to win over the Persian elite, he needed Stateira as a hostage to help bring about Darius' submission, and it was essential to win over Roxane's powerful father to his side.

Chapter Twelve

Alexander's Asian Lieutenants

It was not only Alexander's efforts that won control over Asia. The king was fortunate to have numerous skilled individuals to help him conquer and rule his empire. The great military men played a decisive role on the battlefield: Parmenion, Antigonus and Craterus. These military men, however, did not always share Alexander's vision for the East. In this chapter, we will examine a different group of individuals: those Macedonians and Greeks who assisted Alexander in his pro-Persian policies such as Hephaestion, Peucestas, Tlepolemus and Stasanor. Also the Asians who came over to his side: Mithrenes, Mazaeus, Oxyathres, Artabazos, Oxyartes, Phrataphernes and Atropates. Without the support of these individuals, Alexander's efforts would have been a far more difficult task.

Hephaestion, Chiliarch of Asia

Alexander relied heavily on his companion and lover Hephaestion in running his new Persian-Macedonian state.[1] He awarded Hephaestion the position of chiliarch, the equivalent of the Persian hazarapatis (grand vizier). Historically, in the Persian Empire, the hazarapatis served as the chief assistant to the Persian Great King. He would send messages to officials in the king's name, administer territories and command on the battlefield. The hazarapatis, due to his powerful position, had the potential to betray and depose the reigning king. The two most prominent examples of this are Bagoas, who murdered Artaxerxes Ochus, and Nabarzanes, who helped to depose Darius III.

Under Alexander, the position now referred to as chiliarch took on an expanded role. As Diodorus writes, 'the position and rank of chiliarch had first been brought to fame and honour by the Persian kings and afterwards under Alexander it gained great power and glory at the time when he became an admirer of this and all other Persian customs.' The increased power of the position was likely a convenient step as Hephaestion was closer and more loyal to the king than all others. Alexander relied on his skill as a capable subordinate. Hephaestion had proved himself, heading the royal bodyguards, and was in the thick of the fighting at Gaugamela. He was also able to handle the delicate political situation of selecting a king at Sidon.[2]

Hephaestion played a significant part in Alexander's adoption of native practices. As Plutarch notes, 'among his [Alexander's] closest friends, Hephaestion approved his course and joined him in changing his mode of life.' Due to Hephaestion's exalted position and his open support for his pro-Persian agenda, Alexander came to rely on him in promoting his policies. Plutarch states that Alexander would entrust Hephaestion with matters when it came to 'business with the barbarians'. Hephaestion reportedly read Alexander's mail to him regularly, 'as was his habit'. On one occasion, Hephaestion was even allowed to read Alexander's intimate correspondence with his mother.[3]

Alexander also allowed Hephaestion to undertake important independent actions. During the Indian campaign, Hephaestion and Perdiccas were sent towards the River Indus ahead of the army. Hephaestion was likely allowed to negotiate with the tribes in Alexander's name as chiliarch. During the course of this operation, Hephaestion and Perdiccas suppressed a rebellion, fortified several points along the route and built a bridge over the Indus. When Alexander arrived, he found everything prepared for his crossing of the river.[4]

Hephaestion looks to have been a driving force behind the punishment of Philotas. The chiliarch advocated torturing Philotas for information. According to Plutarch, Philotas begged Hephaestion for mercy during the session. The torture of Philotas demonstrates Hephaestion's intense loyalty to Alexander and his eagerness to purge potential threats.[5]

As chiliarch, Hephaestion played a vital role in the institution of the Persian practice of proskynesis at court. He is even likely to have organized the ritual for Alexander and decided who would submit to the king. As Plutarch records, Hephaestion had gotten a pledge in advance from Callisthenes that he would perform the ritual without issue. Callisthenes broke his word to Hephaestion and derailed the ceremony. Plutarch's account implies that Hephaestion may have secured promises from all the attendees that they would perform the ritual without protest.

It is important to note that Hephaestion could be found at Alexander's side, talking with the king during the proceedings. It was Hephaestion who distracted Alexander with conversation while Callisthenes skipped the ritual bow.[6]

Hephaestion's supreme position as chiliarch and Alexander's lover led to envy and mistrust from others. The chiliarch even clashed with Alexander's mother Olympias, who seems to have written poisonous letters about him. Hephaestion was known to have had a heated rivalry with Alexander's secretary Eumenes. On one occasion Hephaestion, who apparently was in charge of room and board, assigned Eumenes' room to a flute-player. Eumenes was naturally outraged and reported the matter to Alexander. Alexander at first reprimanded Hephaestion, but then changed his mind and turned upon Eumenes.[7]

In another instance, Hephaestion got into a heated confrontation with Craterus. Craterus 'clung fast to his native ways' and does not seem to have embraced Persian customs. Alexander relied on him when dealing with his Macedonian and Greek soldiers. Hephaestion and Craterus' viewpoints on the war in Asia and the Persian issue were likely at opposite ends. It was said that 'Hephaestion loved Alexander, but Craterus loved the king'. The two men eventually came to blows against each other with swords. Alexander intervened and 'abused Hephaestion publicly, calling him a fool and a madman for not knowing that without Alexander's favour he was nothing'. Publicly Alexander gave the impression that Hephaestion was nothing more than his puppet and took Craterus' side, probably to appease the soldiery. However, in a private setting, Alexander decided to rebuke Craterus, reflecting his true feelings on the issue. In reality, Hephaestion was more important to Alexander than anyone else in the regime.[8]

In the autumn of 324, Hephaestion fell ill with a sudden fever and succumbed not long after. Alexander was at that time attending a festival in the Median capital of Ecbatana. When he received word of Hephaestion's state, he hurried to his comrade's side but arrived too late. The sudden death of Hephaestion from fever was a devastating blow to Alexander. It was distressing on a personal level due to them being close friends since childhood and also lovers. Politically, Hephaestion was Alexander's most able subordinate and his right-hand man as chiliarch.

Alexander was inconsolable in his grief. Hephaestion's wife Drypetis, daughter of Darius, entered a period of mourning for her husband.[9]

Alexander 'threw himself into preparations' for the funeral of Hephaestion. The event would be a full display of Alexander's great wealth, costing some 10,000 talents. Perdiccas, now Alexander's closest comrade, was given the body and escorted it for the funeral to be hosted in Babylon. The epicentre of the event was a gigantic funeral pyre seven levels high. Interestingly, one level of the pyre is reported to have been decorated with elaborate hunting scenes and another with Macedonian-Persian arms. Alexander used these to demonstrate his Eastern-style grand hunts and the joint nature of the empire with both people bearing arms. Similar decorations would be present on the elaborate hearse that carried Alexander's body. Alexander had Hephaestion's personal items added onto the pyre, and as noted by Aelian, these included clothing coveted by the Persians. Hephaestion, out of loyalty to the king, had joined him in adopting Eastern dress. The king clearly wanted all to see that Hephaestion had been a loyal supporter of his pro-Persian agenda and thus should be honoured by Macedonians and Asians alike.[10]

The impact of the chiliarch's death on the Asian inhabitants looks to have been significant. Alexander had ordered the regions of Babylonia to contribute funds for the funeral. The holy fires of the Zoroastrian religion were to be put out until the proceedings ended as if a Persian king had died. He then arranged 'a period of mourning to be observed throughout the barbarian land' and 'immediately ordered that the manes and tails of all horses and mules should be shorn in token of mourning'. The city of Ecbatana itself looks to have borne the brunt of Alexander's wrath as he knocked down its walls and acropolis. Alexander may also have had the temple to Asklepios, the god of medicine, destroyed as revenge for Hephaestion, 'a barbaric order, and not in Alexander's way at all; but rather suitable to Xerxes' insolence'.[11]

Justin states that Alexander wished Hephaestion to now be worshipped as a god. He sent for and got the oracle of Ammon's permission for the plans to go forward. Alexander wanted his comrade to be honoured regardless of the obstacles. In his efforts, Alexander was encouraged by his court flatterers, as he had been in the case of the proskynesis controversy. Alexander's Macedonian comrades also paid homage to Alexander's dead lover out of fear, especially Eumenes, who had quarrelled with him.

According to Lucian, if he is not exaggerating, 'it was once the greatest of all slanderous charges to say that a man did not worship Hephaestion or even make obeisance to him' and could result in execution.[12]

Hephaestion held an unequalled role in Alexander's ruling circle. He proved himself to be Alexander's most dependable lieutenant. In the event of Alexander's death, Hephaestion would have been given the empire as regent. His marriage to the sister of Alexander's Persian wife made him a cousin and effectively a member of the royal family. Without Hephaestion, power passed to Alexander's close companion Perdiccas. Alexander did not appoint anyone to the post of chiliarch; Hephaestion was clearly irreplaceable.

Peucestas, Satrap of Persis

Peucestas would emerge as one of Alexander's most faithful lieutenants. Like Hephaestion, he joined Alexander in embracing Persian ways. Peucestas was someone Alexander could count on as a loyal soldier and competent administrator. During the siege of the Indian city of Malloi, Alexander recklessly leaped over the walls into the city, accompanied by only a few men. Unfortunately he proved an easy target: an arrow hit its mark, penetrating the king's breastplate and entering his lung. It was at this moment that Peucestas leaped to defend his incapacitated king. Alexander had entrusted Peucestas with a sacred shield taken from the ruins of Troy, which he now used to protect his king. Peucestas undoubtedly saved Alexander's life and, for his efforts, sustained three wounds from Indian missiles. Alexander would not forget the services Peucestas rendered on that day, elevating him to the elite bodyguards.[13]

When the satrap of Persis was removed and executed by Alexander, the king sought a new man to fill his position. He had left the position to two Persians previously but now wanted a Macedonian for the role. Alexander may have feared giving the job to another Persian as it could lead to a rebellion. At the same time, he probably wanted someone who would not anger the Persians and cause such an insurrection. Due to Persis' critical position in the empire, Alexander certainly wanted someone loyal and capable to fill such an important position. The king turned to Peucestas to be the Persians' new satrap, someone he considered to be trustworthy.[14]

Importantly, Peucestas was also in agreement with Alexander's pro-Persian policies. Unlike other Greeks and Macedonians who viewed the Persians' ways as barbaric, Peucestas fully embraced them. He adopted Persian dress, Persian manners and even learned the Persian language. Alexander 'commended him, and the Persians were gratified that he preferred their ways to those of his own country'. Peucestas was the perfect person to rule Persis and bridge the divide between the two peoples.[15]

It is notable that Diodorus states that Alexander 'permitted him alone of the Macedonians to wear the Persian raiment wishing to please the Persians and believing that through Peucestas he could keep the nation in all respects obedient'. This statement by Diodorus is intriguing because it implies that the Macedonian officers were not allowed to wear 'Persian raiment' of their own accord and had to get special permission. However, our other sources report Alexander's comrades wearing Persian dress and the king forcing the clothes on his companions. It could be that Diodorus is merely mistaken. However, alternatively, perhaps Alexander had some limitation on what his Macedonian satraps could wear.[16]

Peucestas' rule in Persia would be a popular one. As Diodorus writes, 'He [Peucestas] had held the satrapy of Persia for many years and had gained great favour with the inhabitants.' He was everything Alexander would want in one of his governors and likely hoped his other governors would seek to emulate Peucestas' example. When Alexander wished to expand his recruitment of Asian soldiers further, Peucestas stepped up to the task. The satrap was able to assemble 20,000 Persian 'bowmen and slingers' accompanied by a significant number of Cossaeans and Tapourians, 'the most warlike of those whose lands bordered on Persia'. Peucestas marched this small army to Babylon and presented them to Alexander. Alexander 'commended them for their zeal' and praised Peucestas 'for governing his men in an orderly manner'.[17]

According to the *Alexander Romance*, Peucestas was present at the final drinking party for the king before his illness. When Alexander was dying, Peucestas and several of the king's companions slept in the temple to the god Serapis. Peucestas, by this act, showed his devotion to the king to the end.[18]

After Alexander's death, Peucestas continued to hold his satrapy of Persis; a testimony to Peucestas' governance, that the territory was thriving. Control of Persis placed him in a powerful position. Peucestas kept the satrapy in a state of military readiness. He maintained a force of 10,000 Persian archers and slingers, a 3,000-man phalanx of mixed Macedonian-Asian origins, 600 Greek and Thracian cavalry and 400 Persian cavalry. Peucestas had the support of his people and was rich enough to maintain non-Persian forces for the defence of his satrapy.[19]

The goodwill of the population only added to Peucestas' capabilities. The satrap could summon forces promptly from distant parts of the provinces, regardless of the terrain difficulties. Peucestas had in place a series of guard posts manned throughout the region to relay messages by word of mouth. This system allowed everyone in the province to receive the same march orders promptly. The citizens would also inform Peucestas of any invading armies by lighting fires and sending messages by camel.[20]

Peucestas would initially remain out of the Successor Wars but eventually found himself dragged into the conflict. Eumenes, leading the remainder of Perdiccas' faction, was warring with Antigonus for control of Asia. Peithon, satrap of Greater Media, allied himself with Antigonus and claimed sway over the upper satrapies. He had invaded Parthia, executed its satrap and installed his brother in his place. This action by Peithon was a great affront to Peucestas and the other satraps of the region. The satraps of Carmania, Arachosia, Areía and Zarangiane, and Bactria all rallied together. Peucestas, viewed as 'the most eminent of the commanders', was elected leader 'by common consent'. Together the coalition defeated Peithon in a battle and drove him from Parthia.[21]

When Eumenes marched east looking for support, Peucestas joined his efforts. Peucestas, however, lent his aid grudgingly as he thought himself suited for the high command. The armies of Eumenes and Peucestas united and made for Persepolis. On the march, Peucestas had goods distributed to the soldiers, earning him their acclaim. Arriving at Persepolis, Peucestas hosted a great feast for the army. He gathered 'from almost the whole of Persia a multitude of sacrificial animals'. At the banquet, Peucestas symbolically honoured Philip and Alexander, making a sacrifice to them. Similarly to Opis, both Macedonians and Persians attended the affair, 'each of the Persians who was most highly honoured occupied his own couch.' The feast served to further increase Peucestas' popularity with the army, and he hoped to steal their allegiance away from Eumenes.[22]

Eumenes sensed the tide turning against him and had to take action. He fabricated a letter from Orontes, satrap of Armenia, hailing victories for Eumenes' coalition. Eumenes had this letter shown to the soldiers, and it lifted their confidence in him. Orontes was known to have been a friend of Peucestas, which made the letter all the more believable. Eumenes also brought up false charges against Sibyrtius, the satrap of Arachosia. Sibyrtius was also a close friend of Peucestas, and Eumenes thought it would be a way to pressure his rival. Eumenes actually took military action against the satrap, sending cavalry that attempted to capture him.[23]

Eumenes and Peucestas were soon after confronted by the army of Antigonus at Gabiene. The two sides both employed Asian soldiers on their behalf. Antigonus had the support of Peithon, who had brought a large contingent of cavalry including 'mounted archers and lancers from Media and Parthia'. On the other side, Eumenes' phalanx comprised soldiers 'of all races'. In the battle that followed against Antigonus, Peucestas would behave insubordinately to Eumenes. First Peucestas was driven off the field and then refused to rally his men back into the fray when ordered by Eumenes. Peithon would play an important role on the side of Antigonus when he swept into Eumenes' rear and captured his baggage. The battle ended without a clear winner. Eumenes hoped to rally his army to renew the fighting, but the men refused to fight, knowing Antigonus had their valuables and their wives. To get their baggage returned, the men decided to arrest Eumenes and hand him over to Antigonus.[24]

Peucestas hoped to now make a deal with Antigonus. Antigonus set about 'leading him [Peucestas] on to hope for other things and filling him with vain expectations'. However, according to Diodorus, this was a trick, as 'Antigonus, perceiving that Peucestas was enjoying great favour among the Persians, first took his satrapy away from him.' The Persians were said to have been 'angry' at this decision as they genuinely seemed to have loved Peucestas. One Persian man named Thespius declared to Antigonus that 'the Persians would not obey anyone else' but Peucestas. Antigonus had Thespius executed for his outburst. Peucestas' career was over, and though not executed, he took up a much-diminished role in the retinue of Antigonus.[25]

Tlepolemus, Satrap of Carmania and Stasanor, Satrap of Areía and Zarangiane

Like Peucestas, Tlepolemus and Stasanor followed Alexander's example and built an effective relationship with the populace. As Diodorus writes, 'they [Tlepolemus and Stasanor] had conducted themselves well toward the inhabitants and had many supporters.' In 330 Tlepolemus served as a military commander assigned to the satrap of Parthia. Later in 325/324, he was appointed satrap of Carmania in the period after Alexander returned from India. He retained the post after Alexander's death, joining Peucestas' coalition resisting Peithon and later fighting on the side of Eumenes against Antigonus. Antigonus, having defeated Eumenes, allowed Tlepolemus to retain his satrapy due to his popularity with the inhabitants.[26]

Stasanor was a Greek from Soloi on the island of Cyprus. He likely entered Alexander's service after the king invaded Phoenicia and gained the submission of the regional kings. According to Strabo, Stasanor was 'one of the comrades of Alexander, who was thought worthy of a chief command'.[27]

In the spring of 329, Alexander ordered Stasanor to Areía with the mission to arrest its governor, Arsakes, for having neglected his duties. Alexander then confirmed the Cypriot as satrap of Areía in place of Arsakes. It was a difficult region to govern, having been the centre of Satibarzanes' revolt. Cyprus had been Persianized under the Achaemenids. Stasanor would have had a greater understanding of Asian ways and language than the average Macedonian officer. Perhaps Alexander understood this dynamic when he appointed Stasanor to such a critical territory.[28]

Stasanor's holdings later expanded to also include the satrapy of neighbouring Zarangiane. He is known to have arrived to assist Alexander after his return from India, bringing much-needed supplies and reinforcements. The Cypriot attended Alexander's final drinking party before his death. Following the king's demise, Stasanor retained his two satrapies during the division of Alexander's empire. Later he became the satrap of Bactria and Sogdiana. Curiously, another man from Cyprus named Stasander replaced him in Areía and Zarangiane. It seems everyone understood that officials from Cyprus made good governors of

Asian satraps. Antigonus would later confirm his rule over Bactria, and he looks to have still held the post years later.[29]

Mithrenes, Commander of Sardis

Mithrenes was the citadel commander of Sardis, the capital city of Lydia. The city was of great strategic importance, with Plutarch referring to it as 'bulwark of the barbarian dominion on the sea-coast'. Sardis' fortified citadel could have presented difficulties for Alexander had Mithrenes chosen to hold out.[30] One can speculate that the citadel was well-stocked due to the military situation at hand. Other fortifications such as those found at Halicarnassus would later present a significant obstacle to Alexander, only submitting after a long siege.

The satrap of Lydia, Spithridates, had been killed at the battle trying in vain to slay Alexander personally. The death of the satrap looks to have elevated Mithrenes to the highest-ranking Persian official in the region. Should Mithrenes resist Alexander's advance, he would provide valuable service to the Persian Empire, giving them time to recover from the defeat at Granicus. However, the chances of relief should Sardis endure a siege were undoubtedly slim. It is perhaps unsurprising that Mithrenes chose to open negotiations with Alexander using Sardis as an excellent bargaining chip.[31]

As Alexander advanced upon Sardis, Mithrenes and the leading citizens rode out to meet the king. They offered the surrender of not only the city but, more importantly, the citadel and its treasury. Alexander accepted the generous terms, encamping and sending a force to take possession of the city. Sardis was handed over to the Macedonians smoothly and 'without resistance'. The garrison looks to have followed its commander's example and submitted to Alexander rather than resist. It was an impressive coup for Alexander to secure such a critical city without loss of life. To ensure his gains, Alexander installed both a garrison to hold Sardis' citadel and a governor to administer the entirety of Lydia.[32]

Mithrenes was the first significant Persian official to ally with Alexander. The Persian commander's defection to the Macedonians would bring him some infamy. When contemplating his ultimate fate, King Darius would sarcastically remark, 'unless haply it is better to await a victor's will and, like Mazaeus or Mithrenes, to accept sufferance the rule of a single province, supposing Alexander may now prefer to gratify his vanity rather than his anger'. It seems that Mithrenes, along with Mazaeus, came to be viewed as the archetypal traitor by the Persians. Alexander feared letting Mithrenes talk with the Darius family, not knowing how they would react to a traitor.[33]

Alexander kept Mithrenes in a position that befitted 'the honour of his rank'. His Persian language skills likely proved to be beneficial to Alexander. Ultimately Alexander sent Mithrenes to be satrap over Armenia. It's unclear if Armenia was under Macedonian rule or if Mithrenes had to conquer the territory. Alexander's treatment of Mithrenes set an excellent example for future Persian nobles who chose to surrender rather than resist. They would be treated well for their actions and could perhaps expect a reward beyond their former station. As Alexander would state in his message to Darius, 'I hold myself responsible for all of your troops who did not die in the field but took refuge with me; indeed they are with me of their own free will and of their will serve in my army.'[34]

Mazaeus, Satrap of Babylon

Mazaeus was the next significant Persian commander who submitted to Alexander, and his defection was much more significant than that of Mithrenes. While Mithrenes was a minor noble in control of one city, Mazaeus was one of the most important nobles in the entire Persian Empire. Plutarch refers to him as 'the most influential man at the court of Dareius'. Mazaeus was also a capable military leader with years of experience behind him. As testament to his status, Mazaeus was at one time engaged to marry Darius' daughter.[35]

Under Artaxerxes Ochus, Mazaeus served as the governor of Cilicia. In this capacity, he assisted in subduing the rebellious Phoenicians. Mazaeus' holdings were likely at some point expanded to control the entire Trans-Euphrates region. The territory under his sway would have included important centres such as Damascus and Sidon. His son Brochubelus served as his subordinate commander in Syria. By the time of Darius' accession, he was clearly of high standing within the empire. Perhaps Darius hoped to cement Mazaeus' support through marriage to his daughter.[36]

In the war with Alexander, Mazaeus' major role begins in the Gaugamela campaign. Darius tasked Mazaeus with holding the Euphrates-Tigris river lines and devastating the region to rob Alexander of supplies. He set out with a force of 3,000 to 6,000 cavalry accompanied by some 2,000 Greek mercenaries to complete his mission. Mazaeus attempted to hold the two main bridges over the Euphrates River and initially did an excellent job in delaying the Macedonians.[37]

Arriving at the Euphrates, Alexander's men initially feared a potential attack as they attempted to cross. However, as the Macedonians drew closer and in greater force, Mazaeus balked at the thought of battle and retreated from the river. It was a similar situation when Alexander then advanced to the Tigris. Mazaeus did not resist Alexander as he deemed the Tigris River uncrossable due to its depth and current. Alexander was thus able to cross the river without meeting Persian resistance.[38]

While failing to hold the river lines, Mazaeus attempted to complete his additional task of ravaging the area. He ordered the villages burned along with their crops. When news of Mazaeus' plans reached Alexander, he quickened his march. It was a race against time as to whether Mazaeus could burn the foodstuffs before Alexander's arrival. In the end, Mazaeus proved unable to devastate enough of the region before the appearance of Alexander. The Macedonians were able to put out the fires, leaving the villages virtually undamaged. Alexander's soldiers found only the top of the foodstuffs burned, leaving the bulk intact for consumption.[39]

After retreating, Mazaeus was then to use his cavalry to screen Darius' army. These measures would prevent Alexander from gathering useful intelligence on the Persian deployment. Alexander dispatched a small force of only 200 horsemen to try to break the screen. The Macedonian commander feared that his small force would come under attack from superior numbers and he proceeded cautiously. He reported to Alexander that 'he had heard nothing but the noise of men and the neighing of horse'. Mazaeus had in effect succeeded in this new task as the Macedonians failed to gather proper intelligence. He could have potentially attacked and destroyed the small enemy force. Mazaeus, however, after sighting the Macedonians in the distance swiftly retreated to the Persian camp.[40]

Mazaeus' actions during the early portion of the campaign were largely ineffective. Although he initially delayed the Macedonians at the Euphrates, Mazaeus failed to contest either river. He also proved unable to inconvenience Alexander's army by burning his supplies and again failed to screen the Persian army. It's unlikely that Mazaeus was already a traitor as he would soon fight at Gaugamela with great skill. One explanation may be that Darius did not expect Mazaeus to rebuff Alexander at the rivers or force his army to starvation. Mazaeus' actual assignment could have been to draw Alexander onto the open plain found at Gaugamela. It is perhaps telling that he did not receive any punishment for his failure and subsequently had greater responsibilities placed on his shoulders.[41]

At Gaugamela, Mazaeus served as commander of the Persian right wing and fought against Parmenion. Darius allotted Mazaeus a group of his scythed chariots. The Persian commander performed exceedingly well in the battle. On Mazaeus' wing the chariots proved far more effective than those under Darius and Bessus. Mazaeus supported his chariots with cavalry, and they succeeded in doing significant damage to the Macedonians. As the battle progressed, Parmenion fell under intense pressure from Mazaeus.[42]

Mazaeus' attack on the Macedonian camp and baggage presented a significant danger. It could have resulted in the liberation of Darius' family. Capturing the baggage also may have had a demoralizing effect on the Macedonians. As noted earlier, during the Successor Wars, Eumenes was betrayed by his army after Antigonus captured his baggage. The soldiers were not keen on losing their loot and their women. Alexander, however, chose to run the risk of not weakening his front line, believing he could recover the baggage after the battle.[43]

Ultimately, Mazaeus' attacks did prove significant enough for Alexander to call off his pursuit of Darius. Thus, Mazaeus' actions, even if they did not win the battle, helped to facilitate the Great King's escape. Plutarch is very critical of Parmenion's performance at Gaugamela and blamed him for letting Darius escape, writing 'For there is general complaint that in that battle Parmenion was sluggish and inefficient, either because old age was now impairing somewhat his courage.' Perhaps instead of blaming Parmenion, Plutarch should have praised Mazaeus' skilful generalship.[44]

When news reached Mazaeus of Darius' flight, he became alarmed 'at his side's reverse of fortune'. Mazaeus still had superior numbers to Parmenion, but he sensed the way things were turning. Alexander was heading towards his wing, and the morale of his troops must have begun to falter. Mazaeus began to slowly pull back his forces from the battlefield. The Persian general's retreat took a route that was longer but more remote to protect his soldiers. Mazaeus then entered Babylonia and took command of the city.[45]

After Gaugamela, Mazaeus found Babylonia devoid of leadership. The satrap of the region Boupares had fought at Gaugamela at the head of the Babylonian contingent. He disappeared following the battle and likely fell in the melee. With Boupares' demise and the withdrawal of Darius to Media, Mazaeus was the highest authority left in the region. He probably also had a strong connection with the region. The Persian general had a half-Babylonian son named Artiboles, who would later join Alexander's elite mounted bodyguards. Like Mithrenes, Mazaeus had an opportunity to assemble whatever forces were available and attempt to hold off Alexander.[46]

Babylon itself was a major metropolis with intimidating defences. According to Strabo, it had high thick walls and towers. Curtius notes that Alexander recognized the difficulty in taking such a great city. Babylon was also capable of sustaining a long siege as Curtius notes, 'the land is sown and cultivated so that, in the event of an attack from outside, the besieged could be supplied from produce from the soil of the city itself.' However, one significant drawback for Mazaeus was that at least a portion of the Babylonians seemed eager to welcome Alexander. Any amount of Babylonian support for Alexander would surely have complicated Persian efforts to hold the city.[47]

It was not until roughly a month after Gaugamela that Alexander arrived before Babylon. Mazaeus had no intention of resisting the Macedonians. The Persian commander marched out of the city with his relatives to surrender. However, Alexander did not fully trust Mazaeus and felt it could be a trap, so he ordered the Macedonian soldiers to advance in battle formation. When Alexander discovered that Mazaeus was indeed sincere, he granted the Persian general an amnesty. Alexander then entered the city triumphantly in his chariot.[48]

Alexander recognized Mazaeus as 'a man of distinction...who had also gained widespread reputation in the recent battle'. The king knew that Mazaeus' example was likely to induce the others to surrender and wanted to reward him as proof of his benevolence. Alexander took the extraordinary step of appointing Mazaeus as the satrap of Babylon. Mazaeus, a man who a month prior had been killing Macedonians on the battlefield, was now charged by Alexander with governing one of his most important territories. Alexander's gambit proved successful as the Persian satrap of Susa surrendered soon after, encouraged by Mazaeus' example. According to Plutarch, Alexander later attempted to reward Mazaeus further but the satrap declined, stating 'O King, formerly there was one Dareius, but now thou has made many Alexanders.'[49]

Despite the pleasantry, Alexander was not entirely sure of Mazaeus' loyalty. He appointed a military commander and a tax collector to assist Mazaeus. These men likely had the dual role of carrying out their administrative functions and preventing Mazaeus from rebelling. This was similar to the arrangement in Egypt where Alexander didn't want control of the province concentrated in a single individual's hands. Though Alexander may have been suspicious of his new ally, he allowed Mazaeus a significant level of autonomy. During his rule over Alexandrian Babylonia, Mazaeus was even allowed to mint his own coins; the only Persian satrap to whom Alexander awarded such an honour. The Persian commander would loyally serve Alexander until his death several years later.[50]

Oxyathres, Brother of Darius

Oxyathres, the brother of Darius, was perhaps the weightiest Persian figure to pledge his allegiance to Alexander. Oxyathres was a loyal supporter of his brother, the king. The *Alexander Romance* records a fictitious conversation between Oxyathres and his brother. In this tradition, Oxyathres encourages Darius to take command in the field against Alexander, not leaving the war to his satraps, and to take the war into Greece. Darius praises his brother's advice but deems it hopeless to resist Alexander.[51]

The Achaemenid prince makes his first major appearance at Issus in command of Darius' elite cavalry. During the fighting at Issus, Oxyathres fought bravely at the front, personally killing those who advanced towards the king. In Curtius' words he was 'towering high above the rest in arms and bodily strength'. When Alexander and his cavalry drove at Darius, Oxyathres did his best to shield the Great King. The famed Alexander Mosaic found at Pompeii has forever immortalized Oxyathres' defence of his brother. Despite his best efforts, the Persians were still overwhelmed and Darius fled the field. Following the battle, Parmenion captured Oxyathres' daughter at Damascus.[52]

Oxyathres himself was eventually captured or willingly surrendered to the Macedonians after Darius' defeat at Gaugamela. Alexander kept the prince with a large group of prisoners from various social ranks, eventually ordering the nobles among them to be picked out of the group, including Oxyathres and 1,000 others. At some point after the death of Darius, Oxyathres decided to join Alexander's side, acknowledging his kingship. The exact reason behind his submission to Alexander is unknown. The royal family's captivity and the murder of Darius by Bessus undoubtedly impacted on this decision. Oxyathres would show himself eager to avenge his brother by bringing Bessus to justice.[53]

Oxyathres would become enrolled as one of Alexander's companions. He then accompanied the king on his campaign against Bessus. When Alexander captured Bessus he gave him to Oxyathres for punishment. As per Curtius, Oxyathres brought with him a skilled bowman named Catanes. Oxyathres had Bessus hung on a cross and then shot with arrows by Catanes. The carrion birds would then harass the wounded Bessus. Oxyathres would continue serving Alexander, and his daughter Amastris would be married to Alexander's general Craterus at Susa. Craterus was Alexander's greatest general after the murder of Parmenion. The match further demonstrates how Alexander valued Oxyathres' support.[54]

Artabazos, Satrap of Bactria

Artabazos' failed revolt against Artaxerxes Ochus had left him languishing in exile at the court of Philip. Only the military successes of his brother-in-law Mentor, in the service of Ochus, gained Artabazos' amnesty. Artabazos does not appear to have played a prominent role during the remainder of Ochus' reign. The assumption of the throne by Darius presented a new start for the aged satrap. Artabazos would develop a particularly close relationship with Darius. According to Curtius, Artabazos was a loyal supporter of the king and the 'oldest of his [Darius'] friends'.[55]

In the war against Alexander, Artabazos had accompanied the Great King on campaign as his chief courtier. Darius granted Artabazos' son Pharnabazus command of the Asia Minor coast on the death of

Memnon. Before the Battle of Issus, Artabazos left his family in the city of Damascus for safekeeping. After the rout of the Persian army, his close relatives fell into Macedonian hands. Artabazos meanwhile fled to Mesopotamia with Darius and was likely to have been present at Gaugamela. In the aftermath of the defeat, Artabazos remained Darius' friend while others turned on the king.[56]

Darius had lost heart after the defeat and Artabazos tried his best to reinvigorate him. Artabazos was determined to keep resisting the Macedonians. He declared in a speech before the Persian lords: 'We certainly, clad in our richest apparel and adorned with the finest arms that we possess, will follow our king to battle, and that too with the intention of hoping for victory, yet not shrinking from death.' When Bessus and Nabarzanes began to openly question the Great King's leadership, Artabazos advised Darius not to act against them, knowing that it would divide the army.[57]

Darius had fallen into a state of depression and seemed resolved to die. Artabazos personally saw to the king's welfare, encouraging him to eat and not give up. Artabazos took matters in hand, attempting to rally support for Darius. He went around to the soldiers' tents and encouraged them to remain loyal to the Great King. Despite Artabazos' best efforts, Bessus' coup against the king continued to gain momentum.[58]

In a last-ditch effort, Artabazos supported the efforts of the remaining Greek mercenaries to help Darius escape. If the king could escape, he could rally support from other quarters. However, the Persian ruler rejected such a move and he would not abandon his people for the Greeks. Darius now ordered Artabazos to save himself and leave with the Greeks. In their final encounter, Artabazos and Darius shared a tearful embrace and 'bathed in their mutual tears'. Artabazos still refused to give up on Darius, clinging to him, having to be dragged away by the king's servants. Darius covered his eyes so as not to see Artabazos' expression. Having bid his king and friend a final goodbye, Artabazos then left for the safety of the Greek camp.[59]

Subsequently, Artabazos would surrender to Alexander along with the Greeks. Alexander greeted Artabazos as a friend. It's likely that the king viewed Artabazos favourably not only because he was the father of Barsine but also that he had served Darius loyally, not joining Bessus' plot. Alexander recognized that Artabazos was of considerable age, allegedly in his 'ninety-fifth year'. The Macedonian ruler went out of his way to accommodate the old man. Though the king 'generally made a journey on foot, on that occasion he ordered horses to be brought for himself and Artabazos, in order that the old man might not feel ashamed to ride a horse while the king himself went on foot'. Artabazos and his sons would eternally pledge their allegiance to Alexander.[60]

Alexander first assigned Artabazos to escort the Greeks to their new stations. The mercenaries would serve as reinforcements for Alexander's army. Alexander later awarded him the satrapy of Bactria; a difficult position considering its rebellious nature and being the former territory of Bessus. Artabazos would assist in suppressing the rebellions of Satibarzanes and Spitamenes. Alexander, when setting out against Spitamenes, left his baggage 'under guard' with Artabazos. The king trusted Artabazos enough to let him watch over his valuables. Artabazos would also play an important role in subduing the rebel leader Arimazes. Artabazos' son Kophes served as Alexander's ambassador and negotiated the surrender of the rebel and thirty chieftains.[61]

Artabazos eventually requested to retire as satrap due to his advanced age, which the king accepted. His female relatives would later marry into the Macedonian aristocracy. Artabazos' family allied with Eumenes in the Successor Wars, and his son Pharnabazus actively served under Eumenes' command.[62]

Oxyartes, Father of Roxane

The Bactrian nobleman Oxyartes, the father of Roxane, joined Alexander's cause with the marriage of his daughter to the king. He quickly made himself useful in Alexander's campaign against the 'Khorienes Rock'. This Rock was another fortified outcrop resisting Alexander's rule. The defenders were a coalition of local chieftains under the command of a man named Khorienes. Like the Sogdian Rock, the defenders believed their position to be unassailable. Alexander set out to prove him wrong and began siege operations against the mound.[63]

Alexander employed his usual strategy of attempting to negotiate a surrender with the enemy. The king called upon Oxyartes to go and confer with Khorienes. Oxyartes highlighted Alexander's 'honesty and fairness'. He further told the rebel leader that Alexander could conquer any place he wished and that it would be much better to ally with him. Khorienes, likely influenced by Oxyartes' example, chose to surrender his position. Alexander proved true to Oxyartes' claims and awarded Khorienes back his territory. Khorienes, in return, gave Alexander's army much-needed supplies.[64]

Oxyartes would later be appointed satrap of Paropamisadae by the king. Following Alexander's death, he would support the faction loyal to Perdiccas and Eumenes. These two generals best served his daughter's and grandson's interests. Oxyartes was known to have sent a detachment to the assistance of Eumenes. As late as the Partition of Triparadisus in 321 BC, Oxyartes was still maintaining territory for the Macedonian Empire. According to Diodorus, Antigonus did not attempt to remove Oxyartes because it would have required 'a long campaign and a strong army'. This is testament to the powerful position held by Oxyartes in his satrapy.[65]

Phrataphernes, Satrap of Parthia and Hyrcania

Phrataphernes was another Persian who joined Alexander and served him loyally. He led the satrap of Parthia and Hyrcania under Darius and served at Gaugamela. Phrataphernes looks to have joined with Bessus in the overthrow of Darius. However, he did not stay loyal to the usurper for long and surrendered to Alexander with Nabarzanes. Phrataphernes was later awarded back his satrapy by Alexander. He proved active in crushing the revolt of Satibarzanes and rounding up the supporters of Bessus.[66]

Later Phrataphernes brought reinforcements to the aid of Alexander in India. He also rushed supplies to Alexander after his disastrous crossing of the Gedrosian desert while other satraps delayed. His sons would later join Alexander's elite cavalry guard. All in all, while not of the stature of Artabazos or Mazaeus, Phrataphernes nonetheless played an important part in Alexander's efforts in Asia. He would retain his satrapy in the initial period following Alexander's death.[67]

Atropates, Satrap of Media

Atropates served as the satrap of Media under Darius. His Medians were called upon to serve after the disaster at Issus. Darius began to draw on the

Eastern portion of his empire to mobilize more men against Alexander. Atropates led his Medes into battle for the Great King at Gaugamela. Following the defeat and death of Darius, he surrendered to Alexander. The king initially removed Atropates from control over his satrapy, but later reversed his decision and restored him to office.[68]

Atropates would prove to be one of Alexander's most effective subordinates. While Alexander was absent fighting in India and thought by many to be dead, Atropates held the loyalty of Media. Atropates fought against the usurper Baryaxes' attempts to claim power in Media and Persia. The satrap would ultimately capture the rebel and bring him to Alexander.

At a later date, Atropates reportedly brought a group of female warriors to Alexander, but the king declined to take these women into his service. Atropates' women may have led to the birth of legends about Alexander meeting Amazons. The satrap's daughter would marry Perdiccas at Susa. Perdiccas was Alexander's number three and later, with the death of Hephaestion, became the king's right-hand man.

After Alexander's death, Atropates would lose his hold over Greater Media but retain Lesser Media. The satrap would set out to forge his own independent kingdom of Media Atropatene. He would take the title of king and establish a dynasty that would rule the territory for centuries, marrying into many of the region's great royal families.[69]

Alexander's Asian lieutenants were critical to the king's success in Asia. Hephaestion, in his role as chiliarch, was an irreplaceable asset who helped Alexander push forward his Persian policies. Peucestas, Tlepolemus and Stasanor were trusted officers who gained the love of the native people and helped Alexander to secure key regions. Mithrenes delivered him Sardis without loss of life. The alliance with Mazaeus brought Darius' finest general off the battlefield and gave Alexander control over Babylon. Alexander's appointment of Darius' brother Oxyartes to his inner circle helped gain support from the Persian elite. Alexander's pact with Artabazos brought this illustrious figure and his large family into the king's service. The marriage to Roxane and the alliance with Oxyartes had positive military implications. Phratapphernes and Atropates both proved to be able subordinates and provided invaluable assistance to Alexander. The latter's defeat of the usurper Baryaxes is particularly notable.

Chapter Thirteen

Great Reforms and Death

T he period from Alexander's return from India to the end of his life, the winter of 325/324 to summer of 323, holds important significance for the king's pro-Persian policies. Since arriving in Asia, Alexander had fought constantly, but finally, after India, he would have a period of relative peace. The King of Asia could see to managing his empire and pushing forward his pro-Persian reforms. Alexander conducted a series of wide-ranging reforms in his kingdom, impacting the administration, the ruling class and the army. However, the Macedonian veterans did not entirely approve of Alexander's reforms and had to overcome their mutinous opposition.

Gedrosian Disaster

Alexander split his army in two for the march out of India, sending a portion under Craterus on an inland route while he took the coastal route. Alexander's path led him through the barren and sparsely populated Gedrosian desert. As Arrian recounts, Alexander's road was 'both difficult and lacking in supplies; in particular, the army often found no water; but they were obliged to traverse a considerable part of the country by night.' The army soon became desperate for supplies and particularly water. The area was largely uninhabited apart from a few fishermen, and Alexander did not find any native guides capable of assisting him.[1]

The army's desperation only grew worse, and they eventually began killing their horses and pack animals for food. Wagons transporting critical supplies broke down in the sandy terrain. Water, when found, was consumed by some soldiers in very high quantities, causing the men to die. A monsoon rain then raged and destroyed the army's camp. The accompanying women and children, remaining animals and even Alexander's personal effects were lost. Alexander himself set an example by refusing water in order to share his soldiers' problems. In Arrian's opinion, the soldiers suffered more in the crossing than at any other time in Alexander's campaigns.[2]

Many have speculated on Alexander's reasoning for crossing the desert and the disaster that followed. One is that he wanted to punish the army after the mutiny at the Hyphasis. Another is that perhaps he, in part, was motivated by a wish to surpass his illustrious predecessors Semiramis and Cyrus, who also undertook the crossing. As Strabo writes,

> They say that Alexander, although aware of the difficulties, conceived an ambition, in view of the prevailing opinion that Semiramis escaped in flight from India with only about twenty men and Cyrus with seven, to see whether he himself could safely lead that large army of his through the same country and win this victory too.

In admiral Nearchus' opinion, Alexander simply underestimated the difficulties of the crossing.[3] It shouldn't be overlooked that he remained in this harsh land near the coast not for the benefit of the army but for Nearchus' large fleet. The army helped to supply the large navy, not the other way around. As they advanced, Alexander's soldiers had to dig wells and points of anchor for the ships. Alexander earmarked much of the foodstuffs for the sailors and at one point desperate soldiers broke into these stores. Alexander, understanding their plight, ignored this act of disobedience.[4]

Purge of Abusive Officials

Emerging from the desert after sixty days, Alexander ordered his local satraps and administrators to send supplies as soon as possible. He pinned the disaster in part on the failure of his satraps to properly organize supplies and have depots ready for the journey in advance. Alexander swiftly stripped the satrap of Gedrosia and Arachosia from his office. At this moment, the king was looking for scapegoats to explain the disaster. It soon became apparent to Alexander that numerous satraps had committed abuses and neglected their duties in his absence. As Strabo writes, 'the remote distance to which the army of Alexander had advanced, to Bactra and India, gave occasion to the introduction of many disorderly acts.'[5]

News of these abuses has been described as a purge by Alexander of his imperial administration. Many have interpreted the purge as a reign of terror on the part of the king. As Arrian states, Alexander had 'become quicker to accept accusations as wholly trustworthy and to impose severe punishments'. However, Alexander's satraps and officials had truly committed terrible abuses in the king's absence. From his viewpoint, he had every justification for purging these administrators. As Diodorus notes, 'many of his officials who had used their powers arbitrarily and selfishly had committed serious offences.' The officials were well aware of their guilt and 'became alarmed' at the news of Alexander's return. The king's absence had drawn these abusers from out of the shadows and now Alexander could legitimately remove them. Perhaps instead of viewing Alexander's purge as a great crime, we can interpret it as a brutal but beneficial reform to the administration of the empire.[6]

The men who had assassinated Parmenion fell victim to Alexander's purge. They had committed numerous crimes, from plundering to the sexual assault of Asian noblewomen. In Alexander's absence, their actions were so bad that it made the 'barbarians abhor the Macedonian name'. They had acted under the pretext that Alexander was dead and would not be coming back. Alexander could not ignore these crimes despite their previous good service and provided justice for his new Asian subjects. The former assassins were put on trial for their crimes and executed. Some 600 rank-and-file soldiers who participated in the crimes were also sent to their death by Alexander.[7]

The populace of Media stated that Alexander's soldiers 'despoiled the shrines, disturbed ancient tombs and injured their subjects by rash and reckless behaviour'. Alexander responded promptly to these allegations and ordered those responsible executed. He adopted a similar stand when he received word of waves of abuse in Susa. The satrap of Susiana Aboulites along with his son Oxyathres, satrap of Paraitakene, were removed from their posts and executed. Like the other officials purged, they had committed 'offences against temples, tombs and the inhabitants themselves'. Similarly to Parmenion's assassinations, these satraps were said to have committed the abuses because they thought Alexander would not return from India or that he had perished in the desert.[8]

During his homecoming, Alexander would receive word of the abuses committed by his old comrade Harpalus, who Alexander had left as treasurer in Babylon while he embarked for India. This position made Harpalus one of the most influential figures in the empire. Unfortunately for the king, his old friend began to neglect his duties and abuse his office, believing the king would never return. Harpalus, as Diodorus recounts,

> first occupied himself with the abuse of women and illegitimate amours with the natives and squandered much of the treasure under his control on incontinent pleasure. He fetched all the long way from the Red Sea a great quantity of fish and introduced an extravagant way of life, so that he came under general criticism.[9]

Harpalus would spend lavishly on his mistresses, while reportedly doing nothing to honour the soldiery. The treasurer built a statue in honour of his lover Glycera and allowed her to live in the palace of Tarsus. Harpalus made Glycera a queen and allegedly ordered men to perform proskynesis before her. These reports must have been highly embarrassing for Alexander, and he would have to make amends with the populace by punishing Harpalus. Harpalus got word of Alexander's anger and fled Asia with some 5,000 talents and 6,000 mercenaries. First he went to Greece, where he attempted to inflame Athens against Alexander. Failing in this, he went with his mercenaries to Crete, where he was ultimately betrayed and murdered by them.[10]

Overall, Alexander became convinced that his satraps and officials were wielding far too much power. The king issued a decree for 'all his generals and satraps in Asia to disband all their mercenaries instantly'. With this reform, Alexander weakened the power of his satraps and further centralized his rule. By removing these private armies of Greek mercenaries, he limited the possibility of future unrest from his satraps. Alexander's measures were not unlike the actions taken by Artaxerxes Ochus against his wayward satraps. The satraps may very well have revolted at this point against Alexander as they had against Ochus, but instead complied with the command.

The decision by Alexander to disband satrapal mercenaries did have several adverse effects. In the immediate aftermath, the unrestrained Greek warriors took to plundering their way home. Diodorus stated that the decree helped to spur the Greek states' uprising against Macedon after Alexander's death. The Greeks now had a large number of unemployed and well-trained men for hire. It seems that Alexander took this measure to centralize his administration in Asia without considering the effect on Greece.[11]

The period of Alexander's return from India was the most volatile for his administration. The king tackled the internal issues within his empire head-on. By removing those who committed abuses, Alexander set a standard for his empire. The remaining satraps and officials now understood that Alexander valued the relationship he had crafted with the Asians. As Arrian explains, Alexander

> put fear into any other satraps or governors who were left, that if they committed the like crimes they too should suffer the like fate. And this above everything else kept in order the tribes which Alexander had subdued or which had surrendered to him, being as they were so many in number, and so far separated one from another – namely, that Alexander permitted no subjects under his sway to be wronged by their rulers.[12]

Return to Persis

Alexander made his triumphant return to the Persian heartland. It was customary for the Persian kings, when they entered Persis, to pay homage to the populace through the distribution of gifts. Xenophon reports how Cyrus performed the tradition when entering the province. According to Plutarch, King Ochus had avoided visiting Persis because he didn't want to pay! Alexander had money to spare and set about distributing it among the Persians.[13]

While absent in India, Alexander had left Phrasaortes as satrap of Persis, but he had died of an illness during the king's absence. To Alexander's dismay, a nobleman named Orxines had seized the satrapy of his own accord. Orxines was said to have been of Cyrus' bloodline and a man of great wealth. He had led the 'Red Sea tribes' against Alexander at Gaugamela. Orxines pledged his loyalty to Alexander, presenting him and his comrades with numerous gifts. The king, however, was still suspicious due to Orxines' noble lineage and the potential threat he posed.[14]

Bagoas helped to encourage Alexander's feelings against Orxines as the satrap had refused to honour the eunuch with gifts. The satrap chose to ignore warnings about Bagoas' power over Alexander. Due to the insult, Bagoas began to plot Orxines' downfall. Alexander eventually had Orxines executed charged with the desecration of tombs, including that of Cyrus. The satrap was likely innocent and the desecration the work of thieves. However, the elimination of Orxines satisfied both Alexander and Bagoas. It also allowed Alexander to appoint his loyal friend Peucestas to the position of satrap over Persis.[15]

On returning to Persis, Alexander also had to deal with a serious rebellion that had broken out in his absence. A Mede named Baryaxes had declared himself king of the Medes and Persians. Baryaxes, like Bessus before him, adopted the upright tiara. On behalf of Alexander, Atropates, with the assistance of Craterus, put down the rebellion. Baryaxes was brought to Pasargadae before Alexander and executed.[16]

While his previous visit to Pasargadae had been uneventful, Alexander now went to visit the tomb of his idol Cyrus. Alexander had perhaps explicitly chosen not to see the tomb during his first visit to the city. As per Arrian, Alexander had vowed to pay homage to Cyrus' resting-place only after conquering the Persians. Unlike today, the tomb in Alexander's era had elaborate decorations of Persian, Median and Babylonian styles representing the many peoples of Cyrus' empire.[17]

However, the tomb had been thoroughly looted before Alexander's arrival. The Persian king's personal items were missing. The robbers even mutilated Cyrus' body and threw aside the Persian king's corpse. Alexander was furious at this sight and had ordered the tomb's restoration. The king placed his own diadems and cloak on the sarcophagus, honouring the Persian.[18] According to Plutarch, Alexander was deeply affected by an inscription on Cyrus' tomb. The inscription read as follows:

> O man, whosoever thou art and whencesoever thou comest, for I know that thou wilt come, I am Cyrus, and I won for the Persians their empire. Do not, therefore, begrudge me this little earth which covers my body.

These words, then, deeply affected Alexander, who was reminded of the uncertainty and mutability of life.[19]

Alexander ordered the words copied below the original, this time in Greek. The king would not let the crime of despoiling Cyrus' tomb go unpunished. He had to find the guilty parties to appease his Persian subjects, and it is also likely that he wanted to gain justice after such a monstrous crime.

He turned his ire upon the Magi guards of the tomb. The tomb's guardians were a select group who had maintained the role from father to son since Cambyses' reign. Where the tomb guards were at the time of the looting remains a mystery. Alexander had the guards tortured, but got no answers about the desecrators. The Magi likely did not know, and thus Alexander ordered them released. He then turned his attention to other culprits. As noted earlier, he executed the satrap Orxines for involvement in the crime. The king also had a Macedonian named Polymachus executed for taking part in the crime. Polymachus hailed from the Macedonian capital of Pella and may have been from a prominent family. Alexander, however, had no issues about killing a pure Macedonian for a crime against Persians.[20]

Susa Mass Marriages

In the spring of 324 BC, Alexander found himself back in the royal city of Susa. It was in this city that Alexander had left the Achaemenid royal family. Also likely present at Susa was the family of Artaxerxes Ochus, who Parmenion had captured at Damascus. The Persian royals had spent the past years being tutored in the Greek language and learning Greek mannerisms. In this way, Alexander was preparing them for their future role in his empire.[21]

Darius' daughters had grown in Alexander's absence, and they were no longer the children he found sitting on their grandmother's lap. The king now wished to take Stateira II, the eldest daughter of Darius, as his wife. After Issus, she had been offered to Alexander by Darius himself. Alexander, at the time, refused, claiming that he could marry her anytime he wished regardless of Darius' opinion. Alexander felt that now was the proper time to marry the princess. The King of Asia did not stop there and sought to marry another Achaemenid princess, Parysatis, the youngest daughter of Artaxerxes Ochus.[22]

Alexander would not be alone in his marriages as 100 of his companions also wed the daughters of Asian noblemen. This step was taken by Alexander to further bind the noble families of Asia to his top

Macedonian and Greek officers. Hephaestion married Drypetis, the younger daughter of Darius. Craterus married Amastris, the daughter of Darius' brother Oxyathres. Perdiccas wed the daughter of Atropates and Seleucus the daughter of Spitamenes. Ptolemy, Eumenes and Nearchus were linked to relatives of Artabazos.[23]

Hephaestion's marriage to Drypetis strengthened his position as chiliarch and related him to the king by marriage. If Alexander had any children by Stateira, they would be cousins of those Hephaestion had with Drypetis. The marriage of Alexander's top general Craterus to Amastris further served to reinforce the Macedonian hold on the Persian royals. Amastris was known to have been very close to her cousin Stateira as the two had grown up together.[24] Perdiccas' match served to help win over Atropates, who had just proven himself by crushing the usurper Baryaxes. Seleucus' marriage was intended to help mollify Sogdiana. The marriages of Ptolemy, Eumenes and Nearchus further strengthened Alexander's standing with Artabazos' family.

The timing of the wedding, in spring, aligned with the vernal equinox as per Persian marriage custom. Conducted in the 'Persian manner', the preparations were extremely elaborate. Alexander had a pavilion constructed with ninety-two bridal chambers. The structure was massive, held up by huge decorative columns and surrounded by beautiful curtains. Inside were 100 couches for the wedded, 99 made of silver and 1 of gold for Alexander. The brides and grooms sat together and toasted symbolically. Plutarch recounts how Alexander at the ceremony 'was the first to raise the marriage hymn as though he were singing a song to truest friendship over the union of the two greatest and most mighty peoples'.[25]

Alexander invited his friends and also foreign diplomats who brought expensive gifts. Interestingly, it is mentioned that local Greeks also participated in the event. These could be recent colonists of the king or perhaps men who lived in the empire before his invasion. Plutarch records that Alexander generously 'paid himself the debts, which his guests owed, the whole outlay amounting to 9,870 talents'. Alexander also took the step of having the marriages of his soldiers and their Asian concubines made official; some 10,000 in total.[26]

We must ask the question of why Alexander took the step of hosting these mass marriages. Plutarch believed that Alexander married out of 'imperial and political reason, since the union of the two races was highly advantageous'. The biographer is undoubtedly correct in his assessment and the advantages are apparent. Political marriages had worked many times for Philip and recently for Alexander with his union to Roxane, so it's unsurprising that Alexander again turned to this strategy. Having already gained the support of Sisygambis and Darius' brother, Alexander knew the Achaemenids would not oppose the match. The king perhaps also looked to the example of Darius the Great, who married a daughter of Cyrus to increase his legitimacy. The marriage to the daughters of two former Persian kings was the perfect way for Alexander to solidify his position after his campaigns.

The mass marriages at Susa were not an attempt by Alexander to fuse the races. The Macedonians and Greeks were marrying the Asian elite, not the other way around. Alexander did not bring noble Macedonian women to the ceremony and match them to Asian nobles. The lack of Hellenic women suggests that perhaps Alexander's goal was not to mix the races equally but rather to gain greater dominance over the Asian elite. He may have been attempting to dilute the Persian elite by mixing it with Macedonians. The Persians could no longer claim themselves as being pure if their daughters all married Macedonians and Greeks. Alexander thus could weaken the Persian elite and lessen the danger they posed to him.[27]

The fate of these women after the Susa marriages is another interesting subject for discussion. Many have assumed that Alexander's comrades divorced their hated Asian wives after his death. Despite the popularity of this theory, it does not seem to have a legitimate basis. We should not take these women's lack of mention in the source work or the fact that their husbands took other wives as evidence. It's more likely that Alexander's comrades maintained their Asian wives while also pursuing other polygamous marriages.

In some cases, we can say for certain what happened to these marriages. In the case of Craterus, we know that Amastris, likely with his consent, left him to marry the tyrant Dionysus of Heraclea Pontica and later married Lysimachus. Seleucus kept his wife Apama, the daughter of Spitamenes, and had the future Antiochus I by her. She proved a useful asset when Seleucus built his Asian empire. Eumenes maintained his wife Artonis and her brother Pharnabazus fought under his command.[28]

Formation of the *Epigoni*

That same spring following the mass marriages, Alexander christened the formation of a new military unit known as the *epigoni* (offspring). The formation was a phalanx 30,000 strong in number and made up entirely of Asian recruits. Youth and impressive physical attributes were the conditions for their recruitment. Alexander had employed numerous instructors to teach the young men the Macedonian style of warfare and the Greek language. The sarissa was to be the unit's main weapon, not the usual Persian arms. At Susa, the *epigoni* undertook military manoeuvres before Alexander. The king was impressed by their performance and praised the young boys for their efforts.[29]

According to Curtius, it was in 327 BC, before invading India, that Alexander issued orders for the *epigoni*'s formation. As Plutarch notes, while Alexander was fighting in India, the Asian recruits underwent their training regimen. When their training was complete and Alexander had returned, the satraps brought the youths to Susa for review by the king. Some surmise that the *epigoni* assembled at Susa was only a small part of a larger recruitment drive. Perhaps the *epigoni* unit at Susa was the most recent year's allotment of soldiers or an elite subunit. This idea comes from the belief that Alexander had 30,000 men levied yearly. If Alexander indeed recruited on a yearly basis, around 120,000 Asian soldiers in total could have been trained and assembled.[30]

Alexander also specifically had plans to recruit the children of Macedonian soldiers and Asian women. These young men would not burden Macedonia itself with having to send manpower to the East. A portion of them may have been orphans of fathers killed in the war. Having been born in the military camps, they were accustomed to living in Asia. These mixed-race youths would not need to be introduced to the lifestyle like a pure Macedonian recruit. However, this plan of Alexander's looks to have been a long-term project as the children born during his campaigns would be only a few years old.[31]

When Alexander issued the order for the formation of the *epigoni*, his immediate concern was keeping his empire stable in his absence. As Plutarch concludes, Alexander's goal was so that 'his authority would be kept secure while he was far away'. These recruits helped stabilize the empire when Alexander was fighting across the Hindu Kush. The last thing he wanted was a large-scale uprising in his rear when trying to secure his Eastern border. On a more malevolent note, according to Curtius, Alexander wanted the Asian youths to serve 'as hostages and as soldiers'. It seems that in Alexander's mind, the people of Asia would be less likely to rebel if they knew their sons were serving in his army.[32]

On his return from India, Alexander now valued his new Asian soldiers even more. The Macedonian soldiers, tired after years of war and angry at Alexander's pro-Persian policies, were becoming more disgruntled. Alexander could hardly have forgotten the plots against his life and the Indian mutiny. He had even threatened to continue without his Macedonians, using only his Scythians and Bactrians during the latter mutiny. Alexander wanted the *epigoni* to serve as a 'counter-balance to the Macedonian phalanx'. Should he face another mutiny by the Macedonians, he would retain the loyalty of his Asian phalanx.[33]

Alexander also oversaw the formation of mixed units of Asian and Macedonians. Experienced Macedonians would officer them while the Asians would make up the rank and file. Unlike the *epigoni*, they did not adopt Macedonian equipment. The Asian soldiers would keep their traditional weapons such as bows and javelins. As Diodorus explains, 'Alexander placed these in units with other soldiers, and by the novelty of this innovation created a force blended and adjusted to his own idea.' In Xenophon's *Cyropaedia*, we find that King Cyrus adopted a similar arrangement. Cyrus adopted a deployment in which the heavy infantry manned the first line with archers and javelin men supporting them. Since Alexander undoubtedly read Xenophon's work, he would have been familiar with Cyrus' deployment and some speculate that he based this arrangement upon that of the Persian king.[34]

The king's mass recruitment of the *epigoni* and other majority Asian units demonstrates his intentions in Asia. By the last year of his life, Alexander's army had become majority Asian. The fact that Asians now outweighed the Macedonians in the army was not a coincidence but due to the direct policy of the king, who realized that he could not run an empire with the manpower of Macedonia alone. The growing discontent among the Macedonians only added to his determination to raise Asian forces.

Had Alexander lived longer, one can only surmise that the number of Asian soldiers would have increased and the number of Macedonian soldiers in Asia declined further. At the time of his death, Alexander was preparing to go on a campaign to subdue Arabia. Undoubtedly, Alexander's Asian soldiers would have spearheaded future military ventures. It is possible that Alexander raised these Asian forces in such numbers to facilitate numerous future campaigns.[35]

Alexander's River Reforms

One of the more impressive reforms attributed to Alexander is his overhaul of Mesopotamia's irrigation system. Due to the inefficient irrigation system, the soil of the region was lacking water. At the time of Alexander's inspection, 10,000 Assyrians had been toiling in the ground for three months. Alexander allegedly proceeded to alter the course of the Euphrates in order to free them from the intense labour.[36]

Controversially, Alexander also decided to remove the defensive barriers on the Tigris River. The Persians constructed these barriers to keep foreign ships from sailing up the river and penetrating the empire. The Persians allegedly lacked naval skills to combat such an attack, but this is likely just another Greek stereotype. Arrian claims that Alexander viewed the barriers as cowardly and was confident in his navy. Alexander, at this point, was planning to take the offensive against the Arabs in the Persian Gulf. The navy was to play a key role in the campaign and needed to be able to sail freely. Some have criticized Alexander for removing these barriers as they may have damaged the local irrigation system. However, more likely these were light structures that the Persians themselves removed when required for irrigation or naval purposes.[37]

Mutiny of Opis

The mutiny at Opis in the summer of 324 was the last significant incident of Macedonian opposition faced by Alexander. Dissatisfaction with his Persian policies had been growing for years and finally boiled over into open defiance. The immediate causes of this outburst were twofold. Alexander made the decision to further open up his elite cavalry and bodyguards to the Persians. The king also made plans to dispatch some 10,000 Macedonian veterans home.

In keeping with his pro-Persian policies, Alexander began the mass introduction of Asians into the ranks of his elite horsemen. Numerous Asian nobles' children joined, including a son of Artabazos, two sons of Mazaeus, and Itanes, a son of Oxyartes and brother of Alexander's queen Roxane. Similarly to the *epigoni*, these new cavalrymen took up Macedonian spears instead of their usual Persian javelins. Alexander is said to have also 'appointed generals from specially selected Persians and advanced them into positions of responsibility'.[38]

The king began to re-enrol thousands of Asians into his bodyguard. It now seems that he was to be almost exclusively guarded by Persians and Asians. As Plutarch notes, Alexander 'committed his watches to Persians'. Having to pass through Persian guards to meet their king was an affront to Macedonian honour. Cleitus had complained years earlier about having to be beaten by Median rods to see Alexander.[39]

These latest measures by Alexander, combined with the Susa weddings and the formation of the *epigoni*, were too much to bear for the Macedonian veterans. The Macedonian soldiers were 'filled with dejection and fear, thinking that their king would now pay less regard to them'. According to Arrian, they felt that Alexander had converted entirely to Persian ways and abandoned his native customs. It is clear that the king had not properly explained his actions and the purpose of his policies to the rank-and-file soldiers. They felt betrayed and had little understanding of Alexander's complex political manoeuvres with the Asian elite. Alexander may have still been angry with his army for their disobedience in India and happy to honour the Persians.[40]

Macedonian agitation grew when the soldiers heard that many of their veterans had orders to go home. The orders only confirmed to the Macedonians that Alexander no longer needed them and that Asians were replacing them. The orders also implied that Alexander would not be coming home with them but intended to remain in Asia indefinitely. The soldiers became riotous and made mutinous statements about the king.[41]

This discontent exploded at a city called Opis, where Alexander had gathered his soldiers for an assembly. The king rose onto a platform and announced that he was detaching those Macedonians who were aged or unfit for service. Alexander stated that they would be rewarded for their outstanding services in the East and would live splendidly on their return. He may have expected the soldiers to be pleased, but they were clearly outraged. The issue of Alexander's Persian policies was finally boiling over into the open. They now mocked Alexander in the manner he hated most by mentioning the god Ammon. The soldiers said that Alexander should send them all home and fight alone with his 'father' Ammon's help. In Plutarch's account, the soldiers also sarcastically shouted that Alexander didn't need them any more because 'he had these young war-dancers (*epigoni*), with whom he could go on and conquer the world.'[42]

The king furiously jumped down into the crowd of soldiers and sought out the men who dared to question him. He pointed to specific individuals and ordered his guards to arrest them. Thirteen men in total were to 'be led away for execution'. Alexander retook the platform and delivered a dynamic speech about the accomplishments of his father and himself. He then dared his soldiers to go home and abandon their king. According to Curtius, Alexander declared them to be deserters and ungrateful. Alexander then, clearly upset, withdrew into isolation and was not heard of for three days.[43]

When word from the king finally came, it was Alexander calling in a group of Persians, who were awarded higher commands and referred to as 'kinsmen'. The Persians then performed proskynesis and kissed the king. The Macedonians were distraught; the fact that Alexander called upon the Persians first was a great affront to their honour. For all their mutinous behaviour, the men still loved Alexander for leading them to such achievements. The soldiers stormed the palace and voiced their protests to the king. They threw down their weapons, promised to give up those who had mocked Alexander, and vowed not to leave his palace until their duties were met. Alexander went out to meet the soldiers, who he found dejected and visibly depressed. One veteran stepped forward and asked the king why he called the Persians 'kinsmen' and allowed them to kiss him while Macedonian soldiers had not experienced the same honour. Alexander recognized that he must appease the soldiers' cries. The king responded to the assembled soldiers, saying 'But all of you I regard as my kinsmen, and so from henceforth I call you.' The Macedonians were then allowed to kiss Alexander as his 'kinsmen' before they departed.[44]

Following the mutiny, Alexander held sacrifices to the gods and a large banquet with 9,000 in attendance. This was an attempt at reconciliation between all the factions in his empire. Macedonians, Persians and Asians are said to have attended the affair. Arrian describes the ceremonies:

> He himself and his comrades drank from the same bowl and poured the same libations, while the Greek seers and the Magians began the ceremony. And Alexander prayed for all sorts of blessings, and especially for harmony and fellowship in the empire between Macedonians and Persians.

By 'concord and partnership', Alexander likely refers to the fact that both Macedonians and Asians now held military commands and administrative positions. Arrian did not mean that Alexander intended to fuse the two groups together as some have alleged. The guests favourably received Alexander's actions and it helped to calm anger after the mutiny.[45]

Some historical debate has arisen over the seating placement of the guests during the banquet. On the one hand, from reading the account, you can get the impression that Alexander seated the Macedonians closest to him, the Persians more distant and the Asians even further away. This arrangement could signify that Alexander was attempting to appease the Macedonians by seating them closest and distancing himself from the Persians and Asians. Further, his placement could show the class structure of Alexander's empire, with the Macedonians occupying the first position above the Persians and Asians. On the other hand, one can point to the fact that the Macedonians and Persians are seated together around Alexander to prove that the king intended to unite them further. There looks to be no indication that Alexander viewed the Persians as of lower status or meant to exclude them at the event. Alexander, through the banquet, probably sought to bring peace between the factions of his empire and further promote his Persian policies.

The Opis mutiny was a critical point for the king. It was the greatest challenge the Macedonian ever faced to his pro-Persian policies. Alexander, to his credit, did not yield from his position, and in the end the mutinous soldiers had to relent. He would order his veterans – some 10,000 in total – to return home, selecting Craterus to lead them on the march. Craterus is an interesting choice as he was known to have been against Alexander's Persian policies. Alexander was, in effect, getting rid of those who could oppose his new plans by sending them away. In the aftermath of the mutiny, Alexander would have more freedom to pursue his agenda. Unfortunately, any future plans Alexander had would not come to fruition as he would die not long after the events at Opis.

Death of Alexander

In Babylon, on 11 June 323, Alexander the Great breathed his last. The cause of death has remained a mystery ever since. Shortly before his illness, the king had attended a drinking party with his companions. Some have alleged that the king was poisoned, but it remains unproven. Infamously, the dying Alexander, when asked to whom the empire should be left, spoke the likely invented phrase 'to the strongest'. The war that followed between his Diadochi (successors) was his funeral games.[46]

Alexander's lack of an heir proved to be a critical issue for his empire and is a well-trodden criticism of the king. Prior to departing Asia, Parmenion and Antipater had warned the king to sire an heir before setting out, but to no avail. Parmenion and Antipater likely had other motives as either of their daughters would be fitting brides and this would have gained them greater influence. If Alexander had agreed to marry, it would have placed him in the awkward position of choosing between his two chief lieutenants. Also, had Alexander accepted their advice, it surely would have delayed his expedition and only allowed Darius to better prepare for war. Other than possible death in battle, Alexander had no reason to expect his death at such a young age. Many of his contemporaries lived to be old men. He could have expected to have children later in his reign.[47]

While in Asia, Alexander had attempted to rectify his lack of heirs. The king listened to Parmenion's advice and took up a relationship with Barsine which produced Heracles, but few viewed him as legitimate. The marriage to Roxane brought a promise of an heir. While in India, Roxane did give birth to a child but it died soon after. When he arrived back from his Indian venture, Alexander began to think more about building a dynasty. He stated that his marriage to Darius' daughter came partly out of a wish to breed more heirs.[48] At his death, Roxane was pregnant again with another child who would become Alexander IV.

On his deathbed Alexander had, in fact, selected Perdiccas to oversee his empire. Alexander had given his signet ring to Perdiccas who he believed to be his most dependable officer. In the tradition preserved in the *Metz Epitome*, Alexander even went so far as to entrust his friend with Roxane's safety and asked him to marry her, something he would not do. Perdiccas had proved himself loyal to the king, pulling an arrow from his chest in India when no one else would. When Hephaestion died, Alexander had allowed Perdiccas to escort his body for burial in Babylon. It was a clear statement by Alexander that, with Hephaestion dead, Perdiccas was the ranking figure among his officers. Lucian mentions that Perdiccas prevented Alexander from executing a man accused of crying when walking by Hephaestion's tomb. This event is another indication that Perdiccas had a significant influence over the king after Hephaestion's death. Alexander, under the circumstances, picked who he believed to be the best man to hold the empire after his death.[49]

Alexander's Last Plans

Just prior to his demise, Alexander sought to undertake an Arabian campaign along the Persian Gulf. As per Arrian, Alexander's motive was to make himself a god among the Arabs. More importantly, this region of Arabia was rich in spices, over which Alexander surely wished to gain control. The king did not want to annex the area directly to his empire and intended to leave the Arabs to govern themselves after forcing their submission. His fleet had begun reconnaissance operations on the coast, but the king died before the army could set out against the Arabs.[50]

After the king's death, Perdiccas purportedly found among Alexander's personal items his *Hypomnemata* (notebooks). In these writings, Alexander had laid out his intended vision for the empire referred to as his 'last plans'. The plans themselves are breathtaking in their scale. First and foremost, Alexander wanted the extravagant tomb of Hephaestion completed, costing some 10,000 talents. Also it ordered the construction of half a dozen expensive temples at various locations and a large pyramid tomb, equal to those in Egypt, for his father Philip.[51]

Perhaps the most interesting part of Alexander's plans was his supposed intention 'to establish cities and to transplant populations from Asia to Europe and in the opposite direction from Europe to Asia, in order to bring the largest continents to common unity and to friendly kinship by means of intermarriages and family ties'. This writing by Alexander is one of the few instances in which the king encouraged something approaching a 'fusion' policy. These plans stand apart from his usual policy of keeping Macedonians and Asians in parallel structures. As noted before, Alexander at Susa did not have Macedonian women marry Asian noblemen.[52]

Militarily, according to the plans, the king intended numerous further campaigns. Alexander proposed to build a fleet of 1,000 ships for a campaign against Carthage in North Africa. One could speculate that he had his sights on Carthage since he besieged their sister city of Tyre. A road was to be built across Libya to the Pillars of Hercules (Gibraltar) and numerous port facilities to facilitate the campaign. The king also intended to subdue the coasts of Libya, Spain and Sicily.[53]

According to Diodorus, Perdiccas presented Alexander's plans before the Macedonian assembly. When the Macedonians heard the proposals, they 'saw that the projects were extravagant and impracticable and decided to carry out none of those that have been mentioned'. Historians have speculated as to the reliability of the 'last plans'. The plans don't match up with Alexander's policies and strategic ideas present throughout his reign. Perdiccas may have lied about some aspects of the plans. He may have done this simply because he wanted to consolidate his own position and had no wish to undertake costly projects or far-flung military ventures.[54]

If Perdiccas indeed took these steps to exaggerate the plans, it was a critical mistake. Wars can serve to rally people around a unifying cause. Instead of taking it before the assembly, Perdiccas could have declared a great war to fulfil Alexander's dying vision. Had he done this, it could have rallied the Macedonians behind his leadership. Instead, Perdiccas chose to try his best to get the plans cancelled, which perhaps seemed prudent at the time but undoubtedly was a missed opportunity.[55]

It's also notable that all these alleged military plans would have taken Alexander outside the boundaries of the Persian Empire. While in Asia, Alexander had never shown himself keen to cross these boundaries into the unknown. A campaign in the western Mediterranean would have been a fundamental change in strategy on the part of the king. The only Persian precedent for such plans was the Great King Cambyses, who had planned to attack Carthage but proved unable due to opposition from the Phoenicians, who did not want to attack their sister nation. Without the support of the Phoenician fleets, Cambyses' plan proved unfeasible.[56]

Had Alexander undertaken the supposed war against Carthage, the empire undoubtedly would have been extended to its breaking-point. One imagines it would have been extremely challenging for Alexander to maintain an empire running from India to Iberia. A more coherent plan by Alexander would have been to undertake a short Arabian campaign and finish subduing the outlying portions of Asia Minor such as Cappadocia, Bithynia and Armenia.

Conclusion

Was Alexander a Good Empire-Builder?

W as Alexander a good empire-builder? In the final calculation, Alexander was undoubtedly one of the great empire-builders in history. The king mastered the roles of both soldier and politician. In coming to this conclusion, we can review Alexander's policies at the imperial and local level, his approach to borders, his administration and the legacy he left in Asia.

Imperial Policy

From the time he arrived in the East, Alexander tried to present himself as the legitimate ruler of Asia. He understood the expectations of an Achaemenid monarch and tried to abide by them. The king knew he had to give the Persian and Asian elite a reason to support him. He was quick to try and delegitimize Darius to boost his own claim to Asia. Alexander was able to win over several key figures of the Persian Empire to his cause, such as Mithrenes, commander of Sardis, and the great Persian lord Mazaeus. Alexander's favourable treatment of Sisygambis and her becoming his 'mother' was a great propaganda coup. Taken together, these individuals gave Alexander the air of legitimacy he sought.[1]

However, Alexander's initial efforts did not lead to a whole-scale abandonment of Darius by his elite. It was not until after Darius' murder by Bessus that the bulk of the ruling class began to support Alexander. Alexander's painting of Bessus as an evil usurper was a brilliant manoeuvre and helped to draw the Eastern nobles on to his side. The punishment of Bessus, while cruel, served the purpose of appeasing the Asian elite. Alexander would come to gain the allegiance of important figures such as Oxyathres, Artabazos, Phrat8aphernes, Atropates and Oxyartes.[2]

Alexander willingly embraced Eastern ways, modifying his dress and perhaps even wearing the upright tiara of the Persian kings. He altered court practices, introducing Persian institutions such as the harem, eunuchs, ushers, the melophori and the proskynesis ritual. Casting himself in the mould of an Eastern monarch, Alexander held lavish banquets in the Persian style, rode a royal chariot, used Darius' seal, minted coins in the Achaemenid manner and took part in great Eastern hunts. Alexander's closest comrade Hephaestion took on the role of chiliarch and helped the king to propagate his imperial policies.[3]

As Strabo noted, Alexander was a great admirer of Cyrus the Great. Xenophon, in his *Cyropaedia*, casts Cyrus as the perfect monarch and Alexander followed his example. Numerous parallels between the two kings exist, such as their courteous treatment of women, embracing the attire of the vanquished and honouring the people of Persis with gifts. Actions by the king such as crossing the Gedrosian desert have been directly attributed to Cyrus' own attempt. He also honoured the Euergetae due to their former assistance to Cyrus. On his return from India, Alexander visited Cyrus' tomb and restored the site to its former glory.[4]

The marriages at Susa and the formation of the *epigoni* were the apex of Alexander's imperial policies in Asia. At Susa, Alexander linked himself to the Achaemenid royal family. The marriages also connected his comrades to the daughters of the Asian nobility. The unions directly incorporated Alexander and his comrades into the Asian ruling class. The creation of the *epigoni*, an all-Asian phalanx, was an essential step for the king. It gave him an alternative military arm to the numerically declining and mutinous Macedonians. Had Alexander lived, the *epigoni* would undoubtedly have spearheaded his future military campaigns. Taken as a whole, Alexander proved himself to be a flexible and visionary figure at the imperial level.[5]

Local Policy

Alexander's local policies focused on the embracing of local traditions and religious customs. In his relations with the Greek cities of Asia Minor, he arrived under the banner of freeing them from Persian rule. The king disbanded the pro-Persian oligarchies and replaced them with democracies. At Ephesus, Alexander paid homage to the Temple of Artemis, a location connected to his birth. In Caria, the king established a critical local alliance with Queen Ada that helped gain him control of the territory. At the town of Gordion, Alexander undid the famed knot and embraced the kingship of Midas.[6]

Among the Phoenicians, Alexander made critical alliances with local kings. He used the fleets provided by the kings of Phoenicia and Cyprus to help achieve victory at Tyre. During his time in Egypt, Alexander honoured the native gods, particularly the Apis calf. He ventured to the oracle of Ammon at Siwa to gain legitimacy in Egyptian eyes. At Babylon, Alexander paid homage to the local gods as the priests instructed and ordered the temple to Marduk rebuilt.[7]

Borders

Alexander understood that an empire's borders needed to be secured. We get a glimpse of this before he even set out to Asia during his campaign on the Danube. After the defeat of Darius, Alexander set out to secure the northern and eastern borders of his empire. He launched a punitive campaign against the Scythians, bringing them to peace. He founded numerous cities, the most important being Alexandria Eschate, to defend his northern frontier and separate the population of his empire from the nomads. On his eastern frontier, Alexander pushed to the borders of the defunct Persian Empire. He won the Battle of Hydaspes and made his former foe King Porus an ally. Porus ruled the region on Alexander's behalf, allowing him to withdraw with the border region protected by a strong ally.[8]

Administration

Alexander did not set out to destroy the Achaemenid administrative system, but rather brought it under his control. The Persian tribute system was maintained by him, except that the wealth now flowed into his coffers. The king did not scrap the Persian satrapal system and instead appointed his own candidates. Maintaining the satrapal system proved a sensible move as it had endured for centuries and would continue to do so long after Alexander's death.[9]

Alexander's satraps were both Persian and Macedonian. The king showed himself favouring satraps who could get along with the population and did not neglect their duties or exploit the natives. Perhaps

Alexander's favourite satrap was Peucestas, who gained the favour of the Persians through his embrace of their ways. Other appointed satraps such as Tlepolemus and Stasanor performed well and also gained acclaim from the populace. Asian satraps such as Phrataphernes and Atropates proved particularly effective and loyal to the king.[10]

Alexander did not shirk from removing those satraps and officials who proved unsatisfactory. In the aftermath of the Gedrosian disaster, he set out to clean up his imperial administration. Numerous satraps and officials were removed for various crimes. Alexander would not even spare close friends such as the treasurer Harpalus, or men who had assisted him in the past such as Parmenion's assassins. The king's order to disband the mercenaries was an attempt to reign in satrapal power, as Artaxerxes Ochus had in his time.[11]

Legacy

Perdiccas ultimately failed to live up to the exalted position Alexander presented him. He would be murdered in Egypt by his officers after a failed attempt to cross the Nile.[12] The empire fractured into civil war through the following decades. However, despite the years of bloodshed, Alexander's Asian conquests remained largely intact. Rule over the bulk of Asia would ultimately fall to Seleucus.

Seleucus succeeded because he, like Alexander, gained the favour of the Asian populace. Overall, the role of Asians and Persians in the Successor Wars is an overlooked subject. It was in these people's territories that the majority of the great battles occurred. They provided thousands of soldiers to various belligerents and played a significant role in the campaigns. Seleucus understood that Asian support would be essential in bringing him victory over his rivals. As Diodorus writes, 'he [Seleucus] had shown himself generous to all, winning the goodwill of the common people.'[13]

The Battle of Ipsus in 301 BC was the decisive encounter of the Diadochi wars. At this battle, Seleucus faced off against his rival Antigonus for control of Asia. Seleucus' army included many soldiers drawn from Asia, including Iranian cavalrymen and also Indian elephants. These men played a critical role in Seleucus' victory at the battle. It's entirely possible that the javelin that killed Antigonus originated from one of Seleucus' Iranians.[14]

Antigonus, in contrast to Seleucus, had not placed great emphasis on the Eastern satrapies. He angered the Persians by removing Peucestas from his office. He also purged Peithon and crushed a rebellion by his loyal Medes. Instead of Asia, Antigonus placed his focus firmly on the western Mediterranean. He was fundamentally a man like Philip and Parmenion. He probably would have accepted Darius' supposed offer of half the empire. This strategy had the advantage that Antigonus would concentrate his efforts on building a stable Hellenic state in northern Syria. However, neglecting the East provided Antigonus' emerging rival Seleucus with a chance to win over the population.[15]

Following his triumph, Seleucus consolidated his rule over Asia. Antiochus, his half-Asian son by the daughter of Spitamenes, began to take a leading role in the administration of Asia. Seleucus effectively let him rule the upper satrapies where his influence would be strongest. When Seleucus fell to an assassin's blade in 281 BC, Antiochus inherited the empire. The mixed-race dynasty founded by Seleucus would rule Asia for the following centuries until superseded by the rising Parthian and Roman empires.[16]

Appian records a story about Alexander and Seleucus. Shortly before his death, Alexander was travelling the Euphrates when a gust of wind blew off his diadem. Seleucus swam to retrieve the crown, putting it on his head to keep it dry before returning it to the king. Perhaps fate predicted both Alexander's death and Seleucus' rule in Asia?[17]

Notes

Preface
1. General Baron Gourgaud, *Talks of Napoleon at St. Helena with General Baron Gourgaud*, trans. Elizabeth Latimer (Chicago, A.C. McClurg & Company, 1903), 209.
2. Ibid, 208.

Introduction
1. Arrian, *Anabasis* 3.7.6; Plutarch, *Alexander* 34.1.
2. Arrian, *Anabasis* 1.11.3.
3. Curtius, 6.3.10; Diodorus, Contents of the Seventeenth Book; Arrian, *Anabasis* 4.25.4.
4. Curtius, 8.8.9; Polybius, 10.27; Arrian, *Anabasis* 3.18.11–12.
5. Curtius, 8.8.10; 6.3.6; Josef Wiesehöfer, *Ancient Persia* (New York, I.B. Tauris Publishers, 2006), 110; E.N. Borza, 'Ethnicity and Cultural Policy at Alexander's Court' in *Alexander the Great: A Reader*, Second Edition, ed. Ian Worthington (New York, Routledge, 2012), 313–318; Richard A. Billows, *Antigonos the One-Eyed and the Creation of the Hellenistic State* (Berkeley and Los Angeles, California, University of California Press, 1990), 47.
6. Diodorus, 18.48.5; Curtius, 8.8.13.
7. Curtius, 8.8.10–12; Plutarch, *Alexander* 47.5; Justin, 12.12.2.
8. For a proponent of Alexander's supposed fusion policy: W.W. Tarn, *Alexander the Great, Vol. 1: Narrative* (Chicago, Ares Publishers Inc., 1948), 137–138; For rejection of fusion and argument for Alexander's pragmatism: A.B. Bosworth, 'Alexander and the Iranians' in *Alexander the Great: A Reader*, Second Edition, ed. Ian Worthington (New York, Routledge, 2012), 304; Ernst Fredericksmeyer, 'Alexander the Great and the Kingdom of Asia' in *Alexander the Great in Fact and Fiction*, eds A.B. Bosworth and E.J. Baynham (New York, Oxford University Press, 2000), 165. For a successful argument against dismissing Alexander's Asian policies as mere pragmatism: M.J. Olbrycht, 'Alexander the Great Versus the Iranians: An Alternative Perspective', *Folia Orientalia* 42/43 (2006/07), 166.
9. Justin, 13.1.4
10. Diodorus, 17.37.6; Curtius, 5.2.18; 10.5.19–25.

Chapter One
1. Xenophon, *Anabasis* 1.7.6.
2. Herodotus, 1.123; 1.128–130.
3. Herodotus, 1.71–1.84; 1.175–1.177; 1.178–1.191; 1.205–214.
4. Herodotus, 3.31; 3.89.
5. Herodotus, 3.1–16; 3.61–79.
6. Herodotus, 3.89.

7. Herodotus, 5.52; 8.98–99.
8. Herodotus, 3.89; George Rawlinson, *The Story of Parthia* (New York, G.P. Putnam's Sons, 1903), 41.
9. Herodotus, 4.83–142; 5.1–5.27.
10. Herodotus, 5.17.
11. Herodotus, 5.18–20.
12. Herodotus, 5.21; Justin, 7.3.1–9.
13. Xenophon, *Anabasis* 1.9.3–6; Arrian, *Anabasis* 4.13.1; Curtius, 5.1.42; 8.6.4–6; Waldemar Heckel, *The Conquests of Alexander the Great* (New York, Cambridge University Press, 2008), 14; Edward M. Anson, *Alexander the Great: Themes and Issues* (New York, Bloomsbury Academic, 2013), 58.
14. Herodotus, 7.131; Justin, 7.4.1–2; N.G.L. Hammond, *The Macedonian State: Origins, Institutions and History* (New York, Oxford University Press, 1989), 44–45.
15. Herodotus, 6.44–45.
16. Herodotus, 6.94–120; 7.54–57.
17. Justin, 7.2.13–14.
18. Herodotus, 7.131–132; 7.185; Justin, 7.4.1–2.
19. Herodotus, 7.173; 7.178–238.
20. Herodotus, 8.34; N.G.L. Hammond, *The Macedonian State: Origins, Institutions, and History* (New York, Oxford University Press, 1989), 44.
21. Herodotus, 8.136–144; 9.1.
22. Herodotus, 9.31; 9.44–45.
23. Demosthenes, *Philip* 12.20–21; N.G.L. Hammond, *The Macedonian State: Origins, Institutions and History* (New York, Oxford University Press, 1989), 45–46.

Chapter Two
1. Diodorus, 16.1.3; 16.2.4–6; 16.3.1.
2. Justin, 7.5.2; Plutarch, *Pelopidas*, 16.5; Diodorus, 16.3.1.
3. Theophrastus, *Enquiry Into Plants* 3.12.1–2; N.G.L. Hammond, *The Macedonian State: The Origins, Institutions and History* (New York, Oxford University Press, 1989), 102; Diodorus, 16.2.3.
4. Diodorus, 16.74.2–3; Demosthenes, *Philippic 3*, 9.49; N.G.L. Hammond, *The Macedonian State: The Origins, Institutions and History* (New York, Oxford University Press, 1989), 106; Richard A. Gabriel, *Philip II of Macedonia: Greater than Alexander* (Dulles, Virginia, Potomac Books, 2010), 94.
5. Justin, 9.8.8; Diodorus, 16.95.3–4; Athenaeus, 13.557b-e.
6. Diodorus, 16.2.6; 16.4.1; Justin, 7.6.3–6.
7. Diodorus, 16.4.2–7; Justin, 7.6.7.
8. Diodorus, 16.8.2–5; 16.34.4–5.
9. Diodorus, 16.23.
10. Diodorus, 16.35.1–2.
11. Diodorus, 16.35.4–6; Justin, 8.2.3–4.
12. Diodorus, 16.38.1–2; Justin, 8.2.8.
13. Justin, 8.3.6–12.
14. Diodorus, 16.77.2–3; Plutarch, *Alexander*, 9.1.
15. Justin, 9.2.1–16; Justin, 9.3.1–3; Plutarch, *Moralia*, 331B.
16. Diodorus, 16.84–86; Justin, 9.3.1–11.
17. Curtius, 10.5.23; Plutarch, *Artaxerxes*, 30.

18. Curtius, 10.5.23; Diodorus, 16.40.4–5; Plutarch, *Artaxerxes*, 30; Valerius Maximus, 9.2.
19. A.T. Olmstead, *History of the Persian Empire* (Chicago, University of Chicago Press, 1970), 424–425; Diodorus, 16.52.3–4; Demosthenes, *Against Aristocrates*, 23.157.
20. Diodorus, 16.22.1–3.
21. Richard A. Gabriel, *Philip II of Macedonia: Greater than Alexander* (Dulles, Virginia, Potomac Books, 2010), 127; Diodorus, 16.34.1–2; 16.40.1–2; Polyaenus, *Stratagems*, 7.33.2.
22. Diodorus, 16.52.3; Curtius, 5.9.1.
23. Diodorus, 16.52.1–3.
24. Peter Green, *Alexander of Macedon, 356–323 B.C.: A Historical Biography* (Berkeley and Los Angeles, University of California Press, 1991), 52–54, 58–59; Polyaenus, *Stratagems*, 6.48B; Diodorus, 16.52.5–7.
25. Diodorus, 16.40.5–6.
26. Diodorus, 16.41.2–6; 16.42.1–2.
27. Diodorus, 16.45.1–6.
28. Diodorus, 16.42.3–9; 16.46.1–3.
29. Diodorus, 16.46.4–9; 16.47.6–7; 16.49.1–5.
30. Diodorus, 16.47.1–5.
31. Diodorus, 16.47.5–7; 16.48.1; 16.49.7–8; 16.51.1.
32. Peter Green, *Alexander of Macedon, 356–323 B.C.: A Historical Biography* (Berkeley and Los Angeles, University of California Press, 1991), 51–52.
33. Diodorus, 16.74.2–5.
34. Diodorus, 16.75.1–4; Pausanias, 1.29.10.
35. Arrian, *Anabasis*, 2.14.1–6.
36. Aelian, *Varia Historia*, 13.9; 13.11; Polybius, 3.6.13; Diodorus, 16.89.2.
37. Justin, 9.4.1–3; Diodorus, 16.87.
38. Justin, 9.5.1–7; Diodorus, 16.89.1–3.
39. Curtius, 8.1.26; Diodorus, 16.91.2; 17.7.1–10; Polyaenus, *Stratagems*, 5.44.4–5; Justin, 9.5.8.
40. Diodorus, 16.49.4; 50.8; 17.5.3; Plutarch, *Moralia*, 337E.
41. Diodorus, 17.5–6; Curtius, 10.5.19; Justin, 10.3.
42. Arrian, 2.14.5; A.T. Olmstead, *History of the Persian Empire* (Chicago, University of Chicago Press, 1970), 493.
43. Diodorus, 16.91.3; Arrian, *Anabasis*, 2.14.5; Diodorus, 17.6–7.
44. Diodorus, 16.91.2; 17.7.1–10; Polyaenus, *Stratagems*, 5.44.4–5; Justin, 9.5.8.

Chapter Three
1. Plutarch, *Alexander*, 3.5–7; Justin, 12.16.4–5.
2. Plutarch, *Alexander*, 5.1–3; Plutarch, *Moralia*, 342 B-C.
3. Valerius Maximus, 3.3. Ext.1.
4. Diodorus, 16.52.3; Curtius, 5.9.1.
5. Curtius, 6.5.2; 7.5.1; 10.6.11; 3.13.14; Plutarch, *Alexander*, 21.7; Justin, 11.10.2.
6. Curtius, 3.7.11–15.
7. Curtius, 6.4.25; Arrian, *Anabasis*, 3.22.1.
8. Diodorus, 16.74.2.
9. Plutarch, *Alexander*, 10.1–5.
10. Justin, 12.16.8; Plutarch, *Alexander*, 8.4.

11. Aristotle, *Meteorologica*, 1.13.
12. Plutarch, *Alexander*, 7.4–5; Plutarch, *Moralia*, 332E-F; Aristotle, *Politics*, 5.1313A.
13. Justin, 12.3.12.
14. Aristotle, *Politics*, 7.1327B; Diodorus, 18.48.5.
15. Plutarch, *Moralia*, 329B-D.
16. Curtius, 8.8.20–23; Arrian, *Anabasis*, 7.27.1; Plutarch, 77.3.
17. Plutarch, *Alexander*, 8.2–3; 10.7; 26.2; 28.3; Justin, 11.11.12; Homer, *Iliad*, 5.340; Pseudo-Callisthenes, *Alexander Romance*, 42.
18. Arrian, 1.11–12; 6.10.2; Plutarch, *Alexander*, 15.7–9.
19. Plutarch, 5.8; Arrian, *Anabasis*, 1.11–12; Waldemar Heckel, *The Conquests of Alexander the Great* (New York, Cambridge University Press, 2008), ix-x; Pierre Briant, *Alexander the Great and His Empire: A Short Introduction* (Princeton, New Jersey, Princeton University Press, 2010), 25–28.
20. Plutarch, *Moralia*, 331C-D; F.S. Naiden, *Soldier, Priest and God: A Life of Alexander the Great* (New York, Oxford University Press, 2019), 203.
21. Homer, *Iliad*, 12.15–25; Naiden, *Soldier, Priest and God*, 47.
22. Pausanias, 10.31.5–8; Smyrnaeus, *The Fall of Troy*, 2; Herodotus, 5.53; Curtius, 4.8.3.
23. Herodotus, 1.4–5.
24. Arrian, *Anabasis*, 2.7.8–9.
25. Xenophon, *Cyropaedia*, 8.8.27.
26. Plutarch, *Alexander*, 16.7; Curtius, 6.6.7; Justin, 12.3.10; Xenophon, *Cyropaedia*, 7.1.2; 6.3.24; 8.3.1–5; 8.5.21.
27. Xenophon, *Cyropaedia*, 5.1.2–18; Andrew Chugg, *Alexander's Lovers* (USA, AMC Publications, 2012), 201.
28. Curtius, 7.3.1; Plutarch, *Moralia*, 343A; Strabo, 11.11.4; 15.1.5; Arrian, *Anabasis*, 6.29.4–11; Pierre Briant, *Darius In the Shadow of Alexander*, trans. Jane Marie Todd (Cambridge, Massachusetts, Harvard University Press, 2015), 223.
29. Xenophon, *Anabasis*, 1.5.9.
30. Xenophon, *Anabasis*, 1.8.8–10; 1.8.22; Arrian, *Anabasis*, 2.8.11.
31. Xenophon, *Anabasis*, 1.8.24–9.
32. Xenophon, *Anabasis*, 1.4.18; Waldemar Heckel, *The Conquests of Alexander the Great* (New York, Cambridge University Press, 2007), 52.
33. Plutarch, *Alexander*, 8.3; Athenaeus, *Deipnosophistae*, 10.435E; Plutarch, *Moralia*, 338 BC.
34. Diodorus, 14.44.8; Athenaeus, *Deipnosophistae*, 6.251.F; 12.535E; M.J. Olbrycht, 'An Admirer of Persian Ways: Alexander the Great's Reforms in Parthia-Hyrcania and the Iranian Heritage' in *Excavating an Empire: Achaemenid Persia in Longue Durée*, eds Touraj Daryaee, Ali Mousavi and Khodadad Rezakhani (Costa Mesa, California, Mazda Publishers, 2014), 54.
35. Justin, 11.4.5; 11.10.3; Arrian, *Anabasis*, 4.8.3; 4.28; 5.26.5, 7.10.6.
36. Arrian, *Anabasis*, 5.1; 6.3.5; 6.28; 7.10.6.
37. Herodotus, 1.184; 2.155; Diodorus, 2.4.1; Strabo, 15.1.5; Arrian, *Anabasis*, 1.23.7.
38. Arrian, *Anabasis*, 3.3.1; Herodotus, 7.61; 7.150.

Chapter Four

1. Plutarch, *Moralia*, 327C-D; 342C.
2. Curtius, 6.9.17; Justin, 12.6.14.

3. Plutarch, *Alexander*, 9.7; Diodorus, 17.2.3; Curtius, 6.9.17.
4. Diodorus, 17.2.3–5; 17.3.2; 17.5.1–2.
5. Plutarch, *Moralia*, 332F; Diodorus, 17.17.5; 17.73.5.
6. Plutarch, *Alexander*, 9.1–2; Diodorus, 16.86.1–4.
7. Arrian, *Anabasis*, 1.1.4–1.4.8; 1.5.5–1.6.11.
8. Plutarch, *Moralia*, 327C-D; Justin, 11.2.8; Arrian, *Anabasis*, 1.7.1–4.
9. Diodorus, 17.9.4; Arrian, *Anabasis*, 1.7.-1.10.
10. Diodorus, 17.9.5; 17.14.2; Justin, 11.3.6–10.
11. Plutarch, *Alexander*, 11.10; 14.1; Arrian, 1.10.1–6.
12. Aelian, *Varia Historia*, 13.11; Justin, 11.2.6; 11.5.6.
13. Arrian, *Anabasis*, 2.14.4.
14. Diodorus, 17.4.9; Curtius, 3.10.4; Justin, 2.8.4.
15. Curtius, 3.10. 8–10.
16. Arrian, *Anabasis*, 1.16.7; 3.16.7–8; Plutarch, *Alexander*, 16.17–18; 37.5–7.
17. Plutarch, *Alexander*, 51.4; 53.3–6.
18. Curtius, 9.7.16–26; Diodorus, 17.100.1–101.6.
19. Arrian, *Anabasis*, 1.15.6; Plutarch, *Alexander*, 37.5–7; Plutarch, *Agesilaus*, 15.3.
20. Plutarch, *Agesilaus*, 15.3; Arrian, *Anabasis*, 1.16.6.
21. Plutarch, *Alexander*, 16.12–14; Arrian, *Anabasis*, 1.16.2; 2.10.7.
22. Arrian, *Anabasis*, 1.29.6; 3.24.4; 3.6.2.
23. Xenophon, *Cyropaedia*, 7.5.73; Pierre Briant, *Alexander the Great and His Empire: A Short Introduction* (Princeton, New Jersey, Princeton University Press, 2010), 62.
24. Arrian, *Anabasis*, 1.23.4; 4.2.4.; Diodorus, 17.22.3–5.
25. Diodorus, 16.45.5.
26. Plutarch, *Moralia*, 327D-E; J.F.C. Fuller, *The Generalship of Alexander the Great* (New Brunswick, New Jersey, De Capo Press, 1960), 89–90.
27. Arrian, *Anabasis*, 1.17.1–2; Curtius, 6.3.12; Pierre Briant, 'The Empire of Darius III in Perspective' in *Alexander the Great: A Reader*, Second Edition, ed. Ian Worthington (New York, Routledge, 2012), 182–183; for the best summary of Alexander's aims from the Persian perspective see: Josef Wiesehöfer, *Ancient Persia* (New York, I.B. Tauris Publishers, 2006), 105.
28. Waldemar Heckel, *The Conquests of Alexander the Great* (New York, Cambridge University Press, 2008), 85; Waldemar Heckel, 'Alexander the Great and the "Limits of the Civilized World"' in *Alexander the Great: A Reader*, Second Edition, ed. Ian Worthington (New York, Routledge, 2012), 72, 82; Pierre Briant, *Alexander the Great and His Empire: A Short Introduction* (Princeton, New Jersey, Princeton University Press, 2010), 37–38.
29. Plutarch, *Alexander*, 38.6–7; Curtius, 6.2.15–16; 6.3.15; Pierre Briant, *Alexander the Great and His Empire: A Short Introduction* (Princeton, New Jersey, Princeton University Press, 2010), 63–64.

Chapter Five
1. Curtius, 4.1.38; Justin, 11.12.9–16.
2. Diodorus, 17.17.1–2.
3. Plutarch, *Moralia*, 327D-E; Justin, 11.6.4.
4. Xenophon, *Hellenica*, 3.4.3; Fred Eugene Ray Jr, *Greek and Macedonian Land Battles of the 4th Century B.C.* (Jefferson, North Carolina, McFarland & Company Inc., 2021), 172.

5. Diodorus, 17.18.2; Arrian, *Anabasis*, 1.12.8–10.
6. Xenophon, *Anabasis*, 1.6.2; Arrian, *Anabasis*, 1.12.10.
7. Arrian, *Anabasis*, 1.12.8–10.
8. Waldemar Heckel, *The Conquests of Alexander the Great* (New York, Cambridge University Press, 2008), 45.
9. Justin, 11.6.8–9; Pierre Briant, *From Cyrus to Alexander: A History of the Persian Empire*, trans. Peter T. Daniels (Eisenbrauns, 2002), 822–823.
10. Plutarch, *Alexander*, 16.1; Waldemar Heckel, *The Conquests of Alexander the Great* (New York, Cambridge University Press, 2008), 45; Arrian, 1.14.4; Diodorus, 17.19.4.
11. Plutarch, *Alexander*, 16.2.
12. Arrian, *Anabasis*, 1.13.3–5.
13. Arrian, *Anabasis*, 1.13.6–7.
14. Arrian, *Anabasis*, 1.15.3–5; Plutarch, *Alexander*, 16.7.
15. Diodorus, 17.20.3; Arrian, *Anabasis*, 1.15.6.-1.16.2.
16. Justin, 11.6.12; Diodorus, 17.21.6; Arrian, 1.16.3.
17. Arrian, *Anabasis*, 1.17.1–3; Pierre Briant, *From Cyrus to Alexander: A History of the Persian Empire*, trans. Peter T. Daniels (Eisenbrauns, 2002), 233. For a full list of Alexander's satraps, see Waldemar Heckel, *The Conquests of Alexander the Great* (New York, Cambridge University Press, 2008), 164–165.
18. Arrian, *Anabasis*, 1.18.6–9; 1.20.1; Diodorus, 17.23.1.
19. Diodorus, 17.23.4–6.
20. Arrian, *Anabasis*, 1.19.1–6.
21. Diodorus, 1.20.3.
22. Arrian, *Anabasis*, 1.22–23; Waldemar Heckel, *The Conquests of Alexander the Great* (New York, Cambridge University Press, 2008), 51.
23. Arrian, *Anabasis*, 2.1.1–3; 2.2.1.
24. Plutarch, *Alexander*, 17.3–6; Arrian, *Anabasis*, 1.24.3–4.
25. Arrian, *Anabasis*, 1.25.1–10.
26. Arrian, *Anabasis*, 1.29.1–3.
27. Arrian, *Anabasis*, 1.27–29; Jeff Champion, *Antigonus the One-Eyed: Greatest of the Successors* (South Yorkshire, Great Britain, Pen & Sword Military, 2014), 17.
28. Arrian, *Anabasis*, 2.4.5–6; Curtius, 3.4.14–15. Pierre Briant, 'The Empire of Darius III in Perspective' in *Alexander the Great: A Reader*, Second Edition, ed. Ian Worthington (New York, Routledge, 2012), 182–183.
29. Arrian, *Anabasis*, 2.4.7–11.
30. Curtius, 3.6.4; 4.11.18–19.
31. Diodorus, 17.30.
32. Arrian, *Anabasis*, 2.6.3.
33. Diodorus, 17.30.
34. Curtius, 3.8.8; Arrian, 2.6.3–7.
35. Arrian, *Anabasis*, 2.8.6–8; Plutarch, *Alexander*, 18.6; Curtius, 3.2.4–9.
36. Curtius, 3.3.8–25.
37. Curtius, 3.8.12; Xenophon, *Cyropaedia*, 4.2.2; 3.3.67; 4.1.17; Plutarch, *Artaxerxes*, 5.3.
38. Curtius, 3.8.13.
39. Arrian, *Anabasis*, 2.7.1; Curtius, 3.8.15; Waldemar Heckel, *The Conquests of Alexander the Great* (New York, Cambridge University Press, 2008), 58.

40. Curtius, 3.7.8–9; Arrian, *Anabasis*, 2.7.1.

41. Curtius, 3.9–11; Arrian, *Anabasis*, 2.9–11.

42. Curtius, 3.11.7–9; Plutarch, *Alexander*, 20.9; Arrian, *Anabasis*, 2.11.4–6.

43. Pierre Briant, *Darius In the Shadow of Alexander*, trans. Jane Marie Todd (Cambridge, Massachusetts, Harvard University Press, 2015), xiv.

44. Curtius, 3.11.17–18; Diodorus, 17.36.6.

45. Arrian, *Anabasis*, 2.11.9–10; Diodorus, 17.32.3; Curtius, 3.13.1–17.

46. Curtius, 3.13.12–14.

47. Plutarch, *Alexander*, 21.7–9; Justin, 15.2.3.

48. Polyaenus, *Stratagems*, 4.5.

49. Justin, 11.12; Diodorus, 17.39.1–4; 17.54.2; Curtius, 4.5.1–6.

50. Plutarch, *Alexander*, 29.7–9.

51. Justin, 11.12.4; Arrian, 2.14.7–9; 2.25.1–3.

52. Richard Billows, *Before and After Alexander: The Legend and Legacy of Alexander the Great* (New York, The Overlook Press, 2018), 156.

53. Pierre Briant, *From Cyrus to Alexander: A History of the Persian Empire*, trans. Peter T. Daniels (Eisenbrauns, 2002), 832–840.

54. Waldemar Heckel, *The Conquests of Alexander the Great* (New York, Cambridge University Press, 2008), 65.

55. Diodorus, 17.40.3; Pierre Briant, *Darius In the Shadow of Alexander*, trans. Jane Marie Todd (Cambridge, Massachusetts, Harvard University Press, 2015), 58; Arrian, *Anabasis*, 2.16.

56. Arrian, *Anabasis*, 2.17; Curtius, 4.4.1–2.

57. Arrian, *Anabasis*, 2.16; Justin, 9.2.10–13.

58. Arrian, *Anabasis*, 2.24.5–6; Curtius, 4.4.1–2.

59. Curtius, 4.6.7; Arrian, *Anabasis*, 2.25.4–2.27.7.

60. Pierre Briant, *From Cyrus to Alexander: A History of the Persian Empire*, trans. Peter T. Daniels (Eisenbrauns, 2002), 828; Waldemar Heckel, *The Conquests of Alexander the Great* (New York, Cambridge University Press, 2008), 70.

61. Arrian, *Anabasis*, 3.1–5; Curtius, 4.7.4.

62. Curtius, 4.9.1.

63. Arrian, *Anabasis*, 3.24.4; Curtius, 4.1.34–35; Pierre Briant, *Alexander the Great and His Empire: A Short Introduction* (Princeton, New Jersey, Princeton University Press, 2010), 46–47.

64. Fred Eugene Ray Jr, *Greek and Macedonian Land Battles of the 4th Century B.C.* (Jefferson, North Carolina, McFarland & Company Inc., 2021), 156–157.

65. Diodorus, 17.48.1–2; 17.63.1–4; 17.73.5; Curtius, 4.1.39–40; 6.1; Plutarch, *Agesilaus*, 15.4.

66. Arrian, *Anabasis*, 3.8.6; 3.12.5; Curtius, 4.12.13.

67. Diodorus, 17.53.1–4; Arrian, *Anabasis*, 3.8.6; Curtius, 4.3.36.

68. Arrian, *Anabasis*, 3.7.1–5; Curtius, 4.9.7–8.

69. Arrian, *Anabasis*, 3.10.1–4; 3.11.1–2.

70. Arrian, 3.11–12; 3.13.1–4.

71. Curtius, 4.15.23–24; Arrian, 3.13.5–6; 3.14.2.

72. Arrian, *Anabasis*, 3.14.3; Curtius, 4.15.28–32; Plutarch, *Alexander*, 33.8.

73. Curtius, 4.15.5; Plutarch, *Alexander*, 33.9–11; Arrian, *Anabasis*, 3.14–3.15; Stephen English, *Field Campaigns of Alexander* (South Yorkshire, Great Britain, 2011), 143–145.

74. Arrian, *Anabasis*, 3.16.1–5; Curtius, 4.16.8–9.
75. Curtius, 4.16.26; Diodorus, 17.61.3; Justin, 11.14; Plutarch, *Alexander*, 34.1.

Chapter Six
 1. Diodorus, 17.24.1; Waldemar Heckel, *The Conquests of Alexander the Great* (New York, Cambridge University Press, 2008), 43.
 2. Justin, 11.6.1; 11.6.14; Diodorus, 17.24.1; Arrian, *Anabasis*, 1.17.1.
 3. Arrian, *Anabasis*, 1.17.2; 1.22.7; 1.23.4; Diodorus, 17.22.3–5.
 4. Arrian, *Anabasis*, 1.17.11–12.
 5. Arrian, *Anabasis*, 1.17.10; Strabo, 4.1.22.
 6. Arrian, *Anabasis*, 1.23.7–8.
 7. Arrian, *Anabasis*, 1.23.7–8; Diodorus, 17.23.2–3; Plutarch, *Alexander*, 22.8.
 8. Memnon, *History of Heracleia*, 4.1–2.
 9. Arrian, *Anabasis*, 1.24.5–6; 1.27.5–8.
10. Arrian, *Anabasis*, 1.26.3–1.27.4.
11. Herodotus, 8.138.2; Justin, 7.1.11; Mark Munn, 'Alexander, The Gordian Knot And the Kingship of Midas' in *Macedonian Legacies: Studies in Ancient Macedonian History and Culture in Honour of Eugene N. Borza*, Revised Edition, eds Timothy Howe and Jeanne Reames (CreateSpace Independent Publishing Platform, 2016), 109–115.
12. Plutarch, *Alexander*, 18.1–4; Curtius, 3.1.14–18; Justin, 11.7.4.
13. Memnon, *History of Heracleia*, 12.4; Diodorus, 18.22.1.
14. Curtius, 3.4.1; Arrian, *Anabasis*, 2.4.2; Diodorus, 18.16.1–3.
15. Arrian, *Anabasis*, 2.13.7–8; Justin, 11.10.6; Plutarch, *Moralia*, 334E; Pierre Briant, *Alexander the Great and His Empire: A Short Introduction* (Princeton, New Jersey, Princeton University Press, 2010), 9.
16. Diodorus, 16.43.1–4; 16.45.1–6.
17. Diodorus, 17.47.1; Arrian, *Anabasis*, 2.16; Curtius, 4.1.1–20.
18. Curtius, 4.1.1–20; Justin, 11.10.8–9; Diodorus, 47.46.4–5.
19. Arrian, *Anabasis*, 2.21.1; Curtius, 4.4.13–17.
20. Arrian, *Anabasis*, 3.6.3; Curtius, 4.8.14–15.
21. Curtius, 4.8.9–10.
22. Arrian, *Anabasis*, 3.6.4; 3.19.7.
23. Diodorus, 16.51; 17.49.2; Curtius, 4.7.1–2; Herodotus, 3.1–16; 3.28–29; 7.7.
24. Curtius, 4.7.1–2; Diodorus, 1.70; 17.49.2.
25. Arrian, *Anabasis*, 3.1.4; Plutarch, *Isis and Osiris*, 353A; Herodotus, 3.28–29.
26. Pseudo-Callisthenes, *Alexander Romance*, 1.34; Herodotus, 3.2.
27. N.G.L. Hammond, *The Macedonian State: Origins, Institutions and History* (New York, Oxford University Press, 1989), 279; Curtius, 4.7.5; Diodorus, 1.73; Stanley M. Burstein, 'Alexander's Organization of Egypt: A Note on the Career of Cleomenes of Naucratis' in *Macedonian Legacies: Studies in Ancient Macedonian History and Culture in Honour of Eugene N. Borza*, Revised Edition, eds Timothy Howe and Jeanne Reames (CreateSpace Independent Publishing Platform, 2016), 191.
28. Arrian, *Anabasis*, 3.5.2–5; Burstein, 'Alexander's Organization of Egypt' in *Macedonian Legacies*, eds Timothy Howe and Jeanne Reames (CreateSpace Independent Publishing Platform, 2016), 189–190.
29. Arrian, *Anabasis*, 3.5.4; Burstein, 'Alexander's Organization of Egypt' in *Macedonian Legacies*, 186.

30. Arrian, *Anabasis*, 7.23.6.
31. Curtius, 4.8.5; Burstein, 'Alexander's Organization of Egypt' in *Macedonian Legacies*, 187.
32. Curtius, 4.7.9; Diodorus, 17.49.2–3.
33. Arrian, *Anabasis*, 3.3.1; 3.5.2; Herodotus, 3.17; 3.26; Strabo, 17.1.43.
34. Herodotus, 2.55–56; Pausanias, 5.15.11; 9.16.1; Günther Hölbl, *A History of the Ptolemaic Empire*, trans. Tina Saavedra (New York, Routledge, 2001), 10–11, 78.
35. Curtius, 5.1.24; F.S. Naiden, *Soldier, Priest and God: A Life of Alexander the Great* (New York, Oxford University Press, 2019), 127.
36. Curtius, 5.1.19–23; Naiden, *Soldier, Priest and God*, 125.
37. Diodorus, 2.9.9; Herodotus, 1.183; Strabo, 16.1.5.
38. Pierre Briant, *Alexander the Great and His Empire: A Short Introduction* (Princeton, New Jersey, Princeton University Press, 2010), 105–107.
39. Curtius, 5.1.22; Strabo, 16.1.5.
40. Xenophon, *Cyropaedia*, 8.6.22; Arrian, *Anabasis*, 7.17.3–4.

Chapter Seven
 1. Arrian, *Anabasis*, 3.17; Curtius, 5.3.14–15; Diodorus, 17.67.
 2. Plutarch, *Alexander*, 37.1; Curtius, 5.4.5–8; Diodorus, 19.21–22.
 3. Arrian, *Anabasis*, 3.18.2.
 4. Plutarch, *Alexander*, 37.3; Arrian, 3.18.2–9; Curtius, 5.4; 5.7.12.
 5. Curtius, 5.4.33–34; Plutarch, *Alexander*, 37.3.
 6. Diodorus, 17.71; Curtius, 5.7.8.
 7. Diodorus, 17.70.1; Curtius, 5.6.1.
 8. Arrian, *Anabasis*, 3.18.10; Diodorus, 17.69.1.
 9. Diodorus, 17.69; Justin, 11.14.11; Curtius, 5.5.5–24.
10. Curtius, 5.6.2–9; Justin, 11.14.10; Diodorus, 17.70.1–6.
11. Curtius, 5.6.9; 5.6.20.
12. Curtius, 5.6.11–19.
13. Arrian, 3.18.11–12; *Itinerary of Alexander*, 29.
14. Curtius, 5.7.1–11; Plutarch, *Alexander*, 38.
15. Plutarch, *Alexander*, 38; Curtius, 5.7.1–11.
16. Curtius, 5.6–7; Diodorus, 17.72; Plutarch, *Life of Alexander*, 38; *Itinerary of Alexander*, 29.
17. Plutarch, *Alexander*, 38; Curtius, 5.6.1.
18. Curtius, 5.7.9; Diodorus, 19.22; Edward M. Anson, *Alexander the Great: Themes and Issues* (Bloomsbury Academic, 2013), 153.
19. Arrian, *Anabasis*, 3.18.12; Plutarch, *Alexander*, 38.
20. Arrian, *Anabasis*, 3.18.12; 6.30.1; Curtius, 5.7.10–11.
21. Ernst Fredericksmeyer, 'Alexander the Great and the Kingdom of Asia' in *Alexander the Great in Fact and Fiction*, eds A.B. Bosworth and E.J. Baynham (New York, Oxford University Press, 2000), 145, 149. M.J. Olbrycht, 'An Admirer of Persian Ways: Alexander the Great's Reforms in Parthia-Hyrcania and the Iranian Heritage' in *Excavating an Empire: Achaemenid Persia in Longue Durée*, eds Touraj Daryaee, Ali Mousavi and Khodadad Rezakhani (Costa Mesa, California, Mazda Publishers, 2014), 39; Plutarch, *Life of Alexander*, 38; Arrian, *Anabasis*, 3.18.11.
22. Curtius, 5.6.10; Arrian, *Anabasis*, 3.18.10.
23. Plutarch, *Artaxerxes*, 3.1–2.

24. Plutarch, *Demetrius*, 25.3.
25. Josef Wiesehöfer, *Ancient Persia* (New York, I.B. Tauris Publishers, 2006), 29–30; Herodotus, 1.125.
26. E.R. Bevan, 'Antiochus III and His Title "Great-King"' in *The Journal of Hellenic Studies* 22 (November 1902), 241–244.
27. Josef Wiesehöfer, 'The "Accursed" and the "Adventurer"' in *A Companion to Alexander's Literature in the Middle Ages*, ed. Z. David Zuwiyya, 125; Edward M. Anson, *Alexander the Great: Themes and Issues* (Bloomsbury Academic, 2013), 123.
28. Mary Boyce, *Zoroastrians: Their Religious Beliefs and Practices* (New York, Routledge, 2001), 79; Polybius, 10.27.
29. F.S. Naiden, *Soldier, Priest and God* (New York, Oxford University Press, 2019), 168–169.
30. Curtius, 3.12.13; 4.10.23; Diodorus, 17.110–115; Edward M. Anson, *Alexander the Great: Themes and Issues* (Bloomsbury Academic, 2013), 123.

Chapter Eight
1. Diodorus, 17.65.5; Arrian, *Anabasis*, 3.16.3.
2. Arrian, *Anabasis*, 3.16.
3. Curtius, 4.9.13; Arrian, *Anabasis*, 3.19.1–4; 3.21.5; 3.30.4.
4. Arrian, *Anabasis*, 3.19.5–8; 3.20.3.
5. Arrian, *Anabasis*, 3.20.1–4; 3.21.1.
6. Curtius, 5.9.4–5; 5.9.7.
7. Curtius, 5.9.9–10.
8. Curtius, 5.9.12–13; 5.9.16–17; 5.11.8–11.
9. Arrian, *Anabasis*, 3.21.1–5.
10. *Itinerary of Alexander*, 30; Curtius, 5.13.15–16; Arrian, *Anabasis*, 3.21.6–10.
11. Curtius, 5.13.15–25.
12. Justin, 11.15.8; Curtius, 5.13.15–25; Pierre Briant, *Darius In the Shadow of Alexander*, trans. Jane Marie Todd (Cambridge, Massachusetts, Harvard University Press, 2015), 36.
13. Plutarch, *Alexander*, 43; Plutarch, *Moralia*, 332F; Justin, 11.15.14.
14. Plutarch, *Alexander*, 43.7; Justin, 11.15.14; *Itinerary of Alexander*, 30; Briant, *Darius In the Shadow of Alexander*, trans. Jane Marie Todd (Cambridge, Massachusetts, Harvard University Press, 2015), 36–37.
15. Curtius, 6.6.13.
16. Arrian, 3.23.4; Diodorus, 17.72.1–2.
17. Curtius, 6.6.13; Arrian, *Anabasis*, 3.13.3; 3.25.3.
18. Arrian, *Anabasis*, 3.25.5; 3.28.2; Arrian, *Anabasis*, 4.7.1–2; A.B. Bosworth, 'Alexander and the Iranians' in *Alexander the Great: A Reader*, Second Edition, ed. Ian Worthington (New York, Routledge, 2012), 290.
19. Robin Lane Fox, 'Alexander the Great: "Last of Achaemenids?"' in *Persian Responses Political and Cultural Interaction With(in) the Achaemenid Empire*, ed. Christopher Tuplin (Swansea, Great Britain, The Classical Press of Wales, 2007), 296.
20. Curtius, 7.4.1–4.
21. Curtius, 7.4.5–17.
22. Curtius, 7.4.19; Diodorus, 17.83.7.
23. Curtius, 6.3.16–17.
24. Curtius, 6.3.6; 6.3.11; 6.3.15.

25. Curtius, 6.2.11; Curtius, 6.3.13–14; Curtius, 7.3.4.

26. Arrian, *Anabasis*, 3.28.8–10; 3.29.1–4.

27. Arrian, *Anabasis*, 3.30.6.

28. *Metz Epitome*, 5–6; Diodorus, 17.83.7–9; *Itinerary of Alexander*, 34; Arrian, *Anabasis*, 3.29.6–7.

29. Curtius, 7.5.36–37; Arrian, *Anabasis*, 3.30.4.

30. Arrian, *Anabasis*, 3.30.4–5; *Itinerary of Alexander*, 34.

31. Justin, 12.5.10–11; Arrian, *Anabasis*, 4.7.3–4; Plutarch, *Alexander*, 43; *Metz Epitome*, 14.

32. Diodorus, 17.83.9; Xenophon, *Anabasis*, 1.6.11.

33. Peter Green, *Alexander of Macedon, 356–323 B.C.: A Historical Biography* (Berkeley and Los Angeles, University of California Press, 1991), 355.

Chapter Nine

1. Lucian, *Dialogues of the Dead: Philip and Alexander*, 14; Curtius, 6.6.1–2; 8.8.13; Arrian, *Anabasis*, 4.7.4.

2. Curtius, 3.3.17–19.

3. Xenophon, *Cyropaedia*, 8.3.13; Herodotus, 7.61; Plutarch, *Moralia*, 488D-E; M.J. Olbrycht, 'An Admirer of Persian Ways: Alexander the Great's Reforms in Parthia-Hyrcania and the Iranian Heritage' in *Excavating an Empire: Achaemenid Persia in Longue Durée*, eds Touraj Daryaee, Ali Mousavi and Khodadad Rezakhani (Costa Mesa, California, Mazda Publishers, 2014), 42.

4. Curtius, 6.5.32; Plutarch, *Alexander*, 45.1.

5. Arrian, *Anabasis*, 4.7.4.

6. Curtius, 6.6.4.

7. Diodorus, 17.77.5.

8. Justin, 12.3.8–9.

9. Plutarch, *Alexander*, 45.1–2.

10. Lucian, *Dialogues of the Dead: Philip and Alexander*, 14.

11. Diodorus, 17.77.5.

12. Xenophon, *Anabasis*, 2.5.23.

13. For arguments in favour of Alexander wearing an upright tiara, see M.J. Olbrycht, 'An Admirer of Persian Ways: Alexander the Great's Reforms in Parthia-Hyrcania and the Iranian Heritage' in *Excavating an Empire: Achaemenid Persia in Longue Durée*, eds Touraj Daryaee, Ali Mousavi and Khodadad Rezakhani (Costa Mesa, California, Mazda Publishers, 2014), 43–44; M.J. Olbrycht, 'On Coin Portraits Of Alexander The Great and His Iranian Regalia: Some Remarks Occasioned by the Book by F. Smith: *L'immaginedi Alessandro il Grande sulle monete del regno* (336–323)' in *Notae Numismaticae-Zapaski Numizmatyczne* 6 (2011), 13–26; for arguments against Alexander wearing an upright tiara see Collins, Andrew W., 'The Royal Custom and Insignia of Alexander the Great' in *The American Journal of Philology* 133 (Autumn, 2012), 372.

14. Curtius, 10.6.4.

15. Curtius, 6.6.7; Justin, 12.3.8–9; Xenophon, *Cyropaedia*, 8.3.1–5; Herodotus, 3.84.

16. Arrian, 7.29.4; Plutarch, *Alexander*, 45.1; Plutarch, *Moralia*, 330.

17. Athenaeus, *Deipnosophistae*, 12.538–539; Aelian, *Varia Historia*, 9.3; Polyaenus, *Stratagems*, 4.3.24.

18. Curtius, 6.6.4; Plutarch, *Phocion*, 17.6.

19. Diodorus, 17.77.4; Plutarch, *Alexander*, 46.1; Athenaeus, *Deipnosophistae*, 13.575; M.J. Olbrycht, 'An Admirer of Persian Ways: Alexander the Great's Reforms in Parthia-Hyrcania and the Iranian Heritage' in *Excavating an Empire: Achaemenid Persia in Longue Durée*, eds Touraj Daryaee, Ali Mousavi and Khodadad Rezakhani (Costa Mesa, California, Mazda Publishers, 2014), 48.

20. Diodorus, 17.77.6–7; Plutarch, *Artaxerxes*, 27.2; Curtius, 3.3.24; 6.6.8.

21. Diodorus, 17.77.4; Curtius, 7.3.2.

22. Atheneaus, *Deipnosophistae*, 12.538–539; Polyaenus, *Stratagems*, 4.3.24; Aelian, *Varia Historia*, 9.3; A.B. Bosworth, 'Alexander and the Iranians' in *Alexander the Great: A Reader*, Second Edition, ed. Ian Worthington (New York, Routledge, 2012), 292–293.

23. Aelian, *Varia Historia*, 9.3; Curtius, 8.4.17; Valerius Maximus, 5.1. Ext.1.

24. A.B. Bosworth, 'Alexander and the Iranians' in *Alexander the Great: A Reader*, Second Edition, ed. Ian Worthington (New York, Routledge, 2012), 292; Polyaenus, *Stratagems*, 4.3.24.

25. Arrian, *Anabasis*, 3.24.1; 4.17.3. For full discussion see M.J. Olbrycht, 'First Iranian Units in the Army of Alexander the Great' in *Anabasis-Studia Classica Et Orientalia* 2 (2011), 67–84.

26. Curtius, 6.2.17; Diodorus, 17.74.3; Arrian, *Anabasis*, 3.19.5–6.

27. Plutarch, *Alexander*, 4.11; 23.4; Curtius, 8.1.10–18.

28. Noriko Sawada, 'Social Customs and Institutions: Aspects of the Macedonian Elite Society' in *Alexander the Great: A Reader*, Second Edition, ed. Ian Worthington (New York, Routledge, 2012), 49–51. For an in-depth look at Alexander's royal hunts, see James Stephen Mullen, 'The Royal Hunts of Alexander the Great: Engaging with Local Traditions of Kingship Throughout his Empire' (PhD diss., Newcastle University, 2019).

29. Athenaeus, *Deipnosophistae*, 12.537E-538B; Plutarch, *Alexander*, 40.4.

30. Curtius, 8.1.10–18; 8.6.7; Plutarch, *Alexander*, 41.

31. Pierre Briant, *From Cyrus to Alexander: A History of the Persian Empire*, trans. Peter T. Daniels (Eisenbrauns, 2002), 231.

32. Justin, 15.3; Plutarch, *Demetrius*, 27; Curtius, 8.1; Jeff Champion, *Antigonos the One-Eyed: Greatest of the Successors* (South Yorkshire, Great Britain, Pen & Sword Military, 2014), 148.

33. Plutarch, *Alexander*, 20.10; Curtius, 4.6.29; 5.1.23.

34. Waldemar Heckel, *The Conquests of Alexander the Great* (New York, Cambridge University Press, 2008), 95; Arrian, *Anabasis*, 3.30.4.

35. Curtius, 3.3.15–16.

36. Plutarch, *Alexander*, 23.4.

37. Athenaeus, *Deipnosophistae*, 12.537E-538B; Curtius, 3.3.18; James Stephen Mullen, 'The Royal Hunts of Alexander the Great: Engaging with Local Traditions of Kingship Throughout his Empire' (PhD diss., Newcastle University, 2019), 210, 232–233.

38. Justin, 12.3.11.

39. Athenaeus, *Deipnosophistae*, 4.145; 12.514.

40. Curtius, 6.2.2–5; Athenaeus, *Deipnosophistae*, 4.171C; *Itinerary of Alexander*, 29; Arrian, *Anabasis*, 4.8.2.

41. Curtius, 9.7.12–15.

42. Athenaeus, 12.537E-538B.

43. Arrian, *Anabasis*, 6.28.1–2; Diodorus, 17.106.1.
44. Curtius, 9.10.22–28.
45. Plutarch, *Alexander*, 67.
46. Xenophon, *Cyropaedia*, 7.5.61; Diodorus, 16.49.4; 16; 16.50.8; Arrian, *Anabasis*, 3.25.4; Curtius, 4.6.7–29.
47. Curtius, 6.6.8; Arrian, *Anabasis*, 7.24.2–3.
48. Curtius, 7.9.19.
49. Curtius, 6.5.22–23.
50. Curtius, 6.5.22–23.
51. Curtius, 10.1.25–26; Plutarch, *Alexander*, 67; Aelian, *Varia Historia*, 3.23.
52. Waldemar Heckel, *The Conquests of Alexander the Great* (New York, Cambridge University Press, 2008), 98; Andrew Chugg, *Alexander's Lovers* (USA, AMC Publications, 2012), 157.
53. Arrian, *Anabasis*, 4.11.9; Valerius Maximus, 4.7, Ext 2; Xenophon, *Cyropaedia*, 8.5.17.
54. Herodotus, 1.134.
55. Curtius, 8.5.5–9; Justin, 12.7.1–3.
56. Plutarch, *Alexander*, 54.4.
57. Arrian, *Anabasis*, 4.11.6.
58. Plutarch, *Alexander*, 54.1; Homer, *Iliad*, 21.120.
59. Josef Wiesehöfer, *Ancient Persia* (New York, I.B. Tauris Publishers, 2006), 30.
60. Aelian, *Varia Historia*, 1.21.
61. Cornelius Nepos, *Conon*, 3.3.
62. Curtius, 8.5.5; Arrian, *Anabasis*, 4.9.9.
63. Plutarch, *Alexander*, 28; Homer, *Iliad*, 5.340.
64. Justin, 12.7.1–3; Arrian, *Anabasis*, 4.9.9; 4.10.5.
65. Curtius, 8.5.22–24; Plutarch, *Alexander*, 74.1–3.
66. Diodorus, 17.66.1–7.
67. Plutarch, *Alexander*, 48.5–6; Plutarch, *Moralia*, 339F; Arrian, *Anabasis*, 3.26.1–4.
68. Arrian, *Anabasis*, 3.26.1–4.
69. Diodorus, 17.80.4; Justin, 12.5.8; Curtius, 7.2.35–38; Pierre Briant, *Alexander the Great and His Empire: A Short Introduction* (Princeton, New Jersey, Princeton University Press, 2010), 65.
70. Curtius, 6.6.5; 6.6.9–11; Diodorus, 17.78.1.
71. Arrian, *Anabasis*, 4.8.4; 4.8.8; Plutarch, *Alexander*, 51.2.
72. Arrian, *Anabasis*, 4.13.
73. Curtius, 8.7.1; 8.8.10–12.
74. Curtius, 8.7.8–10; 8.8.20–23; Arrian, *Anabasis*, 4.14.3; Plutarch, 55.9.

Chapter Ten
1. Arrian, *Anabasis*, 3.8.4; 3.21.10; 3.25.1–2; Diodorus, 17.83.3.
2. Arrian, *Anabasis*, 3.25.5–7.
3. Arrian, *Anabasis*, 3.28.2–3; Curtius, 7.4.38.
4. Arrian, *Anabasis*, 3.30.6; 4.1.5.
5. Diodorus, Contents of the Seventeenth Book.
6. Arrian, *Anabasis*, 4.1.5; Curtius, 7.6.13–15.
7. Curtius, 7.6.13–15.
8. Strabo, 11.11.4; Arrian, *Anabasis*, 4.2.1–4.3.4; 4.5.2–9; 4.6.1–2; Curtius, 7.7.24; 7.7.29.

9. Arrian, *Anabasis*, 4.6.3–5.
10. Curtius, 7.7.39.
11. Arrian, *Anabasis*, 4.16.1–3.
12. Arrian, *Anabasis*, 4.16.4–7.
13. Arrian, *Anabasis*, 4.17.4–6.
14. Arrian, *Anabasis*, 4.17.6–7; *Itinerary of Alexander*, 43.
15. Curtius, 8.3.1–15; *Metz Epitome*, 20–23.
16. Richard Billows, *Before and After Alexander: The Legend and Legacy of Alexander the Great* (New York, The Overlook Press, 2018), 179; Plutarch, *Moralia*, 328.
17. Plutarch, *Moralia*, 328–329; Strabo, 11.11.
18. Curtius, 4.8.1–6; Valerius Maximus, 1.4, ext 1; *Itinerary of Alexander*, 20.
19. Strabo, 11.11; Curtius, 10.2.8; Diodorus, 17.99.5–6.
20. Michael Iliakis, 'Greek Mercenary Revolts in Bactria: A Re-Appraisal' in *Historia: Zeitschrift für Alte Geschichte* 62, no. 2 (2013), 194.
21. Curtius, 9.7.1–11.
22. Curtius, 9.7.1–11.
23. Diodorus, 18.7.1–3; M.J. Olbrycht, 'Iranians in the Diadochi Period' in *After Alexander: The Time of the Diadochi (323–281 BC)*, eds Victor Troncoso and Edward Anson (Havertown, United States, Oxbow Books, 2016), 163.
24. Diodorus, 18.7.4–8.
25. Curtius, 8.8.7–8.
26. Arrian, *Anabasis*, 3.27.4–5; Curtius, 7.3.1–4.
27. Arrian, *Anabasis*, 5.2.1–7.
28. Herodotus, 6.18–22; Curtius, 7.5.28–35; Strabo, 11.11.4.
29. Curtius, 7.5.28–35; Strabo, 11.11.4.
30. Curtius, 7.5.28–35.
31. Arrian, *Indica*, 40.7–8; Polyaenus, *Stratagems*, 4.3.31.
32. Plutarch, *Alexander*, 72.4; Arrian, *Anabasis*, 7.15.1–3; Arrian, *Indica*, 40.7–8; Diodorus, 17.111.4–6; 19.19.
33. Strabo, 11.11.
34. Curtius, 7.6.25–27; 7.7.2; Polybius, 10.27.3.
35. Arrian, *Anabasis*, 3.30.6–11; 4.1.3.
36. Arrian, *Anabasis*, 4.3.6; 4.4.2–3.
37. Arrian, *Anabasis*, 4.4.3.
38. Arrian, *Anabasis*, 4.4.5–9.
39. Waldemar Heckel, *The Conquests of Alexander the Great* (New York, Cambridge University Press, 2008), 97; Strabo, 11.11; Arrian, 4.5.1.
40. Arrian, *Anabasis*, 4.15.1–6; Curtius, 8.1.9; Richard A. Gabriel, *Philip II of Macedonia: Greater than Alexander* (Dulles, Virginia, Potomac Books, 2010), 16.
41. Arrian, *Anabasis*, 4.15.5–6; Curtius, 7.9.19.
42. Arrian, *Anabasis*, 4.15.6; 4.22.3; Waldemar Heckel, *The Conquests of Alexander the Great* (New York, Cambridge University Press, 2008), 112; Pierre Briant, *Alexander the Great and His Empire: A Short Introduction* (Princeton, New Jersey, Princeton University Press, 2010), 37–38.
43. Arrian, *Anabasis*, 3.8.6; Waldemar Heckel, *The Conquests of Alexander the Great* (New York, Cambridge University Press, 2008), 113.
44. Curtius, 8.5.4; Plutarch, *Alexander*, 66.5.
45. Arrian, 5.12.2; Curtius, 8.14.5; M.J. Olbrycht, 'The Military Reforms of Alexander the Great During His Campaign in Iran, Afghanistan and Central

Asia' in *Understanding Eurasia: From Ancient Times to Present Day* (Krakow, 2007), 316. Robin Lane Fox, 'Alexander the Great: "Last of Achaemenids?"' in *Persian Responses Political and Cultural Interaction With(in) the Achaemenid Empire*, ed. Christopher Tuplin (Swansea, Great Britain, The Classical Press of Wales, 2007), 284.
46. Curtius, 9.5.19–20; *Itinerary of Alexander*, 52; Arrian, 4.25.4.
47. Curtius, 8.10.22; Justin, 12.7.9–11; *Metz Epitome*, 39–45.
48. *Metz Epitome*, 39–45.
49. Curtius, 8.10.33–36; Diodorus, 17.84.1; Justin, 12.7.11.
50. Diodorus, 17.86.4–7; Arrian, *Anabasis*, 3.25.8; Curtius, 8.13.3–5.
51. Curtius, 8.13.1–2; *Metz Epitome*, 53–62; Arrian, *Anabasis*, 5.18.6.
52. Curtius, 8.14.35–36; Arrian, *Anabasis*, 5.19.2–3.
53. Curtius, 8.14.44–45; Arrian, *Anabasis*, 5.19.4–6.
54. Arrian, *Anabasis*, 5.24–29; for full discussion of the Hyphasis 'Mutiny', see Philip O. Spann, 'Alexander at the Beas: Fox in a Lion's Skin' in *The Eye Expanded: Life and the Arts in Greco-Roman Antiquity*, eds Frances B. Titchener and Richard F. Moorton, Jr (Berkeley and Los Angeles, California, University of California Press, 1999), 62–74; Heckel, 'Alexander the Great and the "Limits of the Civilised World"' in *Alexander the Great: A Reader*, Second Edition, ed. Ian Worthington (New York, Routledge, 2012), 71–88; Waldemar Heckel, *The Conquests of Alexander the Great* (New York, Cambridge University Press, 2008), 120–125; Pierre Briant, *Alexander the Great and His Empire: A Short Introduction* (Princeton, New Jersey, Princeton University Press, 2010), 37–38.
55. Waldemar Heckel, *The Conquests of Alexander the Great* (New York, Cambridge University Press, 2008), 126–131.

Chapter Eleven
1. Curtius, 5.6.8; 6.2.8; Plutarch, *Alexander*, 22.
2. Plutarch, *Alexander*, 12.1–6.
3. Curtius, 6.2.5–10.
4. Curtius, 3.11.20–22; Diodorus, 17.35.7.
5. Plutarch, *Themistocles*, 36.3–4; Diodorus, 17.35.7.
6. Curtius, 3.3.24; 4.14.22; Diodorus, 17.36.4.
7. Diodorus, 17.36.5.
8. Curtius, 3.12.4–12; Diodorus, 17.37.3.
9. Arrian, *Anabasis*, 2.12.3–5; Diodorus, 17.37.3; Justin, 11.9.12–16.
10. Diodorus, 17.37.5–6.
11. Diodorus, 17.38.1–2; Curtius, 3.12.24.
12. Curtius, 4.15.9–10.
13. Diodorus, 17.67.1; Curtius, 5.2.17–22.
14. Curtius, 5.3.11–15.
15. Diodorus, 17.38.3–4.
16. Curtius, 3.12.22–23; Arrian, *Anabasis*, 4.19.6; Plutarch, *Alexander*, 21.7; 21.10; 22.1–5; Justin, 11.12.7.
17. Andrew Chugg, *Alexander's Lovers* (USA, AMC Publications, 2012), 201.
18. Justin, 11.12.6; Curtius, 4.10.19; Diodorus, 17.54.7.
19. Curtius, 4.10.18–22; Plutarch, *Alexander*, 30.12–13; Plutarch, *Moralia*, 33E-F.
20. Waldemar Heckel, *The Conquests of Alexander the Great* (New York, Cambridge University Press, 2007), 85; Plutarch, *Alexander*, 30.1; Justin, 11.12.6–7.

21. Curtius, 4.10.18–19; 4.14.22–23; 8.4.26.
22. Arrian, *Anabasis*, 4.18.4–7; 4.19.1–4; Curtius, 8.4.1–17.
23. Plutarch, *Life of Alexander*, 47.7; Arrian, *Anabasis*, 4.19.5; Diodorus, Contents of the Seventeenth Book; *Metz Epitome*, 28–31; Curtius, 8.4.25.
24. Plutarch, *Alexander*, 47.7–8; Sabine Müller, 'The Female Element of the Political Self-Fashioning of the Diadochi: Ptolemy, Seleucus, Lysimachus and Their Iranian Wives' in *After Alexander the Time of the Diadochi (323–281 BC)*, eds Victor Troncoso and Edward Anson (Havertown, Pennsylvania, Oxbow Books, 2016), 200; Worthington, 'Alexander the Great, Nation Building and the Creation and Maintenance of Empire' in *Alexander the Great: A Reader*, Second Edition, ed. Ian Worthington (New York, Routledge, 2012), 209.
25. Arrian, *Anabasis*, 4.19.5; 4.20.4; Curtius, 8.4.21–30.
26. *Metz Epitome*, 70, 112, 118; Plutarch, 77.6–7; Sabine Müller, 'The Female Element of the Political Self-Fashioning of the Diadochi: Ptolemy, Seleucus, Lysimachus and Their Iranian Wives' in *After Alexander the Time of the Diadochi (323–281 BC)*, eds Victor Troncoso and Edward Anson (Havertown, Pennsylvania, Oxbow Books, 2016), 203.
27. Plutarch, *Alexander*, 77.4; Diodorus, 19.105.1–4.

Chapter Twelve

1. Andrew Chugg, *Alexander's Lovers* (USA, AMC Publications, 2012), 133.
2. Diodorus, 18.48.5; Curtius, 4.16.32.
3. Plutarch, *Alexander*, 39.5; 47.
4. Arrian, *Anabasis*, 4.22.7–8; 4.28.5; 5.3.5; Curtius, 8.12.4.
5. Curtius, 6.11.10–11; Plutarch, *Alexander*, 49.6.
6. Plutarch, *Alexander*, 55.1; 54.4–5.
7. Plutarch, *Eumenes*, 2.1.
8. Plutarch, *Alexander*, 47.5–7.
9. Arrian, *Anabasis*, 7.14.8–10; Curtius, 10.5.20.
10. Diodorus, 17.110–115; 18.37.1; Aelian, *Varia Historia*, 7.8; Andrew Chugg, *Alexander's Lovers* (USA, AMC Publications, 2012), 124.
11. Diodorus, 17.110–115; Plutarch, *Alexander*, 72.3; Aelian, *Varia Historia*, 7.8; Arrian, *Anabasis*, 7.14.5.
12. Arrian, *Anabasis*, 7.14.10; Plutarch, *Eumenes*, 2.4–5; Lucian, *Slander*, 17.
13. Curtius, 9.5.14; Arrian, *Anabasis*, 6.30.2.
14. Arrian, *Anabasis*, 6.30.2.
15. Arrian, *Anabasis*, 6.30.2–3.
16. Diodorus, 19.14.5.
17. Diodorus, 19.14.4–5; Arrian, *Anabasis*, 7.23.1–2; Diodorus, 17.109.2.
18. Pseudo-Callisthenes, *Alexander Romance*, 3.31.8; Arrian, *Anabasis*, 7.26.2.
19. Diodorus, 19.14.4–5; 19.21.2–3; 19.22.
20. Diodorus, 19.17.4–7; Plutarch, *Eumenes*, 15.4.
21. Diodorus, 19.14.
22. Diodorus, 19.22–23.
23. Diodorus, 19.23.
24. Diodorus, 19.27.6; 19.29.2.
25. Diodorus, 19.48.5.
26. Diodorus, 19.14.6; 19.28.3; 19.48.1; Arrian, 6.27.1.
27. Strabo, 14.6.3.

28. Arrian, *Anabasis*, 3.29.5; M.J. Olbrycht, 'Iranians in the Diadochi Period' in *After Alexander the Time of the Diadochi (323–281 BC)*, eds Victor Troncoso and Edward Anson (Havertown, United States, Oxbow Books, 2016), 161–162.
29. Arrian, *Anabasis*, 4.18.3; 6.27.3; Diodorus, 18.3.3; 18.39.5; 19.48.1; Pseudo-Callisthenes, *Alexander Romance*, 3.31.8.
30. Plutarch, *Alexander*, 17.1; Diodorus, 17.21.7.
31. Pierre Briant, *From Cyrus to Alexander: A History of the Persian Empire*, translated by Peter T. Daniels (Eisenbrauns, 2002), 843.
32. Arrian, *Anabasis*, 1.17.3–4; 1.17.7; Diodorus, 17.21.7.
33. Curtius, 3.12.6–7; 5.8.12.
34. Arrian, *Anabasis*, 1.17.3–4; 2.14.7; 3.16.5.
35. Plutarch, *Alexander*, 39.9; Curtius, 4.11.20.
36. Diodorus, 16.42.1; Pierre Briant, 'The Empire of Darius III in Perspective' in *Alexander the Great: A Reader*, Second Edition, ed. Ian Worthington (New York, Routledge, 2012), 177–178.
37. Arrian, *Anabasis*, 3.7.1–2; Curtius, 4.9.7–8.
38. Diodorus, 17.55.1–2; Curtius, 4.9.7–8.
39. Curtius, 4.9.7–8; 4.10.11–14.
40. Curtius, 4.12.1.
41. Waldemar Heckel, *The Conquests of Alexander the Great* (New York, Cambridge University Press, 2008), 74–75.
42. Diodorus, 17.58.2; Curtius, 4.16.1.
43. Curtius, 4.15.6–8.
44. Plutarch, *Alexander*, 33.9–11.
45. Curtius, 4.16; Arrian, *Anabasis*, 3.15.1.
46. Arrian, *Anabasis*, 7.6.4; Naiden, *Soldier, Priest and God* (New York, Oxford University Press, 2019), 236.
47. Curtius, 5.1.17; 5.1.27; Strabo, 16.1.5.
48. Curtius, 5.1.17–19; Pierre Briant, 'The Empire of Darius III in Perspective' in *Alexander the Great: A Reader*, Second Edition, ed. Ian Worthington (New York, Routledge, 2012), 183.
49. Plutarch, *Alexander*, 39.9; Curtius, 5.1.17–18; Arrian, *Anabasis*, 3.16.6–7.
50. Arrian, *Anabasis*, 4.18.3; Curtius, 8.3.17; Pierre Briant, 'The Empire of Darius III in Perspective', 183.
51. Pseudo-Callisthenes, *Alexander Romance*, 7.
52. Curtius, 3.11.8; 3.13.12–14; 6.2.9.
53. Curtius, 6.2.9.
54. Curtius, 7.5.40; Plutarch, *Alexander*, 43; Arrian, *Anabasis*, 7.4.5.
55. Curtius, 5.9.1.
56. Arrian, *Anabasis*, 2.1.3; 2.2.1; Curtius, 3.13.12–14; 10.6.11; Plutarch, *Alexander*, 21.7; Justin, 11.10.2.
57. Curtius, 5.9.1; 5.9.12.
58. Curtius, 5.9.17.
59. Curtius, 5.12.8; 5.12.18.
60. Arrian, 3.23.7; Curtius, 6.5.1–5.
61. Arrian, 3.24.9; 3.28.2; 3.29.1; 4.15.5; 4.16.3; Curtius, 6.5.6–10; 7.5.1; 7.11.23–29.
62. Plutarch, *Eumenes*, 7.1.
63. Arrian, *Anabasis*, 4.21.1–2.

64. Arrian, *Anabasis*, 4.21.6–10.
65. Diodorus, 19.14.6; 19.48.2.
66. Arrian, *Anabasis*, 3.8.4; 3.23.4; 3.28.2.
67. Arrian, *Anabasis*, 5.20.7; 6.27.6; 7.6.3; Diodorus, 18.3.3.
68. Arrian, *Anabasis*, 3.8.4; 4.18.3.
69. Arrian, *Anabasis*, 6.29.3; Diodorus, 18.3; Strabo, 11.13.1.

Chapter Thirteen
 1. Arrian, *Anabasis*, 6.22.3; 6.23.1–2.
 2. Arrian, *Anabasis*, 6.24–25.
 3. Strabo, 15.2.5; Arrian, *Anabasis*, 6.24.1–3.
 4. Arrian, *Anabasis*, 6.23.1–6.
 5. Arrian, *Anabasis*, 6.27.1–2; Diodorus, 17.105.6–9; Plutarch, *Alexander*, 66.7; Curtius, 9.10.22; Strabo, 15.3.7.
 6. Arrian, *Anabasis*, 7.4.1–3; Diodorus, 17.106.2.
 7. Curtius, 10.1.1–9.
 8. Arrian, *Anabasis*, 6.27.3–5.
 9. Arrian, *Anabasis*, 3.6.8; Diodorus, 108.4.
10. Athenaeus, *Deipnosophistae*, 13.594D-596B; Diodorus, 17.108.4–8.
11. Diodorus, 17.106.2–3; 17.111.1.
12. Arrian, *Anabasis*, 6.27.4.
13. Xenophon, *Cyropaedia*, 8.5.21; Plutarch, *Alexander*, 69.1–2.
14. Arrian, *Anabasis*, 3.18.11; 6.29.2.
15. Curtius, 10.1.22–26; Strabo, 15.3.7.
16. Arrian, *Anabasis*, 6.29.3; Curtius, 10.1.1–9.
17. Arrian, *Anabasis*, 6.29.4–6; 6.29.9.
18. Curtius, 10.1.32.
19. Plutarch, *Alexander*, 69.4–5.
20. Arrian, *Anabasis*, 6.29.9–11; 6.30.1–2; Plutarch, *Alexander*, 69.3.
21. Diodorus, 17.67.1.
22. Curtius, 4.11.20; Arrian, *Anabasis*, 2.25.1.
23. Arrian, *Anabasis*, 7.4.4–6; Justin, 12.10.9–10; Plutarch, *Alexander*, 70.2.
24. Memnon, *History of Heracleia*, 4.4.
25. Strabo, 15.3.17; Atheneaus, *Deipnosophistae*, 12.538B-539A; Plutarch, *Moralia*, 329E.
26. Aelian, *Varia Historia*, 8.7; Atheneaus, *Deipnosophistae*, 12.538B-539A; Plutarch, *Alexander*, 70.2; Arrian, *Anabasis*, 7.4.7–8.
27. Ian Worthington, *By the Spear: Philip II, Alexander the Great and the Rise and Fall of the Macedonian Empire* (New York, Oxford University Press, 2014), 277.
28. Branko F. van Oppen de Ruiter, 'The Susa Marriages: A Historiographical Note' in *Ancient Society* 44 (2014), 25–41.
29. Diodorus, 17.108.1–3; Plutarch, *Alexander*, 47.5; 71.1.
30. Curtius, 8.5.1; Plutarch, 71.1; Arrian, *Anabasis*, 7.6.1; N.G.L. Hammond, 'Royal Pages, Personal Pages and Boys Trained in the Macedonian Manner during the Period of the Temenid Monarchy' in *Historia: Zeitschrift für Alte Geschichte* 39, no. 3 (1990), 279.
31. Justin, 12.4.5–11.
32. Plutarch, *Alexander*, 47.5; Curtius, 8.5.1.

33. Curtius, 9.2.33; Diodorus, 17.108.1–4; Arrian, *Anabasis*, 7.6.2–5.

34. Arrian, *Anabasis*, 7.23.3–4; Diodorus, 17.109.2; Xenophon, *Cyropaedia*, 6.3.24; M.J. Olbrycht, 'The Military Reforms of Alexander the Great During His Campaign In Iran, Afghanistan and Central Asia' in *Understanding Eurasia: From Ancient Times to Present Day* (Krakow, 2007), 318.

35. Olbrycht, 'The Military Reforms of Alexander the Great During His Campaign In Iran, Afghanistan and Central Asia', 319; N.G.L. Hammond, *The Genius of Alexander the Great* (Chapel Hill, North Carolina Press, 1997), 184.

36. Arrian, *Anabasis*, 7.21.5–6.

37. Arrian, *Anabasis*, 7.7.7; Pierre Briant, *Alexander the Great and His Empire: A Short Introduction* (Princeton, New Jersey, Princeton University Press, 2010), 91–92.

38. Arrian, *Anabasis*, 7.6.3–6; Diodorus, 109.3.

39. Justin, 12.12; Plutarch, *Alexander*, 71.4; 51.2.

40. Plutarch, *Alexander*, 71.1; Arrian, *Anabasis*, 7.6.2–5; Justin, 12.4.1.

41. Curtius, 10.2.12; Justin, 12.11.5.

42. Arrian, *Anabasis*, 7.8.1–2; Plutarch, *Alexander*, 71.3.

43. Arrian, *Anabasis*, 7.8.3; 7.9–10; 7.11.1–4; Curtius, 10.2.27–28.

44. Arrian, *Anabasis*, 7.11.1–7.

45. Arrian, *Anabasis*, 7.11.8–9; A.B. Bosworth, 'Alexander and the Iranians' in *Alexander the Great: A Reader*, Second Edition, ed. Ian Worthington (New York, Routledge, 2012), 287.

46. Diodorus, 17.117.4.

47. Diodorus, 17.16.2; Elizabeth Carney, *Olympias: Mother of Alexander* (New York, Routledge, 2006), 48.

48. Curtius, 10.3.12.

49. *Metz Epitome*, 112, 118; *Heidelberg Epitome*, 1.2; Lucian, *Slander*, 18.

50. Arrian, *Anabasis*, 7.20.1–2; 7.20.7–10.

51. Diodorus, 18.4.2–6; Plutarch, *Alexander*, 72.5.

52. Diodorus, 18.4.2–6.

53. Diodorus, 18.4.4.

54. Diodorus, 18.4.3–6; Pierre Briant, *Alexander the Great and His Empire: A Short Introduction* (Princeton, New Jersey, Princeton University Press, 2010), 38–41; A.B. Bosworth, 'Alexander and the Iranians' in *Alexander the Great: A Reader*, Second Edition, ed. Ian Worthington (New York, Routledge, 2012), 287.

55. Waldemar Heckel, *The Conquests of Alexander the Great* (New York, Cambridge University Press, 2008), 150.

56. Herodotus, 3.17–19.

Conclusion

1. Arrian, *Anabasis*, 1.17.3; 3.16.4; Diodorus, 17.37.6; Curtius, 5.2.18.

2. Peter Green, *Alexander of Macedon, 356–323 B.C.: A Historical Biography* (Berkeley and Los Angeles, University of California Press, 1991), 355; for a more complete list of significant Persians and Asians who joined Alexander, see Edward M. Anson, *Alexander the Great: Themes and Issues* (Bloomsbury Academic, 2013), 161–162.

3. Ernst Fredericksmeyer, 'Alexander the Great and the Kingdom of Asia' in *Alexander the Great in Fact and Fiction*, eds A.B. Bosworth and E.J. Baynham (New York, Oxford University Press, 2000), 15–152; M.J. Olbrycht, 'An Admirer of Persian Ways: Alexander the Great's Reforms in Parthia-Hyrcania and the Iranian

Heritage' in *Excavating an Empire: Achaemenid Persia in Longue Durée*, eds Touraj
Daryaee, Ali Mousavi and Khodadad Rezakhani (Costa Mesa, California, Mazda
Publishers, 2014), 43–44; M.J. Olbrycht, 'On Coin Portraits Of Alexander The
Great and His Iranian Regalia: Some Remarks Occasioned by the Book by F.
Smith: *L'immaginedi Alessandro il Grande sulle monete del regno (336–323)*' in *Notae
Numismaticae-Zapaski Numizmatyczne* 6 (2011), 13–26; Waldemar Heckel, *The
Conquests of Alexander the Great* (New York, Cambridge University Press, 2008), 95;
Arrian, *Anabasis*, 3.30.4; James Stephen Mullen, 'The Royal Hunts of Alexander
the Great: Engaging with Local Traditions of Kingship Throughout his Empire'
(PhD diss., Newcastle University, 2019), 210, 232, 232–233; Andrew Chugg, *Alexander's
Lovers* (USA, AMC Publications, 2012), 133.

4. Curtius, 7.3.1; Plutarch, *Moralia*, 343A; Strabo, 11.11.4; 15.1.5; Arrian, *Anabasis*,
6.29.4–11; Plutarch, *Alexander*, 69.1–2.

5. Arrian, *Anabasis*, 7.4.4–8; 7.6.1; 7.8.2.

6. Arrian, *Anabasis*, 1.17.10; 1.18.2; 1.23.7–8; 2.3.1–4; Mark Munn, 'Alexander, The
Gordian Knot and the Kingship of Midas' in *Macedonian Legacies: Studies in Ancient
Macedonian History and Culture in Honour of Eugene N. Borza*, Revised Edition,
eds Timothy Howe and Jeanne Reames (CreateSpace Independent Publishing
Platform, 2016), 109–115.

7. Arrian, *Anabasis*, 2.20.1–3; 2.24.1–2; 3.16.4–5; Curtius, 5.1.22; Strabo, 16.1.5.

8. Pierre Briant, *Alexander the Great and His Empire: A Short Introduction* (Princeton,
New Jersey, Princeton University Press, 2010), 37–38; Josef Wiesehöfer, *Ancient
Persia* (New York, I.B. Tauris Publishers, 2006), 105; Waldemar Heckel, *The
Conquests of Alexander the Great* (New York, Cambridge University Press, 2008), 85.

9. Arrian, *Anabasis*, 1.17.1–2.

10. Arrian, *Anabasis*, 6.30.2–3; 7.6.3; M.J. Olbrycht, 'Iranians in the Diadochi Period'
in *After Alexander the Time of the Diadochi (323–281 BC)*, eds Victor Troncoso and
Edward Anson (Havertown, United States, Oxbow Books, 2016), 160–162.

11. Diodorus, 17.106.2; 17.108.4–8; Curtius, 10.1.1–9.

12. Diodorus, 18.36.5.

13. Diodorus, 19.91.2.

14. M.J. Olbrycht, 'Iranians in the Diadochi Period' in *After Alexander the Time of
the Diadochi (323–281 BC)*, eds Victor Troncoso and Edward Anson (Havertown,
United States, Oxbow Books, 2016), 169–170.

15. Richard A. Billows, *Antigonos the One-Eyed and the Creation of the Hellenistic State*
(Berkeley and Los Angeles, California, University of California Press, 1990), 321,
324; M.J. Olbrycht, 'Iranians in the Diadochi Period' in *After Alexander the Time
of the Diadochi (323–281 BC)*, eds Victor Troncoso and Edward Anson (Havertown,
United States, Oxbow Books, 2016), 168.

16. M.J. Olbrycht, 'Iranians in the Diadochi Period' in *After Alexander the Time of
the Diadochi (323–281 BC)*, eds Victor Troncoso and Edward Anson (Havertown,
United States, Oxbow Books, 2016), 171.

17. Appian, *Syrian Wars*, 56.

Bibliography

Ancient Sources

Aelian, *Historical Miscellany*, translated by N.G. Wilson (Cambridge, Massachusetts, Harvard University Press, 1997)

Appian, *Roman History*, Volume II, translated by Horace White (Cambridge, Massachusetts, Harvard University Press, 1999)

Aristotle, *Meteorologica*, translated by H.D.P. Lee (Cambridge, Massachusetts, Harvard University Press, 1952)

Aristotle, *Politics*, translated by H. Rackham (Cambridge, Massachusetts, Harvard University Press, 1932)

Arrian, *Anabasis of Alexandri*, Books I-IV, translated by E. Iliff Robson (Cambridge, Massachusetts, Harvard University Press, 1947)

Arrian, *Anabasis of Alexandri*, Books V-VII, Indica Book VIII, translated by E. Iliff Robson (Cambridge, Massachusetts, Harvard University Press, 1944)

Athenaeus, *The Deipnosophistae*, translated by C.B. Gulick (Cambridge, Massachusetts, Harvard University Press, 1930)

Ctesias, *History of Persia: Tale of the Orient*, translated by Lloyd Llewellyn-Jones and James Robson (New York, Routledge, 2010)

Curtius, Quintus, *History of Alexander the Great of Macedon*, Books VI-X, translated by John C. Rolfe (Cambridge, Massachusetts, Harvard University Press, 1976)

Curtius, Quintus, *History of Alexander the Great of Macedon*, Books III-V, translated by John C. Rolfe (Cambridge, Massachusetts, Harvard University Press, 1971)

Demosthenes, *Against Aristocrates*, translated by A.T. Vince (Cambridge, Massachusetts, Harvard University Press, 1939)

Demosthenes, *Philippic*, translated by J.H. Vince (Cambridge, Massachusetts, Harvard University Press, 1930)

Demosthenes, *Philip*, translated by C.A. and J.H. Vince (Cambridge, Massachusetts, Harvard University Press, 1926)

Heckel, Waldemar and J.C. Yardley, *Historical Sources in Translation: Alexander the Great* (Oxford, Blackwell Publishing, 2004)

Herodotus, *The Persian Wars*, Books 8-9, translated by A.D. Godley (Cambridge, Massachusetts, Harvard University Press, 1925)

Herodotus, *The Persian Wars*, Books 5-7, translated by A.D. Godley (Cambridge, Massachusetts, Harvard University Press, 1922)

Herodotus, *The Persian Wars*, Books 3-4, translated by A.D. Godley (Cambridge, Massachusetts, Harvard University Press, 1921)

Herodotus, *The Persian Wars*, Books 1-2, translated by A.D. Godley (Cambridge, Massachusetts, Harvard University Press, 1920)

Homer, *The Iliad*, Books 13-24, translated by A.T. Murray (Cambridge, Massachusetts, Harvard University Press, 1925)

Homer, *The Iliad*, Books 1–12, translated by A.T. Murray (Cambridge, Massachusetts, Harvard University Press, 1924)

Jacoby, Felix, *Fragmente der griechischen Historiker I–III* (1923–1959)

Justin, *Epitome of the Philippic History of Pompeius Trogus*, Books 1–44, translated by Rev. John Selby Watson (London, Henry G. Bohn, York Street, Covent Garden, 1853)

Lucian, *The Works of Lucian of Samosata*, Volume IV, translated by H.W. and F.G. Fowler (Oxford, Clarendon Press, 1905)

Lucian, *The Works of Lucian of Samosata*, Volume I, translated by H.W. and F.G. Fowler (Oxford, Clarendon Press, 1905)

Maximus, Valerius, *Memorable Doings and Sayings*, Books 6–9, translated by D.R. Shackleton Bailey (Cambridge, Massachusetts, Harvard University Press, 2000)

Maximus, Valerius, *Memorable Doings and Sayings*, Books 1–5, translated by D.R. Shackleton Bailey (Cambridge, Massachusetts, Harvard University Press, 2000)

Nepos, Cornelius, *Conon*, translated by Albert Fleckeisen (Leipzig, Teubner, 1886)

Pausanias, *Description of Greece*, Books 8.22–10, translated by W.H.S. Jones (Cambridge, Massachusetts, Harvard University Press, 1935)

Pausanias, *Description of Greece*, Books 3–5, translated by W.H.S. Jones (Cambridge, Massachusetts, Harvard University Press, 1926)

Pausanias, *Description of Greece*, Books 1–2, translated by W.H.S. Jones (Cambridge, Massachusetts, Harvard University Press, 1918)

Plutarch, *Plutarch's Moralia V*, translated by F.C. Babbitt (Cambridge, Massachusetts, Harvard University Press, 1936)

Plutarch, *Plutarch's Moralia IV*, translated by F.C. Babbitt (Cambridge, Massachusetts, Harvard University Press, 1936)

Plutarch, *Plutarch Lives, V: Agesilaus and Pompey. Pelopidas and Marcellus*, translated by Bernadotte Perrin (Cambridge, Massachusetts, Harvard University Press, 1926)

Plutarch, *Plutarch Lives, IX: Demetrius and Antony. Pyrrhus and Gaius Marius*, translated by Bernadotte Perrin (Cambridge, Massachusetts, Harvard University Press, 1920)

Plutarch, *Plutarch Lives, VII: Demosthenes and Cicero. Alexander and Caesar*, translated by Bernadotte Perrin (Cambridge, Massachusetts, Harvard University Press, 1919)

Plutarch, *Plutarch Lives, XI: Aratus. Artaxerxes. Galba. Otho*, translated by Bernadotte Perrin (Cambridge, Massachusetts, Harvard University Press, 1917)

Plutarch, *Plutarch Lives, VIII: Sertorius and Eumenes. Phocion and Cato the Younger*, translated by Bernadotte Perrin (Cambridge, Massachusetts, Harvard University Press, 1919)

Plutarch, *Plutarch Lives, II: Themistocles and Camillus. Aristides and Cato Major*, translated by Bernadotte Perrin (Cambridge, Massachusetts, Harvard University Press, 1914)

Polyaenus, *Stratagems*, Books 1–8, translated by R. Shepherd (1793)

Polybius, *The Histories*, Volume IV, Books 9–15, translated by W.R. Paton (Cambridge, Massachusetts, Harvard University Press, 1925)

Pseudo-Callisthenes, *The Greek Alexander Romance*, translated by Richard Stoneman (New York, Penguin Books, 1991)

Siculus, Diodorus, *Diodorus Siculus, Library of History Books 16.66–17*, translated by C. Bradford Welles (Cambridge, Massachusetts, Harvard University Press, 1963)

Siculus, Diodorus, *Diodorus Siculus, Library of History Books 15.20–16.65*, translated by Charles L. Shepard (Cambridge, Massachusetts, Harvard University Press, 1952)

Siculus, Diodorus, *Diodorus Siculus, Library of History Books 18–19.65*, translated by Russel M. Geer (Cambridge, Massachusetts, Harvard University Press, 1947)

Smyrnaeus, Quintus, *The Fall of Troy*, translated by A.S. Way (Cambridge, Massachusetts, Harvard University Press, 1913)

Strabo, *The Geography of Strabo*, Books 15–16, translated by H.L. Jones (Cambridge, Massachusetts, Harvard University Press, 1930)

Strabo, *The Geography of Strabo*, Books 10–12, translated by H.L. Jones (Cambridge, Massachusetts, Harvard University Press, 1928)

Strabo, *The Geography of Strabo*, Books 3–5, translated by H.L. Jones (Cambridge, Massachusetts, Harvard University Press, 1923)

Theophrastus, *Enquiry into Plants*, Volume I, Books 1–5, translated by Arthur Hort (Cambridge, Massachusetts, Harvard University Press, 1916)

Xenophon, *Cyropaedia*, Books 5–8, translated by Walter Miller (Cambridge, Massachusetts, Harvard University Press, 1914)

Xenophon, *Cyropaedia*, Books 1–4, translated by Walter Miller (Cambridge, Massachusetts, Harvard University Press, 1914)

Xenophon, *Anabasis*, Books 1–7, translated by Carleton Lewis Brownson (Cambridge, Massachusetts, Harvard University Press, 1922)

Secondary Sources

Anson, Edward M., *Alexander the Great: Themes and Issues* (New York, Bloomsbury Publishing, 2013)

Badian, Ernst, 'Alexander the Great and the Unity of Mankind' in *Historia: Zeitschrift für Alte Geschichte* 7, no. 4 (October 1958), 425–444.

Bevan, E.R., 'Antiochus III and His Title "Great-King"' in *The Journal of Hellenic Studies* 22 (November 1902), 241–244.

Billows, Richard, *Before and After Alexander: The Legend and Legacy of Alexander the Great* (New York, The Overlook Press, 2018)

Billows, Richard, *Antigonos the One-Eyed and the Creation of the Hellenistic State* (Berkeley, University of California Press, 1997)

Borza, E.N., 'Ethnicity and Cultural Policy at Alexander's Court' in *Alexander the Great: A Reader*, Second Edition, edited by Ian Worthington (New York, Routledge, 2012) 313–318.

Bosworth, A.B., 'Alexander and the Iranians' in *Alexander the Great: A Reader*, Second Edition, edited by Ian Worthington (New York, Routledge, 2012), 286–312.

Bosworth, A.B., *Alexander and the East: The Tragedy and Triumph* (Clarendon Press, 1998)

Bosworth, A.B., *Conquest and Empire: The Reign of Alexander the Great* (Cambridge, Cambridge University Press, 1988)

Branko, F. van Oppen de Rutter, 'The Susa Marriages: A Historiographical Note' in *Ancient Society* 44 (2012), 25–41.

Briant, Pierre, *Darius in the Shadow of Alexander*, translated by Jane Marie Todd (Cambridge, Massachusetts, Harvard University Press, 2015)

Briant, Pierre, *Alexander the Great and His Empire: A Short Introduction*, translated by Amélie Kuhrt (Princeton, New Jersey, Princeton University Press, 2010)

Briant, Pierre, 'The Empire of Darius III in Perspective' in *Alexander the Great: A New History*, edited by Waldemar Heckel and Lawrence A. Tritle (Oxford, Blackwell Publishing Ltd, 2009) 171–188.

Briant, Pierre, *From Cyrus to Alexander: A History of the Persian Empire*, translated by Peter T. Daniels (University Park, Pennsylvania, Eisenbrauns, 2002)

Brunt, P.A., 'The Aims of Alexander' in *Greece & Rome 12*, no. 2 (October 1965), 205–215.

Burn, A.R., *Alexander the Great and the Hellenistic Empire* (London, English Universities Press, 1947)

Burstein, Stanley M., 'Alexander's Organization of Egypt: A Note on the Career of Cleomenes of Naucratis' in *Macedonian Legacies: Studies in Ancient Macedonian History and Culture in Honour of Eugene N. Borza*, Revised Edition, edited by Timothy Howe and Jeanne Reames (CreateSpace Independent Publishing Platform, 2016), 183–194.

Carney, Elizabeth, *Olympias: Mother of Alexander* (New York, Routledge, 2006)

Champion, Jeff, *Antigonus the One-Eyed: Greatest of the Successors* (South Yorkshire, Great Britain, Pen & Sword Military, 2014)

Chugg, Michael Andrew, *Alexander's Lovers* (USA, AMC Publications, 2012)

Collins, Andrew W., 'The Royal Custom and Insignia of Alexander the Great' in *The American Journal of Philology* 133 (Autumn 2012), 371–402.

Dandamaev, M.A., *A Political History of the Achaemenid Empire*, translated by W.J. Vogelsang (Brill, 1989)

De Mauriac, Henry, 'Alexander the Great and the Politics of "Homonoia"' in *Journal of the History of Ideas 10*, no. 1 (January 1949), 104–114.

English, Stephen, *Field Campaigns of Alexander* (South Yorkshire, Great Britain, Pen & Sword Military, 2011)

English, Stephen, *The Sieges of Alexander the Great* (South Yorkshire, Great Britain, Pen & Sword Military, 2009)

Fredricksmeyer, E.A., 'Alexander's Religion and Divinity' in *Alexander the Great: A Reader*, edited by Ian Worthington (New York, Routledge, 2012), 203–215.

Fredricksmeyer, Ernst, 'Alexander the Great and the Kingship of Asia' in *Alexander the Great in Fact and Fiction*, edited by A.B. Bosworth and E.J. Baynham (New York, Oxford University Press, 2000), 136–137.

Fuller, J.F.C., *The Generalship of Alexander the Great* (New Brunswick, New Jersey, Da Capo Press, 1960)

Gabriel, Richard, *The Madness of Alexander the Great and the Myth of Military Genius* (South Yorkshire, Great Britain, Pen & Sword Military, 2015)

Gabriel, Richard, *Philip II of Macedonia: Greater than Alexander* (Dulles, Virginia, Potomac Books Inc., 2010)

Gourgaud, General Baron, *Talks of Napoleon at St. Helena with General Baron Gourgaud*, translated by Elizabeth Latimer (Chicago, A.C. McClurg & Company, 1903)

Green, Peter, *Alexander of Macedon: A Historical Biography* (Berkley and Los Angeles, University of California Press, 1991)

Hamilton, J.R., *Alexander the Great* (Pittsburgh, University of Pittsburgh Press, 1973)

Hammond, N.G.L., *The Macedonian State: The Origins, Institutions and History* (Oxford, Clarendon Press, 1989)

Hammond, N.G.L., *The Genius of Alexander the Great* (Chapel Hill, North Carolina Press, 1997)

Hammond, N.G.L., 'Royal Pages, Personal Pages and Boys Trained in the Macedonian Manner during the Period of the Temenid Monarchy' in *Historia: Zeitschrift für Alte Geschichte 39*, no. 3 (1990), 261–290.

208 Alexander the Great and Persia

Heckel, Waldemar, 'Mazaeus, Callisthenes and the Alexander Sarcophagus' in *Historia: Zeitschrift für Alte Geschichte 55*, no. 4 (2006), 385–396.

Heckel, Waldemar, *The Conquests of Alexander the Great* (New York, Cambridge University Press, 2008)

Heckel, Waldemar, 'Alexander the Great and the "Limits of the Civilized World"' in *Alexander the Great, A Reader*, edited by Ian Worthington (New York, Routledge, 2012), 147–174.

Hölbl Günther, *A History of the Ptolemaic Empire*, translated by Tina Saavdra (New York, Routledge, 2001)

Iliakis, Michael, 'Greek Mercenary Revolts in Bactria: A Re-Appraisal' in *Historia: Zeitschrift für Alte Geschichte 62*, no. 2 (2013), 182–195.

Karunanithy, David, *The Macedonian War Machine: Neglected Aspects of the Armies of Philip, Alexander and the Successors* (South Yorkshire, Great Britain, Pen & Sword Military, 2013)

Lane Fox, Robin, 'Alexander the Great: Last of the Achaemenids' in *Persian Responses: Political and Cultural Interaction with(in) the Achaemenid Empire*, edited by Christopher Tulpin (Swansea, Wales, The Classical Press of Wales, 2007), 267–313.

Lane Fox, Robin, *Alexander the Great* (New York, Penguin Books, 2004)

Mullen, James Stephen, 'The Royal Hunts of Alexander the Great: Engaging with Local Traditions of Kingship Throughout his Empire' (PhD diss., Newcastle University, 2019)

Müller, Sabine, 'The Female Element of the Political Self-Fashioning of the Diadochi: Ptolemy, Seleucus, Lysimachus and Their Iranian Wives' in *After Alexander: The Time of the Diadochi*, edited by Victor Troncoso and Edward Anson (Havertown, PA, Oxbow Books, 2013), 199–214.

Munn, Mark, 'Alexander, The Gordian Knot and the Kingship of Midas' in *Macedonian Legacies: Studies in Ancient Macedonian History and Culture in Honour of Eugene N. Borza*, Revised Edition, edited by Timothy Howe and Jeanne Reames (CreateSpace Independent Publishing Platform, 2016), 107–143.

Naiden, F.S., *Soldier, Priest and God: A Life of Alexander the Great* (New York, Oxford University Press, 2019)

Narain, A.K., 'Alexander and India' in *Greece & Rome 12*, no. 1 (October 1965), 155–165.

Olbrycht, Marek Jan, 'An Admirer of Persian Ways: Alexander the Great's Reforms in Parthia-Hyrcania and the Iranian Heritage' in *Excavating an Empire: Achaemenid Persia in Longue Durée*, edited by Touraj Daryaee, Ali Mousavi and Khodadad Rezakhani (Costa Mesa, California, Mazda Publishers, 2014), 37–62.

Olbrycht, Marek Jan, 'Parthia, Bactria, India: The Iranian Policies of Alexander of Macedon' in *With Alexander in India and Central Asia: Moving East and Back to West*, edited by Claudia Antonetti and Paolo Biagi (Oxford, Oxbow Books, 2017), 194–212.

Olbrycht, Marek Jan, 'Iranians in the Diadochi Period' in *After Alexander the Time of the Diadochi (323–281 BC)*, edited by Victor Troncoso and Edward Anson (Havertown, United States, Oxbow Books, 2016), 159–182.

Olbrycht, Marek Jan, 'On Coin Portraits of Alexander The Great and His Iranian Regalia: Some Remarks Occasioned by the Book by F. Smith: *L'immaginedi Alessandro il Grande sulle monete del regno (336–323)*' in *Notae Numismaticae-Zapaski Numizmatyczne* 6 (2011), 13–26.

Olbrycht, Marek Jan, 'First Iranian Units in the Army of Alexander the Great' in *Anabasis-Studia Classica Et Orientalia* 2 (2011), 67–84.

Olbrycht, Marek Jan, 'The Macedonian Mutiny at Opis and Alexander's Iranian Policy in 324 BC' in *The Children of Herodotus: Greek and Roman Historiography and Related Genres*, edited by Jakub Pigon (Cambridge Scholars Publishing, 2008), 231–252.

Olbrycht, Marek Jan, 'The Military Reforms of Alexander the Great During His Campaign In Iran, Afghanistan and Central Asia' in *Understanding Eurasia: From Ancient Times to Present Day* (Krakow, 2007), 309–321.

Olbrycht, Marek Jan, 'Alexander the Great Versus the Iranians: An Alternative Perspective' in *Folia Orientalia* 42/43 (2006/07), 159–172.

Olmstead, A.T., *History of the Persian Empire* (Chicago, University of Chicago Press, 1970)

Rawlinson, George, *The Story of Parthia* (New York, G.P. Putnam's Sons, 1903)

Ray, Fred Eugen Jr, *Greek and Macedonian Land Battles of the 4th Century B.C.* (Jefferson, North Carolina, McFarland & Company Inc., 2012)

Robinson, Charles A., *Alexander the Great: Conqueror and Creator of a New World* (New York, Franklin Watts, 1963)

Robinson, Charles A., 'The Extraordinary Ideas of Alexander the Great' in *The American Historical Review 62*, no. 2 (January 1957), 326–344.

Room, James, 'Alexander's Policy of Perso-Macedonian Fusion' in *The Landmark Arrian: The Campaigns of Alexander*, edited by James Room (New York, Anchor Books, 2012), 380–387.

Sawada, Noriko, 'Social Customs and Institutions: Aspects of the Macedonian Elite Society' in *Alexander the Great: A Reader*, Second Edition, edited by Ian Worthington (New York, Routledge, 2012), 44–70.

Spann, Philip O., 'Alexander at the Beas: Fox in a Lion's Skin' in *The Eye Expanded: Life and the Arts in Greco-Roman Antiquity*, edited by Frances B. Titchener and Richard F. Moorton Jr (Berkley and Los Angeles, University of California Press, 1999), 62–75.

Tarn, W.W., *Alexander the Great*, 2 Vols (Chicago, Ares Publishers Inc., 1948)

Wheatley, Pat, 'The Heidelberg Epitome: A Neglected Diadoch Source' in *After Alexander: The Time of the Diadochi*, edited by Victor Troncoso and Edward Anson (Havertown, PA, Oxbow Books, 2013), 17–29.

Wiesehöfer, Josef, *Ancient Persia* (New York, I.B. Tauris Publishers, 2006)

Wiesehöfer, Josef, 'The "Accursed" and the "Adventurer"' in *A Companion to Alexander's Literature in the Middle Ages*, edited by Z. David Zuwiyya (Leiden, The Netherlands, Brill, 2011), 113–132.

Wilcken, Ulrich, *Alexander the Great*, translated by G.C. Richards (New York, W.W. Norton & Company, 1967)

Worthington, Ian, *By the Spear: Philip II, Alexander the Great, and the Rise and Fall of the Macedonian Empire* (New York, Oxford University Press, 2014)

Worthington, Ian, 'Alexander the Great, Nation-Building and the Creation and Maintenance of Empire' in *Alexander the Great: A Reader*, Second Edition, edited by Ian Worthington (New York, Routledge, 2012), 203–215.

Index